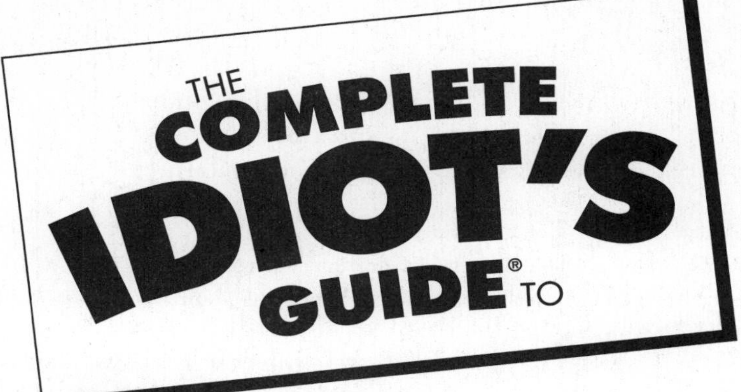

Project Management

Fourth Edition

by G. Michael Campbell, PMP, and Sunny Baker, Ph.D.

ALPHA
A member of Penguin Group (USA) Inc.

ALPHA BOOKS

Published by the Penguin Group

Penguin Group (USA) Inc., 375 Hudson Street, New York, New York 10014, USA

Penguin Group (Canada), 90 Eglinton Avenue East, Suite 700, Toronto, Ontario M4P 2Y3, Canada (a division of Pearson Penguin Canada Inc.)

Penguin Books Ltd., 80 Strand, London WC2R 0RL, England

Penguin Ireland, 25 St. Stephen's Green, Dublin 2, Ireland (a division of Penguin Books Ltd.)

Penguin Group (Australia), 250 Camberwell Road, Camberwell, Victoria 3124, Australia (a division of Pearson Australia Group Pty. Ltd.)

Penguin Books India Pvt. Ltd., 11 Community Centre, Panchsheel Park, New Delhi—110 017, India

Penguin Group (NZ), 67 Apollo Drive, Rosedale, North Shore, Auckland 1311, New Zealand (a division of Pearson New Zealand Ltd.)

Penguin Books (South Africa) (Pty.) Ltd., 24 Sturdee Avenue, Rosebank, Johannesburg 2196, South Africa

Penguin Books Ltd., Registered Offices: 80 Strand, London WC2R 0RL, England

International Standard Book Number: 978-1-59257-598-5
Library of Congress Catalog Card Number: 2006934449

12 11 10 09 8 7 6 5 4

Interpretation of the printing code: The rightmost number of the first series of numbers is the year of the book's printing; the rightmost number of the second series of numbers is the number of the book's printing. For example, a printing code of 07-1 shows that the first printing occurred in 2007.

Printed in the United States of America

Publisher: *Marie Butler-Knight*
Editorial Director: *Mike Sanders*
Managing Editor: *Billy Fields*
Acquisitions Editor: *Michele Wells*
Development Editor: *Lynn Northrup*
Production Editor: *Kayla Dugger*
Copy Editor: *Nancy Wagner*
Cartoonist: *Shannon Wheeler*
Cover Designer: *Bill Thomas*
Book Designer: *Trina Wurst*
Indexer: *Brad Herriman*
Layout: *Brian Massey*
Proofreaders: *Mary Hunt, Kayla Dugger, and John Etchison*

Contents at a Glance

Contents

Introduction

Many project managers guess as a way to estimate the level of effort for a project. However, there is a better way to manage projects, and you don't need to be a genius or even have an MBA to understand how. It doesn't take a special certification to manage a project, but it does take special skills to bring projects in on time and within budget. Yes, some planning and charting is involved in moving projects from start to finish, but this book takes a practical approach to the process and puts you in control. The following pages map the road to successful project management.

The Complete Idiot's Guide to Project Management, Fourth Edition, explains in easy-to-understand language how the power of time-proven project management methods can help your mission-critical projects come in on time, on budget, and on target. You'll learn how to point project teams, in spite of politics and personalities, in the same direction; and how to manage changes, no matter how frequent, to keep projects on track. You'll learn that it's skill, not luck or fancy degrees, that makes the difference in making your project a success.

How to Use This Book

The book has seven parts, which we recommend you read from beginning to end. The parts work together to provide you with the steps and tools behind successful project management and offer practical advice you can adapt to the needs of today's fast-moving, ever-changing organizations.

Part 1, "Project Management Power," explains how to balance all the different needs all project managers must satisfy. We'll introduce you to steps you can use to bring any project to a successful conclusion on time and within budget and the three secrets to success behind any project: the project manager, the team, and the plan.

Part 2, "The Project Definition Phase," presents techniques to start a project off on the right foot with a clear scope and a motivated project team. This part is especially important because the way a project starts off usually defines the way it will end up.

Part 3, "The Project Planning Phase," explains the basic planning processes central to successful project management. You'll observe how to define, schedule, and budget tasks using powerful charting and analysis tools that can help you scope out projects of all shapes and sizes. This is the most technical part of the book, so you might want to read it twice. Mastering the information in this part is important because no project is ever better than the plan used to manage the effort.

Part 4, "The Execution Phase," presents proven techniques to transform the plan into action focused toward meeting the project requirements. This is key to successful project management. The end result of a project is always related to the way the plan is translated into actual work in the real world.

Part 5, "The Controlling Processes," talks about ways to monitor, track, and adjust each project so that you can keep everything on schedule, within budget, and with the right quality. You'll also find easy-to-follow guidelines for dealing with the most common project problems and for minimizing the impact of the changes and conflicts that are part of almost every project.

Part 6, "The Close-Out Phase," shows you how to finish your project and reap the rewards of a job well done. This is often the most ignored part of project management, but you'll see why it is so important.

Part 7, "The Organization and Tools to Make Project Management Prosper," introduces some software packages that can help you find out how to put the discipline of project management to work throughout your organization.

Extras

To add to the material in the main text, a series of sidebars throughout the book highlight specific items that can help you understand and implement the material in each chapter:

Time Is Money

Use the suggestions in these boxes to keep your schedule up-to-date and your budget under control. Hopefully the advice will spare you the embarrassment of running out of money before the project is completed. You'll also pick up on a variety of tips used by veteran project managers to run projects of all sizes and kinds.

def•i•ni•tion

These boxes define the most important concepts in project management. Use these words in meetings to impress your boss and your co-workers because it will demonstrate that you know what you are talking about.

Along the Critical Path

Stories or information related to project management appear in these boxes as examples from experienced project managers.

Words from the Wise

These quotes and tips include observations from our experience and other experts that may help inspire you to greater achievements or simply help keep you motivated to do your best, even when the project seems impossible.

Risk Management

Sometimes things just go wrong, no matter how well you plan your project. Luckily, there are usually warnings before things get too bad if you know how to recognize them. In these boxes, you'll learn how to read the danger signs before you get swamped with problems.

Acknowledgments

All of the people at Alpha Books—especially Michele Wells and Lynn Northrup for their professionalism, skill, and good ideas—deserve our thanks. We've appreciated the opportunity to work with them.

Just as important, we want to thank you, the reader, for purchasing this book. We understand how important your projects are to your personal and professional success, and we feel a deep sense of gratitude that you believe we can teach you something about becoming a better project manager.

In addition, Mike Campbell would like to thank Stephen Schwarz and Dave Feineman at BP, and Greg Ranft and Cliff Halverson at TXDOT for providing great examples of project managers in action.

And any acknowledgement would be incomplete without recognizing Michael's wife, Molly, and her undying patience as he worked to complete this book. Her support, and the love of his children, is the rock upon which everything else is built.

Trademarks

Part 1

Project Management Power

Each year, organizations launch mission-critical projects involving millions of dollars in capital investment plus significant requirements for project-savvy human capital. The processes and methods of project management provide the structure, focus, flexibility, and control to help guide these significant investments to outstanding results, on time and within budget.

In this part, you'll be introduced to the processes and life-cycle phases of the project management discipline and the successful techniques of experienced project managers. You'll also learn the nine key knowledge areas of project management, the first step in consistently bringing your projects in on time and within budget. If you can do this, you'll be a rising star within your organization. That's the power of project management.

Chapter 1

Linking Projects to Strategy and Performance Results

In This Chapter

- Ways projects meet business needs
- A different approach to managing change
- Balancing time, resources, results, and perceptions
- What makes a great project manager
- Defining project success
- All projects great and small

The twenty-first century is here along with tighter budgets, less time to get things done, and fewer resources. Sure, building warp drives that allow faster-than-light travel are still *Star Trek* fantasies, but rapid change, expanding technologies, and global marketing are real today.

To compete, you need to do more with less. Generally, you undertake projects because they are a part of the plan to take your organization to a new level of performance. However, to captain your business in the future, you'll need to build things faster, cheaper, and better. And you'll need to get things done right the first time.

Projects are becoming the way of the working world. Computers and automation have eliminated many types of repetitive work, freeing people to focus on building new products and services and improved organizations. And where things need to be created, collected ideas are organized as projects.

Projects Meet a Business Need

Projects are usually begun to address one or more demands from inside or outside the company. The drivers might be:

- A market demand to expand production of products
- An organizational need to train people with new skills
- A specific request from a key customer
- A legal requirement from the government or regulatory body

def•i•ni•tion

A **project** is defined by the Project Management Institute as a temporary endeavor undertaken to create a unique product, service, or result. This means that a project produces something that has never existed before; has a deadline or target date for when the project must be done; and has a budget that limits the amount of people, supplies, and money that can be used to complete the project.

Projects may take many different forms. For example, they may be projects around:

- Technology implementations, such as automation equipment
- Information technology or systems that will change computers
- Business development initiatives
- Human resource performance, such as training projects
- Strategy initiatives, such as introducing a whole new product line

Any and all of these projects usually start with a decision about what the customers will require from the company in the future and focus on meeting or exceeding these customer requirements or needs. These requirements are then put into a strategic plan that will be carried out over a period of anywhere from a few months to as many as five years. In addition, to execute these requirements, various projects are created. These projects may have a variety of outcomes in the forecast, but one constant is the same—the need to improve performance in the future.

The project manager—the person who takes overall responsibility for coordinating a project regardless of size and for making sure the desired end result comes in on time and within budget—must understand this link. The project manager must also make sure that each member of the project team understands the link to the future of the organization and the performance results the business is trying to achieve. Why, you may ask? The answer is relatively simple as a concept, but much harder to execute. As the project proceeds, the project manager and the project team will be making numerous decisions as they work to overcome a wide variety of technical and business problems that were unforeseen at the start of the project. If these people do not have an understanding of the strategy and how their project helps fulfill the desired performance results, the team could make decisions that would not allow the project deliverables to maximize the business value intended at the beginning of the project.

Viewing Change from a Different Perspective

When project managers think of *change management*, they probably relate it to something an individual goes through during the course of a change. Such theories are very popular, and you may even think of change in this way. Many theories equate change with the death of something familiar and suggest that organizations and people in them will experience a similar process when going through a significant change. This meshes well with theories that organizations are "living organisms" that take on a life of their own. The major problem for project managers in these theories is "how do I and my projects fit in?" Good question! I would like to propose a different approach.

In today's fast-paced world, project managers need to be good at handling change. The best way to control coming changes is to use a disciplined approach—plan the project and then execute against that plan.

> **def•i•ni•tion**
>
> When a project causes organizational changes, a project manager should view those changes as an engineering problem that requires the alteration of concrete parts of the organization. **Change management** is getting the organization prepared for those alterations effectively and efficiently.

The basic problem with the project approach most companies use is that less than 30 percent of the projects companies employ to change their businesses are successful. *Less than 30 percent!* That is clearly unacceptable. Those projects include mergers and acquisitions, major technology initiatives, or reengineering, to name a few. According to research by the Gartner Group, over 30 percent of IT projects are cancelled. Over

50 percent of projects will experience cost overruns. And only about 16 percent will be completed within the desired time frame and budget and achieve the desired results. Amazing!

The dual perspective is needed for simultaneously running the business today and changing the business to meet future needs.

Adapted from Change Is the Rule *by W.E. "Dutch" Holland, Ph.D. (Dearborn Press, 2000)*

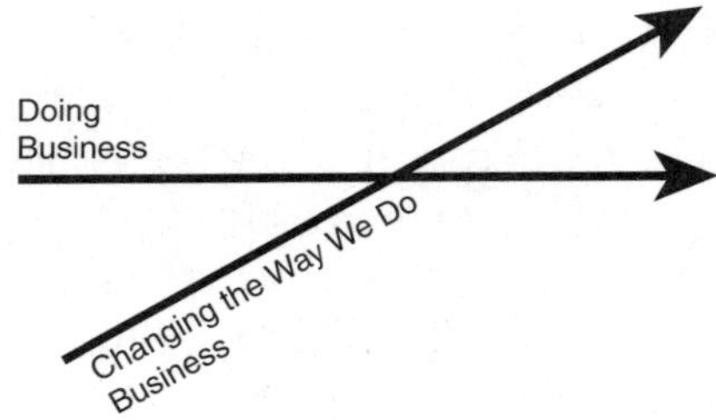

The good news for you is that if you master the techniques in this book, your company will see you as a rising star. Why? Because you will be successful in completing a project, and the contrast of the completed project with so many other failed projects will be striking.

That's why many people see the advantage to becoming a project manager. The Project Management Institute (PMI), an international organization dedicated to the advancement of project management, has nearly 100,000 members at the time we are writing this book and will probably exceed that number by the time you read it. This institute has established standards and certificates to raise the knowledge and professionalism of project managers worldwide.

A Balance Among Time, Resources, Results, and Perceptions

One of the hardest tasks any project manager will face is balancing a project's time, cost, and quality. By looking at the three elements in the accompanying pyramid, you can clearly see that if the time begins to slip (meaning you may miss your deadline), this impacts the other two elements. For example, you can get the project back on track by getting more people involved (and increasing your costs), by reducing the quality that was originally designed into the project, or by asking for more time!

A good project manager will make sure that he or she understands which of these three elements is paramount. In other words, what is most important—the deadline, the budget, or the quality? Once you establish this, you can work to keep the other elements in balance as the project progresses.

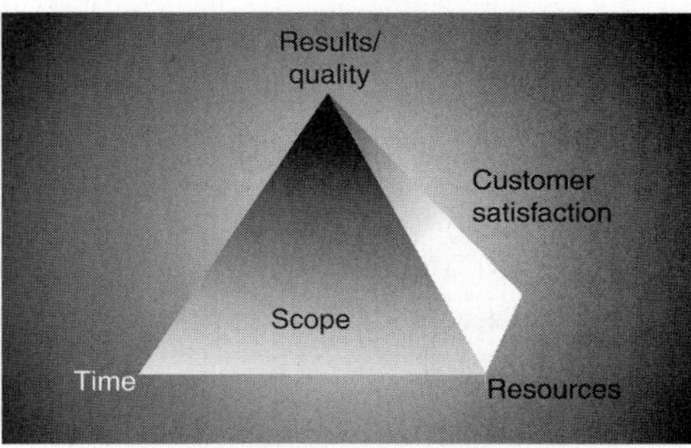

The Universal Project Pyramid

This pyramid demonstrates the balance between time, resources, results, and customer satisfaction that is required to bring a project to a successful conclusion. If you change one of the elements in the pyramid, you automatically change the scope of the project.

This brings us to the factors essential to the success of all projects:

- **Agreement among the project team and the stakeholders (which include internal and/or external customers and management) on the goals of the project.** Without clear goals and agreement among everyone involved, the results can be devastating. No project can be a success unless everybody agrees that he wants the same thing produced. In this book, you'll learn ways to develop clear, agreed-upon goals.
- **Support from management to supply the resources and to remove organizational obstacles.** Without management support, project managers rarely have enough authority of their own to execute the decisions and policies necessary to complete a project. To get that support, you'll need to manage "upward" as well as manage the project team. You'll also learn ways to do this as you read through this book.
- **Communication that is effective, appropriately delivered, and ongoing throughout the project**. Almost every project management technique involves some form of communication. Without clear, concise communication, the people on a project team will never be able to agree on goals and then meet them. The project plan is one major component of this communication, but many other components are required for project success. This book not only explains how to plan a project, it also examines the ongoing communication necessary to keep a project focused and on schedule.

Defining Project Success

Great project managers are made, not born. They have learned to use methods that have been successful for other project managers and adapt them to their particular situations. Sometimes they were lucky and had an opportunity to watch a great project

> **Words from the Wise**
>
> Project management methods are useful if they can be placed in the context of today's trends, impacts, and technology. If we merely forge ahead and use them as they were used 30 years ago, we will meet with, at most, limited success.
>
> —From *Project Management for the 21st Century,* by Bennet P. Lientz and Kathryn P. Rea (Academic Press, 2002)

manager at work or even have one as a mentor. However, most of us are not that lucky. So we can either muddle through it by trial and error, or we can use tried-and-true techniques.

Remember that our information presents the most successful techniques of hundreds of project managers, not just one! And because all projects share similar features and require a balance between time, resources, and results, similar formal project management techniques—the science of the great project managers—are also necessary to bring your projects to successful conclusions. You learn about all these techniques in this book.

The tools and techniques for project management were originally developed to handle construction projects. However, these same methods will work whether you're training a team of new employees, creating an ad campaign, developing a new software product, or reorganizing a corporation. You can also use project management tools to correct midcourse problems that would otherwise go undetected and undermine the success of any project.

In spite of their similarities, all projects are unique. Projects involve different goals, employ different people with distinctive personalities, take place over varying time frames, and produce different results. No two projects, even projects with the same general objectives, are ever identical in planning or implementation. People who manage projects successfully quickly learn to become managers of change because there are always plenty of surprises, even in small projects. Thankfully, the project management toolbox found in this book offers techniques for identifying and managing the unique attributes of every project.

If the project manager understands the business requirements that are driving the project, the project will succeed. If not, it won't. In the long term, the project will be judged not only on how well it met the targeted objectives, but also on whether it achieved its overall business objectives and the anticipated business value the project was supposed to capture. The project manager must seek regular feedback from the client to ensure that the project, as currently defined, still achieves the business objectives. Several things may change during the course of a project, such as:

- Business conditions
- Company objectives
- Management personnel
- Relative priorities
- Risk factors that materialize, requiring intervention to handle them

When you master the techniques of project management, you'll see that the project of setting up a national sales meeting and the project of building a major freeway expansion depend on many of the same project management tools, even though the projects are on vastly different scales.

It's usually easy to identify the most complex projects in business, such as developing a new model automobile, installing a new financial reporting computer application like Enterprise Resource Planning (ERP) tools, or building an overseas manufacturing facility. But smaller and more mundane business endeavors can also be projects, even though they may not be labeled by that name.

Words from the Wise

Project management skills transcend industry boundaries and add a lot of opportunities for people who are willing to learn the ropes. These additional skills are added job security for those who are worried about their current job or company.

Consider the job of hiring a new marketing manager for your company. Most experienced managers wouldn't consider this a project because they know how to plan and schedule all the steps in their head. You simply put an ad in the paper, interview some people, and make a choice. But hiring a new marketing manager involves deadlines, people, money, and time because you'll probably use a team of people to interview the candidates. And when you're done with the project, you'll also have something you didn't have before—a new marketing manager.

When viewed this way, hiring a marketing manager is a project and deserves to be treated like any other project. Good project management will help you hire the right marketing manager in the shortest period of time, which could make a big difference to your company.

Sure, it won't take as long to plan the project of hiring a marketing manager as it will to plan how to build a new bridge across the Potomac. You probably won't have to use a computer program to create the schedule or to manage the budget (although you might). But using good project management techniques is still important because the choice of the marketing manager is important to your business.

You can't afford to treat even a small project, such as hiring a new employee, like ordinary work. Now would be a good time to identify two small but important projects you have been postponing. For practice, you can apply the techniques you learn in this book to them.

The Next Step

In the following pages, we'll take you step-by-step through the fundamentals of planning, scheduling, tracking, and controlling the costs and resources of any project—whether it is mundane or technical or multifaceted and complex. These practical techniques are applicable to projects that people in sales, marketing, human resources, finance, and general management positions are responsible for, yet are based on the same general, accepted methods employed by engineering project managers in building skyscrapers, satellites, or software systems.

After learning about project management techniques, you'll be able to answer questions like these:

- How can I best define the work that needs to be done to make the project a success?
- How can I gain ongoing consensus about the goals and scope of the project?
- How long should the project really take to complete, and how much should it cost?
- How will I attain enough authority to get things done?
- Who should I put on my project team?
- How much work can I expect of each person on the project?
- How can I control cost overruns?
- What are the risks that might cause the project to fail?

If you can answer all these questions, who knows? Maybe with good project management you really can build that next new hot product!

The Least You Need to Know

- All projects meet a business need.
- Use an engineering approach to managing changes brought on by projects.
- Balancing time, resources, results, and perceptions is key to project management.
- Great project managers use the time-tested fundamentals for managing their projects.

Chapter 2

What Does It Mean to Be a Project Manager?

In This Chapter

- Understanding the link between project manager and business strategies
- The role of the project manager
- The knowledge areas possessed by effective project managers
- The skills of successful project managers
- Seven traits of effective project managers

Regardless of what your business card says, if you manage projects, your company is depending on you to deliver a successful project. In this chapter, you'll learn what it takes to be a good project manager.

The Business Connection

Most companies decide to begin a project for one reason and one reason only: they hope to make more money. So this means that every project is linked to the business strategy in some way, as we discussed in Chapter 1.

A project is usually begun to meet the future business requirements of customers. And the final end result is better performance from the business. What does this mean for you as the project manager? It means you must understand the business context or strategy that prompted your management to hand you the project in the first place. Without that understanding, you are like an architect who is designing a building without knowing what the business to be housed in it will do!

What Are My Responsibilities?

As a project manager, you are the one person assigned to lead the project management process, and in most cases, you alone are ultimately responsible for the project's success. (The project sponsor is often the person paying the bill for the project and so wants to make the project a success, too, but we'll talk more about that in Chapter 6.) Even if you have other work to do or if you manage the project as part of a project team, you need to make sure the project gets done as specified.

So how does a project manager do this? First of all, he or she must work with the customer to determine the requirements. When we use the term "customer," we are not necessarily referring to someone outside the company who will buy the product or service. If I am the project manager for a project that is designed to reconfigure the warehouse to get the products boxed and shipped faster, my "customer" may well be my company's manufacturing general manager. And I want to make sure that I have a steering committee of *all* the potential customers (or stakeholders) so that I can confirm they all approve of my plan. (We'll talk more about steering committees and stakeholders and how to define them in Chapter 6).

Time Is Money

According to the Project Management Institute (PMI), project managers must integrate nine areas of knowledge: cost, time, scope, quality, communications, human resources, procurement, risk, and integration management. Whew! That's a lot of stuff to handle. No wonder someone invented project management.

As project manager, once you have the requirements from the customer, you must make sure the steering committee is onboard with the requirements (we'll cover the steering committee in more detail in Chapter 6).

What Do You Need to Do?

Being a successful project manager means that you must master two very different skills. First, you must be very creative in solving problems because all projects, by definition, are unique. However, you must also be very self-disciplined in your approach and employ technology, charting techniques, and budgeting tools to monitor the project. The bottom line is that to be truly successful as a "project" manager, you must first establish yourself as a competent manager.

Learn to Plan and Act

Project management evolved as a discipline because of a need to coordinate resources and technology to secure predictable results. The common project management tasks include establishing objectives, breaking work into well-defined tasks, charting the sequence of tasks, scheduling, budgeting, coordinating a team, reporting, and communicating throughout the project. These tasks involve two general types of activities: planning and definition activities, and implementation and control activities.

As we go through this book, we will look at each of these areas in more detail so you will know exactly how to plan and act at each stage in the project.

Words from the Wise

The world will belong to passionate, driven leaders—people who not only have an enormous amount of energy but who can energize those whom they lead.

—Jack Welch, former CEO of General Electric

Focus on the Project's End

In the 1990s, Stephen Covey's *The 7 Habits of Highly Effective People* became a bestselling book. Covey wrote that one key to success was keeping the end result in mind as you decide what to do and how to do it. Successful project managers should develop this essential habit. Instead of looking at a project as 50 tasks, always keep the end result in mind. That way, the project is less likely to stall midstream. It also makes you a stronger project leader. If you have a clear vision in your mind about how the product will look at the completion of the project, you will be able to steer your project through difficult times and still succeed.

Be a Manager and a Leader

Good project managers can handle both the authority and the responsibility necessary to guide the project. Management of the project and leadership go hand in hand. As a leader, your team will expect you to be honest, competent, and inspirational as well as skilled in the use of project management techniques. On the individual level,

> **Time Is Money**
>
> A project manager who views the responsibility of managing a project as one of guiding, facilitating, negotiating, and coordinating will do better than one who views the project management responsibility as one of ordering, dictating, and coercing.

you will need to motivate, delegate, mentor, and coach at various times. So having those skills plus the ability to help your team members resolve conflicts will be critical elements to your success (and the success of the project).

You must develop administrative procedures to ensure that work is getting done on time and within budget (more on that in Chapter 20), but more importantly, you must gain the trust and respect of the project team so that people feel comfortable taking your direction.

But most of all, to be an effective project manager, you need to lead the project with energy and a positive attitude, which will make you the catalyst for moving your project forward. Never put the techniques of project management above your attitude. Your attitude gives you power!

Let's take a closer look at project managers as leaders.

The Leadership Roles of the Project Manager

As part of your responsibility for leading the various phases of the project, you'll need to assume a variety of roles with other people. Accomplished leaders move effortlessly among these various roles.

Interpersonal Roles

To be perceived as a leader, you must be regarded as honest, capable, and dependable—as well as personable. In your interpersonal roles, you'll need to do these kinds of things:

- Deal effectively with people from various professional backgrounds.
- Solve team disputes and create team unity.
- Focus and motivate team members to achieve milestones on the way to achieving the project goal.
- Build positive relationships with project stakeholders.
- Be sure to listen carefully to others' opinions when making decisions.

Informational Roles

You need to assume informational roles to keep people up-to-date and on track. When you do so, you'll need to accomplish these sorts of tasks:

- Arrange and lead team meetings.
- Create and maintain work schedules for other people.
- Communicate project vision to upper management.
- Provide feedback regarding results, quality, and project deliverables.

Along the Critical Path

After a seminar on project management, one of the attendees (a joker, obviously) ran up to us and told us that, after listening to our presentation, she had finally figured out how to be the perfect project manager. "All you have to do is have the intelligence of Einstein, the patience of Job, the integrity of a Supreme Court judge, the negotiating skills of a Mongolian horse trader, the savvy of James Bond, the appeal of Marilyn Monroe, the charisma of Sir Ralph Richardson, the communication skills of Tom Peters, the ideas of Stephen King, the planning skills of Colin Powell, the personal drive of Bill Gates, the financial acumen of Alan Greenspan, the skin of an armadillo, and the ego of Mother Teresa." Maybe she's right. Maybe we should shorten our seminars to give attendees less time to think up stuff like this.

Decisional Roles

To move forward, projects demand that countless decisions be made, ranging from trivial to critical, at every phase of the project. When a decisional role is required, you'll need the expertise to do the following without alienating the people who may be affected by your choices:

- Distinguish between features and benefits.
- Appropriately allocate resources if a project falls behind schedule.
- Strike a balance between cost, time, and results.
- Prevent *scope creep* and budget "slippage" (when the money starts running out).

def•i•ni•tion

Scope creep is the process of adding work to a project, little by little, until the original schedule and cost estimates are completely meaningless.

The Other Business Management Roles

In addition to the roles already detailed, project managers will need all the general skills required of any competent business manager. Human resource management is one of the most critical requirements.

The Seven Traits of Good Project Managers

In addition to having knowledge of project management processes and an understanding of your various roles as a project manager and leader, research and experience point to seven additional traits that can help you become a successful project manager. The following figure shows these seven success traits, which we will discuss in more detail.

Trait 1: Enthusiasm for the Project

Good project managers want to do a good job. Your enthusiasm for the project will spread to other people on the team, making it easier to keep people motivated and involved.

As successful project managers gain experience, they develop these traits to make their work easier and more satisfying.

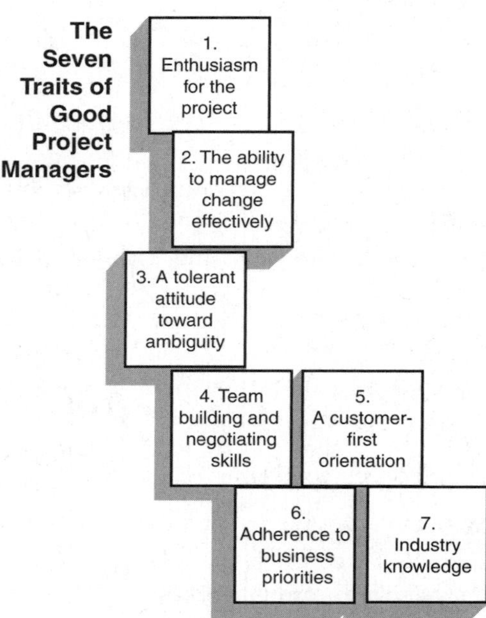

Trait 2: The Ability to Manage Change Effectively

Change is inevitable in projects. Customers change their minds about the end results. Managers decide to make changes to the scope of the project. Team members need to change their schedules. People who manage projects successfully learn to become managers of exceptions because surprises will occur, even in small projects.

Trait 3: A Tolerant Attitude Toward Ambiguity

Project managers often have ambiguous authority because people may have other bosses to report to during the project and may not consider you a manager (unless you earn their respect as a leader). In fact, many of the roles in large projects are not clear-cut.

Some of the team members may make more money or have more senior jobs than the project manager; customers may get involved as team members; other departments may have a stake in the project. A good project manager must feel comfortable with these ambiguous roles and expectations and must learn how to manage them to see the project to a successful conclusion. If you need clear authority and an absolute plan, your project management days are numbered.

Time Is Money

Talk to experienced project managers. They'll tell you (if they'll admit it) that at least one of their first projects was a dismal failure. If a project fails for you, don't kick yourself. Instead, pick up the pieces, learn from your mistakes, and move on.

Trait 4: Team-Building and Negotiating Skills

A project manager needs to build coalitions among the various stakeholders in a project: management, customers, the project team, and suppliers. Power is only granted to a project manager who builds these relationships. Project managers must negotiate authority to move the project forward, so the success of any project depends on the project manager's ability to build a strong team among internal and external players.

Trait 5: A Customer-First Orientation

In projects that involve customers or clients (and most do), a good project manager puts the customer first and understands the customer's perspective regarding the project. After all, the ultimate measure of the project's success is the customer's satisfaction with the results. In a partnership with a customer or client, a skilled project manager crafts a vision for the project that he can communicate to the rest of the project team. Through alliances, team building, and empathy with the customer or client, the project manager is ultimately able to turn changing expectations into satisfaction with the completed project.

Trait 6: Adherence to the Priorities of Business

Earlier we talked about the project's connection to the overall business strategy. You'll also hear this called a "bottom-line" orientation, but paying attention to the budget and costs is only part of the business equation. Other business priorities involve maintaining competitive advantage, integrating the project into the culture of the organization, managing stakeholder issues, and ensuring both productivity and excellence as the project proceeds. However the business connection is served up, never lose sight of it during the project. Make it your compass point that tells you that you are heading in the right direction.

Trait 7: Knowledge of the Industry or Technology

Even though most project management skills are industry-independent, as a project manager, you'll need to have both project management skills and some experience or specific knowledge relevant to the industry you're working in. For example, if you're managing software projects, you'll need experience with programming concepts. If you're managing the development of a new shopping mall, you'll need a background in construction. However, you don't need to be an expert in the field because you shouldn't be doing the work but rather managing it. We once worked with a project manager who insisted on supervising every move his project team made because he knew so much about the topic. However, he was actually a hindrance to the projects he managed because, for all practical purposes, he was doing everything himself!

> **Words from the Wise**
>
> The elevator to success is out of order. You'll have to use the stairs and climb one step at a time.
>
> —Joe Girard, listed in the *Guinness Book of Records* as the world's greatest salesman

Be the Best Leader You Can Be

Of course, project managers would be wise to develop other traits, such as written and verbal communication skills, computer literacy, and above all, dependability.

When you make a commitment to a stakeholder or team member, your reputation is at stake. Don't take that type of commitment lightly, or you will damage your credibility and put the entire project at risk.

If you work at being all the things we've talked about here, you'll reap the rewards of your labor with the help of project teams that respect your efforts as a leader. As a result, your projects will meet their goals more often than not. Remember our advice from Chapter 1: great project managers are made, not born!

The Least You Need to Know

- It is the responsibility of the project manager to lead and manage the project.
- There are key knowledge areas that you must be familiar with before starting a project.
- You need people skills, communication skills, business skills, and technical skills to be an effective project manager.
- There are seven traits that define the successful project manager.
- Being a good project manager takes ongoing, enthusiastic effort.

Chapter 3

The Rules of the Project Game

In This Chapter

- Universal project success criteria revisited
- The seven causes of project failure—and how to avoid them
- The 12 golden rules of project management success
- Simple ways to help you follow the rules for success

We know you're just chomping at the bit to get started managing your projects. But before you are convinced that project management is more about process than substance, you need to know that all the ingredients that make up the project management recipe for success boil down to only 12 rules.

All kinds of project managers responsible for all types of projects in diverse managerial and political environments have honed these 12 golden rules through years of experience. So whether your projects involve building spaceships or building ships in bottles, you'll get better results by following these rules from the project definition phase to the closing phase.

Universal Project Success Criteria

For almost all projects, success is defined as meeting these three criteria:

1. Finishing the project on schedule.
2. Keeping costs within budget.
3. Meeting quality outcomes (or goals) that have been agreed upon by the project team and the project stakeholders.

Quality may be difficult to define in some cases, but in project management, quality is always defined as meeting the requirements of the customer. If our project is to design a container that can hold an internal pressure of 500 pounds per square inch (psi), then a quality bottle will meet that expectation. A bottle will not meet the quality standard if it holds 400 psi or 600 psi.

Project Failure: The Reasons Are Simple

According to research done by the Project Management Institute, projects fail for seven key reasons; in addition, people can employ some basic strategies to avoid these problems. The problems and solutions are as follows:

- **Poor project and program management discipline.** To avoid this problem, develop a well-defined project plan using a proven methodology, and use project management tools to track and control your project.
- **Lack of executive-level support.** This is an all-too-frequent project killer. To avoid this problem, you must enlist executive leadership (we'll talk more about this in Chapter 4). Provide the executive team with regular communications, and constantly reinforce the need for their involvement at the appropriate times.
- **No linkage to the business strategy.** Provide a clear business direction that can be understood by everyone who is impacted by the project. Make sure everyone knows *why* this project is important, *what* it will mean when it is complete, and *how* you plan to implement that finished product.
- **The wrong team members.** Sometimes people are selected for a project because they "have the time." This should be the last criteria for choosing someone for the team. Pick the best players, and give their day-to-day workload to those who "have the time." If the right people aren't available, hire contractors or consultants who do have the knowledge and experience. You'll be glad you did!

- **No measures for evaluating the success of the project.** Too often, no one has determined exactly how the team will know if the project is a success. These measures should be contained in the business case for the project (we'll discuss the business case in Chapter 7). If you haven't been given those measures, then develop them yourself and get the project sponsor and the steering committee to agree to them before you get too far into the project plan.
- **Lack of a robust risk strategy.** All good projects have a well-defined risk plan. Identify as many potential risks as possible, and develop a plan for mitigating them.
- **Inability to manage change.** All too frequently the organization is simply not prepared to accept the changes a project might entail. For example, if the project is to install a new software system to capture orders and schedule delivery, you will likely meet with major resistance to this change. You will need to develop a robust communications and change management plan to get the organization ready to use the new system.

Words from the Wise

Most people think of success and failure as opposites, but they are actually both the products of the same process.
—From *A Whack on the Side of the Head,* by Roger von Oech (Warner Books, 1990)

People don't start a project hoping it will fail. Yet projects fail all too often because project managers disregard the 12 basic project management rules that can help them avoid the seven reasons for failure.

Twelve Golden Rules of Project Management Success

The 12 basic rules of project management define the focus you'll need to get things done on time, within budget, and to the expectations of the stakeholders. As you read this book, you'll see how project management techniques are designed to help project managers put the 12 golden rules into action over and over again.

In the sections that follow, we'll guide you to the chapters of this book that offer specific advice related to the rule being discussed. Of course, if you consistently break or ignore the rules of project management—regardless of your diligent use of our recommended charts, plans, and reports—you'll probably doom your project to failure anyway, or at least cause a lot of problems you otherwise might have avoided.

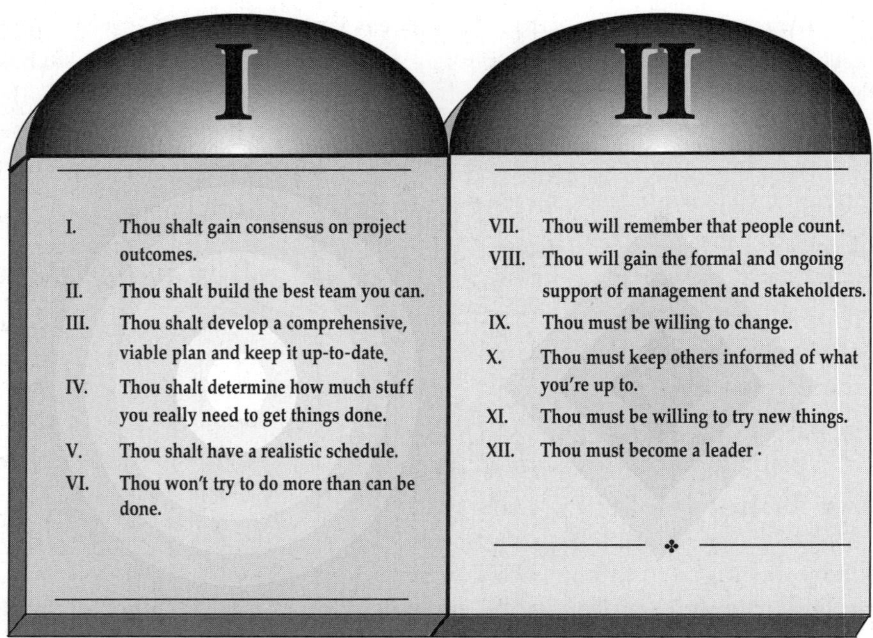

The 12 Rules of Project Management

You'd be wise to keep this list of rules in front of you throughout your projects.

Rule 1: Thou Shalt Gain Consensus on Project Outcomes

If you don't know what you intend to accomplish, you probably won't accomplish anything of value. A project without clear expectations is really just a bunch of work without a purpose. To be considered a success, a project must have clearly defined goals that specify the results the project is to achieve when it's finished.

However, to know exactly what you want to do is not enough. You also have to reach consensus with the stakeholders and team members on the project to make sure that the goals and expectations are the right ones. In Chapter 7, you'll learn how to set clear project goals and expectations, and you'll get tips for gaining the consensus required to ensure the project you finally finish is the project people wanted to get done.

Rule 2: Thou Shalt Build the Best Team You Can

A willing, skilled, appropriately organized project team is the key to success. You'll have to develop this group of people because the perfect team almost never starts out that way. A good team starts with good choices on your part; however, sometimes the people you pick may turn out to be total dummies or uncooperative blockheads.

Your challenge is to make sure the project team gets smart very quickly and stays ambitious in spite of inadequate experience and training, family problems, or conflicting priorities. If people must be trained to get things done right, that's one of your responsibilities as project manager. Of course, the people must also be willing to work on the project and learn new skills. That means you'll have to use your best management skills and motivational tactics to guide them in the right direction. (That's the direction you want them to go!)

Time Is Money

Review the 12 golden rules at least once a week and you'll have a much better chance of getting things done the right way, on time; within budget; and to the specifications agreed upon by customers, management, or other stakeholders. Of course, the schedule and budget may change over time, but as long as people agree on the changes, you're still getting things done the right way. A review of the rules will remind you of that.

Rule 3: Thou Shalt Develop a Comprehensive, Viable Plan and Keep It Up-to-Date

A complete, appropriately detailed project plan is central to successful completion of any project. The plan helps you guide the project. This document communicates the overall intentions, tasks, resource requirements, and schedule for the project. Without a plan, it's almost impossible to lead a group to achieve a common goal. You'll learn about creating the various parts of the project plan in Chapters 9 through 16.

Of course, creating a plan isn't enough. Because you can't see into the future any better than a fortune teller with a broken crystal ball, the plan you develop and get approved will probably change many times from project initiation to project completion. As you gain more information about the realities of the project, and as the stakeholders change their minds about what they need, your plan will have to be reevaluated. Be forewarned, if you don't update the project plan and negotiate these changes with the stakeholders, you will be responsible for the budget and schedule of the original plan (you'll hear about this again in Chapter 24).

Along the Critical Path

Think about all the really smart people who use project management techniques, develop detailed plans, and still seem to fail in getting projects done on time and within budget. Consider the project in Boston, Massachusetts, nicknamed "the Big Dig." Construction on the project began in late 1991, and it is still not completed as of this writing. Furthermore, there is considerable debate as to when, exactly, it will be finished. The project was designed to replace the six-lane highway called the Central Artery that runs through the center of downtown Boston with an underground expressway of eight to ten lanes. At the time of the project initiation, the budget was $11 billion and the project was scheduled to be completed before the end of the decade. That budget has grown to $14.6 billion. This project is similar in scale to the building of the Panama Canal or the English Channel Tunnel (dubbed the Chunnel). However, for the poor citizens of the Boston area, this has been an expensive, inconvenient project that must seem like it will take forever to finish.

Rule 4: Thou Shalt Determine How Much Stuff You Really Need to Get Things Done

No matter what your boss says, you can't squeeze blood from a turnip. Without adequate people, capital, and equipment to complete a project, there is no way can you make it happen. You must get sufficient resources allocated to the project, or you must renegotiate what can be done so that fewer resources are required (refer to Rule 1). In most companies, getting sufficient resources (including equipment, people, and supplies) for a project is an ongoing problem and one of the most important responsibilities for all project managers. In Chapter 15, you'll learn how to scope out what you really need to get a project done. In Chapter 24, you'll discover some techniques for negotiating when you don't get everything you need the first time around.

Words from the Wise

Time waits for no one, and nowhere is that more true than when managing a project.

—Project manager and project management instructor Jim MacIntyre

Rule 5: Thou Shalt Have a Realistic Schedule

Without a realistic schedule, you'll never succeed, and you'll run out of time before you get to try again. You may be able to bring more people on board and buy more supplies, but you can't produce more time no matter what you do. There's no faster way to lose credibility as a project manager than to change the schedule without a really good reason. Then again, if you follow Rules 1 and 8, you can get more time for yourself by getting a new schedule approved. In Chapters 11 and 12, you'll learn how to develop a schedule you can meet and how to change it when necessary.

Rule 6: Thou Won't Try to Do More Than Can Be Done

You must have an appropriate scope for the project. The scope of the project involves more than goals. For example, the goal could be to build a two-story building on the location of the back parking lot by next December. But the scope of the project could range from putting up a prefabricated metal building with a cement floor to building a miniature Taj Mahal for the chairman of the board. While the first scope is feasible, the second is not. Make sure the objectives and the scope of the project are clear to everyone if you want to be considered a success when the project is done. While *gold plating* the project might score you bonus points, don't make it one of your primary goals.

def•i•ni•tion

In project management jargon, doing more than the project requirements call for is called **gold plating** the project.

Rule 7: Thou Will Remember That People Count

Learning to work with people takes a lifetime, and in the end, you'll still be wondering how people really work. Even with all the good advice in this book, people will surprise you in mysterious and wonderful ways. That's what keeps project management interesting.

Sometimes, in focusing on the process of project management, you may forget that projects are mostly about people. Project success depends on people, not on reports or charts or even computers. To be a successful project manager, you must accommodate people's needs and priorities. People manage the project. People do most of the work. People enjoy (or curse) the end results. Projects also put stresses on these people because projects almost always involve new group structures, deadlines, and extra work. If a project's end results don't serve people, then the project has failed.

Another way of stating Rule 7 is this: Do no damage to the people on the project! Don't overwork the staff; don't demand the impossible; never lie to anyone even if it seems like a way out of a tight situation.

Projects almost always incorporate built-in priority conflicts between ordinary work and project work. The bad news is that you must eventually satisfy people's needs, priorities, and conflicts for the project to come to a happy ending. The good news is that, in Chapter 23, we'll show you some techniques to help you deal with the inevitable conflicts between the people and the priorities in your projects.

Rule 8: Thou Will Gain the Formal and Ongoing Support of Management and Stakeholders

It's obvious (or at least it should be) that you must have approval from management and the key stakeholders before you initiate a project. This involves not only communication skills but also negotiation skills. This rule is much like Rule 1, except that it means you must add a formal approval stage to the general consensus you gained in keeping Rule 1. You need to get everyone who has to contribute resources (time or money) or who may be impacted by a project (if it will change his job or life) to formally endorse your project and to agree that the project is worth doing. You also need to get formal agreement from the stakeholders on some basic rules for dealing with issues of authority, changes in project scope, and the handling of basic communications.

For many of the stakeholders, support requires signed approval, but it doesn't stop with a signature. Keeping this rule also demands that you ensure the stakeholders' ongoing interest in your project. If you start a project for your boss who has no real interest in the project even after he has signed on the dotted line, it's unlikely you'll get any praise for finishing the feat. Remember to review Chapters 6, 23, and 24 whenever support wanes for your projects.

Rule 9: Thou Must Be Willing to Change

This rule goes along with Rule 3. You must be willing to adapt the project plan and implementation to guide the project where it needs to go. Sometimes things change for justifiable reasons, such as a rainstorm that stops the work on a construction project. Sometimes things change because you get new information—like when researchers in Utah discovered cold fusion in a test tube, which changed the whole perspective on building fusion reactors and, for a while at least, stopped projects worldwide. As one researcher put it, "It was like we were trying to invent the biplane and someone shows us up with a 747." Sometimes changes are simply the result of peoples' whims, like the advertising agency's customer who now wants a

> **Words from the Wise**
>
> Graham's Law: If they know nothing of what you are doing, they suspect you are doing nothing.
>
> —*Understanding Project Management,* by Robert J. Graham (Jossey-Bass, 2001)

TV commercial instead of a brochure to promote his new product, even though the brochure is almost ready to go to the printer.

You'll also learn in Chapter 24 that change is an important part of controlling a project. The main thing to remember here is that it is *not* the project manager's job to say "no" to a change. Rather, it is her job to inform the stakeholders of the impact the change will have on the time, cost, and quality of the project and to let them make the decision about the change.

Rule 10: Thou Must Keep Others Informed of What You're Up To

You must keep all the relevant stakeholders informed of your progress, problems, and changes. The way to obey this rule is simple: communicate, communicate, communicate. As things change on the project (and they always do), you'll find through your communications that the stakeholders may want or need to introduce their own changes into the project. You'll find several specific techniques for communication in Chapter 21. While adhering to Rule 10, you'll have to refer frequently to Rule 9.

Rule 11: Thou Must Be Willing to Try New Things

Because every project is different, with different people, goals, and challenges involved, using the exact same methods, software, charts, graphs, or other aids on every project would simply be inappropriate. You can use the standard methods and tools with all projects, but not all projects involve the same risk or complexity. Thus, not all the techniques in this book should be used on all projects.

Large, complex projects will likely use more methods or tools than smaller projects. Too many methods *or* too few tools can doom a project. You must adapt the processes, technologies, tools, and techniques to the needs of the project at hand. For example, you would obviously need to put more detail into the network diagram (see Chapter 10 for more on these) for building a new corporate headquarters from scratch than you would for setting up a new sales office in a rented building.

Rule 12: Thou Must Become a Leader

Leadership is an art that comes naturally to some, but the rest of us have to work at it. Chances are, you have to work on your leadership role, too. Reading management books won't be enough to bring your projects in on time and within budget. As a project manager, you must put what you read into action. You need to become a leader as well as a team member. You must not only plan, track, and control the project, you must also be a source of wisdom and motivation for the team members and stakeholders. Without leadership, even a well-coordinated project can fail to meet its goals if people in the project don't feel they have the support or guidance they need to make things happen. That's your job as the project manager. Chapter 2 details the skills and traits of a good project manager, and Chapter 18 will expand on leadership.

Keep Your Eyes on the Prize

Projects help further personal goals as well as those of companies and organizations. If you keep the 12 golden rules of project management in front of you throughout the project phases, you can minimize if not eliminate project failures.

Yes, sometimes fate plays a role, and you can't do everything to everyone's satisfaction. But if you remember the 12 golden rules throughout the five phases of the project management process, you'll succeed more times than you fail. Keep working at it. The prize for your effort will be projects done on time, within budget, and with less stress on mind and body.

The Least You Need to Know

- When projects fail, it is usually due to one or more identifiable reasons.
- Follow the 12 golden rules of project management to help guide projects of all sizes and complexity to more successful conclusions.
- Your first loyalty is to your project even though you may be pressured from all sides for change.
- Keep a list of the 12 golden rules of project management on your desk or, better yet, put the list on your office wall to keep you focused on the success factors during the tough times of a project.
- Remember that the success of a project always depends more on people than on process, but our processes and structures are important in helping people stay on track.

Chapter 4

The Nine Knowledge Areas of Project Management

In This Chapter

- The nine knowledge areas
- The core knowledge areas
- The support knowledge areas
- Project time management and the triple constraints—time, cost, and quality
- The importance of integrating all knowledge areas

Based on their best practice research on projects worldwide, the Project Management Institute (PMI) has established a guide for *project managing* called *A Guide to the Project Management Body of Knowledge* or PMBOK (pronounced *pim bock*). In the PMBOK, PMI has defined the fundamental areas a project manager should address during the course of a project. We introduce each of these nine knowledge areas in this chapter and will elaborate on each of them in the chapters that follow.

The PMBOK is important for many reasons. First, the definitions given in the PMBOK are used universally in the project management field. As we all know, using the right terms identifies us immediately as insiders within

def•i•ni•tion

PMI defines **project management** as the application of knowledge, skills, tools, and techniques to project activities to meet project requirements.

a given community, and the project management field is no different. Second, although much of the material in the PMBOK is theoretical (unlike this book, which we designed to be much more practical), its framework is still very useful for planning and managing projects. It provides a comprehensive picture of what a project manager should be working to achieve as he or she delivers a project.

1. Project Integration Management

As you read in Chapter 1, all projects are meant to address some business need. Otherwise, it would not have been approved in the first place. When the project begins, you will have several people working on a variety of things, often at the same time and only occasionally together.

Eventually, someone will have to bring all this work together in a coherent way, and that is the job of the project manager. In many ways, the project manager can be described as the conductor of an orchestra. Many different types of instruments are playing music at the same time. However, everyone in the orchestra is watching the conductor for his cues, which keep the musicians together to produce the beautiful sounds. So, think of yourself as the conductor! You will need to make sure all the work fits together to produce the results that were promised by the project in its business case.

Finally, when the project is complete (successfully!), the product or service produced by the project will need to be integrated into the company's ongoing operations. That will be your job, too! (We'll cover that in Chapter 23.)

Integration Management as Part of Planning

Much of the work around successful project management is planning your project. The next part of the book covers planning in detail. Your planning will consider how the people in the team will work together, particularly where coordination is concerned. For example, often team members will require information from other people, some inside the project team and others outside the team, to complete their work. Planning for this type of integration will be important as you develop your plans.

Words from the Wise

Luck is a matter of preparation meeting opportunity.

—Oprah Winfrey, TV personality and humanitarian

Integration Management During Project Execution

Here the focus changes from planning to managing the processes. During project execution, the project manager works to ensure that the product or service the project will produce will be acceptable to the customers by carefully managing the written plan and following the outlined procedures.

One of the key procedures, which we will present in Chapter 20, is the Work Authorization System, a formal process for approving project work that makes sure the right work is being done at the right time in the right way. The other key is maintaining a control system that is visible through a reporting system that identifies the status of the project.

Integration Management of Project Changes

During the course of a project, things will always change. A project manager's job is not to prevent change, but to manage it effectively. In Chapter 24, you will see how to manage changes by pulling together a change control plan.

Sometimes you can almost predict which changes will be requested. In those situations, the process you put into place will become a lifesaver and a face-saver. You will need to include specific steps, one of which will be an impact analysis of the change on the project.

Finally, when you do follow the process, the last step will be to revise your project plan. The new plan will reflect the change and the corrections to schedule and budget. You will also need to keep a record of changes made so you can document them at the conclusion of the project.

Words from the Wise

Most bold change is the result of a hundred thousand tiny changes that culminate in a bold product or procedures or structure.

—Tom Peters, author and business guru

2. Project Scope Management

During the project, managing the scope of the project will be extremely important, as one of the leading causes of project failure is the problem of "scope creep," when the project keeps getting bigger and more complex.

One of the first planning exercises in any project will be to define the project scope. You will need to clarify what is included in the project, as well as what is *not* included in the project. Project managers can get into trouble if they make assumptions about what is not included in the project but never confirm those assumptions.

It is good practice to write a clear, definitive scope statement and to have your sponsor and the key customers review it. If any adjustments need to be made, it is best to know that earlier rather than later.

During the planning phase, you begin to define the scope in great detail as you plan for all the tasks that will need to be completed to finish the project.

When you finish the project, you will want to verify that you have indeed completed the scope and your sponsor and your key customers accept it as completed. (See Chapter 6 for more on the role of the project sponsor.)

3. Project Time Management

Many people often refer to project management as a detailed time management exercise. However, time is only one component you must control during a project. Time management is one of three elements referred to as the triple constraints (the other two are cost and quality, which are coming up soon!).

Sometimes time management, as defined by the project schedule, is the key driver for a project. For example, if you are developing a new product, time may be of the essence since there is always the fear a competitor will move into the market ahead of you. On other occasions, time is important but not the key driver. For example, we had a customer for a software installation state he was willing to sacrifice the schedule if the software worked when we finished. In other words, quality was more important to him, and he was willing to make some concessions on schedule.

Just remember, even if time is not the key driver, extending the time on a project usually means costs will also increase.

Time and the Schedule

In simple terms, you manage time during a project if you develop an accurate schedule and manage the project to that schedule. You may also set *milestones* for your project as a way to track how well you are doing in meeting the schedule.

def•i•ni•tion

A **milestone** is a clearly definable point in a project that summarizes the completion of a related or important set of activities. Milestones are often used to summarize important events in a project and help key customers keep track of the project when they don't want to know all the details.

Controlling the Schedule During Execution

You will spend important time developing and establishing the schedule for completing that work. However, all that time and effort will go to waste if you don't manage the time your team uses as they execute the work. Most project managers use a baseline schedule as a way to manage the time. By comparing the way the schedule is progressing versus the baseline schedule, the project manager can see trends and make course corrections before things get out of hand.

4. Project Cost Management

One of the key questions a project manager is always addressing is "So, how are you doing against the budget?" You will always be asked to report how much money you are spending to complete the project.

Financial Issues Outside of Your Control

There are times when the project manager can't control all the factors that influence his or her project. For example, a project manager in Houston budgeted a certain amount of money for renting generators as part of the project plan. Then a series of hurricanes hit (Katrina and Rita), and all the generators became much more expensive to rent (if they could even find any). You should build contingency funds into the budget, but be careful you don't burn that money up too fast. As any manager knows, asking senior management for more money is never fun!

Competing for Funds with Other Projects

Most companies have a limited amount of funds to invest, in projects and other investments, such as new equipment. Remember that you are always in competition with these other initiatives for money. If you need more money, you will need to make the case because you may be taking money from another project or initiative. And if your project is perceived as not being well managed, don't be surprised if your budget shrinks unexpectedly.

5. Project Quality Management

Quality is a key component in any project. We have all seen projects that were completed but the results were disappointing because the quality of the product or service was poor.

The processes for quality in a project are:

- Planning to determine what the quality objectives need to be and how you are going to achieve them.
- Enforcing quality assurance to measure that the project is producing against the requirements.
- Checking quality control to ensure quality standards are met and that any deviations are identified and corrected.

As you will see in Chapter 25, defining the scope of your project correctly is *the* key ingredient in developing a quality plan. We will give you several ideas for managing quality.

6. Project Human Resource Management

In a large project, and even some smaller projects, managing human resources over the course of the project will be one of the most important aspects of a successful project. If you think about it, this makes sense. People do all the work on the project, whether they are under your direct control (as part of the project team itself) or not (as contract labor or workers for one of your vendors). We devote Chapter 6 to stakeholders of your project, and there you will recognize the broad impact people will have on your project.

Organizational Planning

Depending on the size of your project, you will probably want to develop an organizational chart that shows who reports to whom and the teams or groups that sit in across the project. A chart will certainly help clarify reporting relationships, and you will begin to have some vision on the span of control your different team leaders have to contend with.

You will also want to clarify role definitions for the team since you will often be "borrowing" people from operations to fill out part of your project team. These people will have a clear understanding of their role as part of their department or function, but that same intuitive clarity may not be there for the project. And you may need to think about how you will do performance appraisals for a project team. That brings us to where and how you get the people to staff your project.

Staff Acquisition

Getting the people you need will always be a challenge—as will keeping them for the duration of a long project. In Chapter 14, we show you how to think through the type of people you want (their skills, knowledge, and experience), but you also need to understand how to acquire them. To do this, you need to be familiar with the procurement policies and procedures within your company. If you want to hire consultants, for example, you need to know how to make that happen within the time frame you have available (see "Project Procurement Management" later in this chapter).

Making Them a Team

Finally, as part of your human resources management for the project, you'll need to mold this group of people into a team. You will want to consider both broad topics, such as operating procedures within the team, and details, such as the seating chart and who you want to sit next to whom and why it may help promote teamwork.

7. Project Communications Management

Communication is a key success factor in all projects. You can predict how successful a project will be by assessing how well the project team members communicate and how well the project manager communicates with the key stakeholders. If strong communication is evident, you can be sure that success will follow, and poor communications will almost always lead to a failed project. The Project Management Institute has determined that over 89 percent of a project manager's time may be spent in various forms of communication, from meetings to e-mails and progress reports. In Chapter 21, we tell you how to build a communications plan that will help you with this important aspect of project management.

8. Project Risk Management

Many people think project management is all about managing risks, and risk management is one of the key areas of focus for a project manager. While you will never be able to control everything around your projects, using a strong project management methodology, whether from PMI or *PRINCE2*, will help you manage risks effectively.

> **def•i•ni•tion**
>
> PRINCE2 was originally developed by the British government as a way to handle their large information technology projects. Many companies in the UK have since adopted it as their methodology of choice. The official website is www.ogc.uk/prince2/.

In handling risks, you must think about what may go wrong during a project and develop a strategy to either prevent it from happening at all or reduce the negative impact on the project if it does happen. We identify risks and give you tips on how to address them in Chapter 8.

9. Project Procurement Management

Almost all projects will need goods or services from outside the company. This usually includes negotiating contracts and payment schedules and can potentially involve locations all over the world. So you must know how to get the help you need to buy necessary materials. If you have a procurement department in your company, start talking to them as soon as you begin planning your project. You will want to develop a good relationship with them so they can assist you through some of the more difficult procurement aspects.

> **Time Is Money**
>
> PMI has a professional designation, the Project Management Professional (PMP), for those who have the right experience and knowledge and can pass the test on the information contained in the PMBOK.

Debates will always arise about whether it is cheaper to make or buy a product and whether to use an inside source for a service or go outside to get it. There are no easy answers to these questions. As you plan your project, you will want to do a cost-benefit analysis of the options available to you and decide which one makes sense in light of your budget and schedule.

The Least You Need to Know

- As a project manager, you will be expected to manage the time, costs, scope, and quality of the work.
- To manage a project effectively, you will need to manage risks, people, communications, and procurement.
- To be a successful project manager, you will be expected to integrate all the knowledge areas.
- Become familiar with *A Guide to the Project Management Body of Knowledge* (PMBOK).

Chapter 5

Starting Off on the Right Foot

In This Chapter

- Learning the project life cycle
- Differences between a project life cycle and a product life cycle
- The All-Star Cable case study
- Project life cycle phase one: defining your project

No matter how big or how small a project is, the simple fact is that as a project manager you are operating within a larger context. That context is the environment and styles that exist within the organization where you work. Any project manager who doesn't recognize how significant these things can be is in for a rude awakening. In this chapter, we'll take a look at how to organize the project and factor in the environment, too!

The Project Life Cycle

We can break all projects into distinct phases. Taken together, these phases comprise the project life cycle.

Since every project is unique by definition, each has a large degree of uncertainty associated with it. Remember you are creating something that has never existed before. One of the techniques that can help us develop our project plans effectively is to use the project life cycle as a guide.

Project Phases and the Project Life Cycle

Four phases define the project life cycle, as you can see from the following diagram. Normally, each phase of the project will be terminated by a *stage gate*. We have labeled the four phases according to what occurs in them:

> **def•i•ni•tion**
>
> The conclusion of a project phase is generally marked by a review of both key deliverables and project performance to date, to determine if the project should continue. These phase-end reviews are usually called **stage gates**.

- **Phase 1: Project Definition Phase.** This phase of the project defines what the project will attempt to accomplish when it is finished.
- **Phase 2: Project Planning Phase.** In its simplest form, during this phase the project manager and key project team members are planning all the work they must finish to make the project successful.
- **Phase 3: Project Execution Phase.** During this phase, the greatest amount of effort, time, and money are expended to complete all the activities defined during the planning phase.
- **Phase 4: Project Close-Out Phase.** After a project has been successfully completed, the project manager and sometimes key team members capture what they have learned and complete all the administrative tasks that officially end the project.

> **def•i•ni•tion**
>
> The **deliverable** for each project phase is a tangible, measurable, or concrete result that must be produced as part of a project.

In each phase, a *deliverable* marks the end of the current phase and gives the project manager authority to continue. To better understand the project life cycle, let's take a look at our primary case study. Once we've introduced it, we can use it to follow through the four phases of the project life cycle.

① **Project Definition Phase**

- Initiate the project
- Identify Project Manager
- Identify initial project concept
- Develop Project Charter
  - Describe Project Strategy
    - Establish Initial Direction
    - High-level Project Outcomes
    - Project Guiding Principles
  - Define Project:
    - Refine Project Concept
    - Concept Scope Planning
    - Strategic Plan Fit
    - Business Rationale
    - Opportunities/Benefits
    - High level risks
- Conduct Feasibility Study
- Define Planning Phase Schedule & Budget
  - Identify Planning Team Members
  - Determine contracts, as needed
- Deliver Project Charter Memorandum to Decision Authority

② **Project Planning Phase**

- Organize and Staff Project
- Develop Project Plan
  - Finalize Scope Definition
    - Project objectives
    - Project requirements and specifications
  - Develop Work Breakdown Structure (WBS)
    - Identify work activities required
  - Develop Organizational Breakdown Structure
    - Match project work activities and performing organization
  - Project Scheduling and Cost Estimating
    - Identify activity dependencies
    - Sequence activities
    - Develop Project Schedule
    - Estimate costs
    - Develop budget/funding profile
    - Determine scheduled start dates
    - Set project milestones
    - Establish measurement baselines for schedule and cost performance (project metrics)
  - Originate Subsidiary Management Plans
    - Risk Plan
    - Project Change Control Plan
    - Issues Resolution Plan
    - Quality Assurance Plan
    - Organization and Human Resources Plan
    - Procurement Plan
    - Monitoring and Reporting Plan
  - Develop Organization Transition Plan
    - Project Communications Plan
    - Change Leadership Plan
- Deliver Project Plan Memorandum to Decision Authority

③ **Project Execution Phase**

- Execute Project Plan
  - Manage the project scope
  - Monitor and report project status
- Manage Project Plan
  - Execute and refine management plans:
    - Risk Plan
    - Quality Assurance Plan
    - Project Change Control Plan
    - Issue Resolution Plan
    - Organization & HR Plan
    - Procurement Plan
  - Activate Project Controls
    - Scope - Cost - Schedule - Quality
  - Maintain Project Plan:
    - Incorporate Lessons Learned.
    - Add approved Scope Changes
- Implement Project Results
  - Verify Scope Completion
  - Execute Organizational Transition Plan
  - Transition to operations
- Deliver Project Completion Memorandum to Decision Authority

④ **Project Close-Out Phase**

- Document Project Lessons Learned
- Schedule After-implementation Review
- Provide performance feedback
- Close-out contracts (as needed)
- Complete administrative close-out
- Deliver Project Completion Report to Decision Authority

The four phases of the project life cycle. Note the deliverable at the end of each phase.

Project Life Cycle versus Product Life Cycle

As you can see from the following two diagrams, a distinct difference exists between a project life cycle and a product life cycle. In a product life cycle, there is a natural progression from the introduction of a new product as it goes through growth and maturity and into decline. In a project life cycle, you can see the majority of the money and time is spent during the execution phase of the project. As we go through the following chapters, you will see why that is the case.

The classic model of a product life cycle.

Product Life Cycles

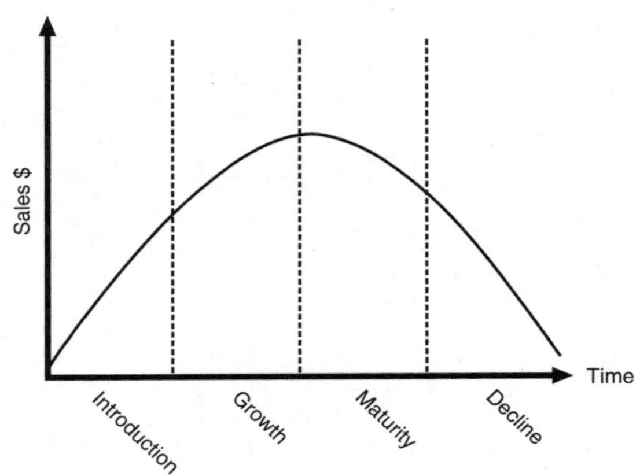

There are four phases in the project, and it takes time and money to accomplish each phase.

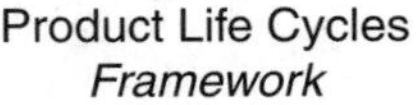

- Four Phases of a Project:
  - Definition
  - Planning
  - Execution and Control
  - Close-out

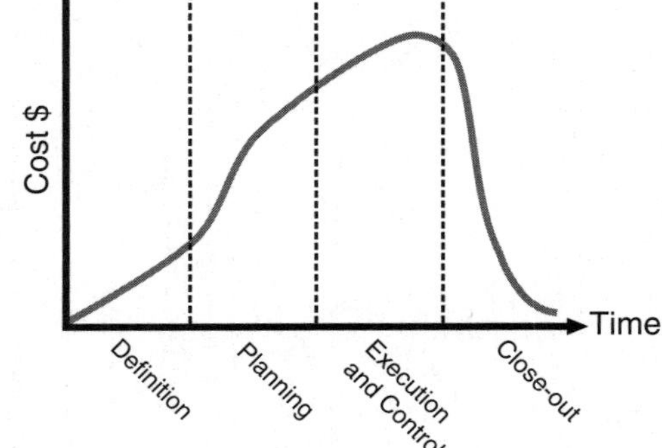

A Case Study: All-Star Cable

All-Star Cable is a 30-year-old company that originated in South Texas. It began as a basic cable company offering standard television channels but with better, more consistent transmissions than traditional reception methods. As a result of deregulation of the industry, it was able to take advantage of larger companies' equipment and lines. It was an excellent business that grew rapidly because it offered great, simple service at a better price than the larger companies. All-Star prided itself on being a small company that could respond very quickly to customers, both in problem resolution and installations.

In the mid-1980s, All-Star realized its growth had virtually stopped and it was starting to lose established customers. But the company was slow to respond to this trend. So by the time managers studied the market and their customer base, All-Star was almost bankrupt. Its problems centered on a few key issues:

- Its customer base was doing better economically and wanted more options than All-Star could offer.
- It was perceived as the "cheap" company, the one you went to when you couldn't afford anything else.
- Its competitors had geared their sales efforts to tiered offerings that attracted the same customer base All-Star previously had relied on.

All-Star hired a marketing manager and an information technology manager, who remapped company strategy and operations and developed new product offerings that turned the company around. The company contracted with premium channel companies to offer their subscribers HBO, Showtime, ESPN Sports, and a host of packages that customers were seeking. By reducing standard margins, they were able to offer these options at a cost below the larger companies, thinking that volume business would offset their declining customer base. It started working immediately.

In addition, the information technology (IT) manager was able to automate the company's billing system and office functions, allowing All-Star to run its business operations more efficiently and cheaply. Its fortunes rose, and All-Star was soon regarded as the "best deal" company. The marketing manager and IT manager were promoted to vice presidents.

Within a few years, managers at All-Star saw Pay-for-View as the coming attraction. The company invested in new equipment, upgraded current equipment, and expanded its IT department. It took a while to become efficient and have customers start using the service. The marketing VP took aggressive action, and revenues and profitability increased. This was the first service All-Star offered that it didn't have to discount to be competitive. Its customer base grew to the point that it was no longer the small competitor. It had become one of the largest cable companies in South Texas and was expanding its market further.

The Project

Now All-Star has identified Movies-on-Demand as the new direction for the company to take. Movies-on-Demand (MOD) is a revolutionary concept. Whereas Pay-for-View allows a viewer to key a code into his controller box to "turn on" a movie that is being broadcast globally, MOD allows a customer to view menus of movies, pick the movie he wants to watch, and watch it at a time he designates.

These movies will be stored digitally in a data warehouse owned by All-Star. And customers will be able to sift through menus that list movies by title, actor/actress, or genre, then drill down to the specific movie they want to order.

The marketing director and the company president believe that their MOD service will make All-Star an industry leader. They have suffered through the pains of catching up in a market, and they've seen the benefits of delivering new products. This time, they have an idea that is a conglomeration of ideas from nationwide cable companies. But not everyone in the company agrees with this vision. They are concerned about their internal IT capability to develop it, and they're very concerned about development costs.

The current system allows customers to access their billing information, make traditional pay-for-view movie selections, and access the Internet using their All-Star controller box. The controller box will also be the access device to the new menu-driven selections.

The billing system will require modification to include the cost to the customer of viewing these digitally stored movies. Menus will have to be built. The anticipated cost of viewing any single movie will be $6.00. No discount is planned for customers who order large numbers of movies.

The Project Manager (That's You)

The president and marketing director have introduced the concept to you, the project manager. They want you to find out how feasible the concept is and to determine what this project might cost to rollout. After acceptance by the board of directors, the project will start. Unfortunately, the president and marketing director have established a go-live date of six months from now.

Next week you will be presenting the concept to the board of directors. While you have come to believe that this move is essential to the company's growth and long-term survival, you have many concerns. These concerns are based on the fact that you don't have a lot of information you feel you need. You are feeling the pressure of "carrying the ball" on this project, without all the information you'd like, with a specific time deadline. It's time to start planning this project and getting ready for the board of directors' presentation.

Time Is Money

According to the Project Management Institute (PMI), project managers must conduct a feasibility study in the Project Definition Phase that will provide some evidence that the project can be successful. In a feasibility study, project managers should evaluate the alternative solutions along with the associated costs and benefits. The objective is to provide predictable results for a specific project. (See Chapter 7 for details.)

Project Definition Phase

For the All-Star Cable project to make Movies-on-Demand a reality, you, the project manager, will now be responsible for defining the project. The first thing you'll need to do is make sure you understand what the project is about and whether or not it can even be done! You will need to interview key people, some of whom will be stakeholders but others who may be experts in information systems, to see if it will be possible to deliver movies through All-Star's cable system using the existing cable boxes that customers already have. You will need to interview the president and vice president of marketing to find out if All-Star is going to offer "adult" videos as part of the selection that its customers can order. As you and your project team continue to work on the project, you will undoubtedly come up with more questions that you will need to research or ask others about.

At the same time, you need to think about the various risks involved in this project. While you can't anticipate all of them, you can certainly think of some. For example, what if you miss your schedule and another competitor introduces the idea first? *Remember, this has never been done before* and, therefore, it is, by definition, a project. Essentially, at this point, you are trying to build a case that allows the board of directors to decide if they should go ahead with the project or drop the idea right now before they spend any more money.

Time Is Money

As part of the project definition phase, you will need to …

- Identify the basic idea behind the project.
- Develop a project charter that defines what the project will include and what it will not include.
- Conduct a feasibility study to see if it's even possible.
- Plan a preliminary budget and schedule for delivery.

The definition phase of the project moves from the space where you don't know what you will do or how you will do it, to the space where you have defined what you will do. In the planning phase of the project, you will move to the space where you know what you will do to how you will do it. During the execution phase, you move the project into the space where the solution resides.

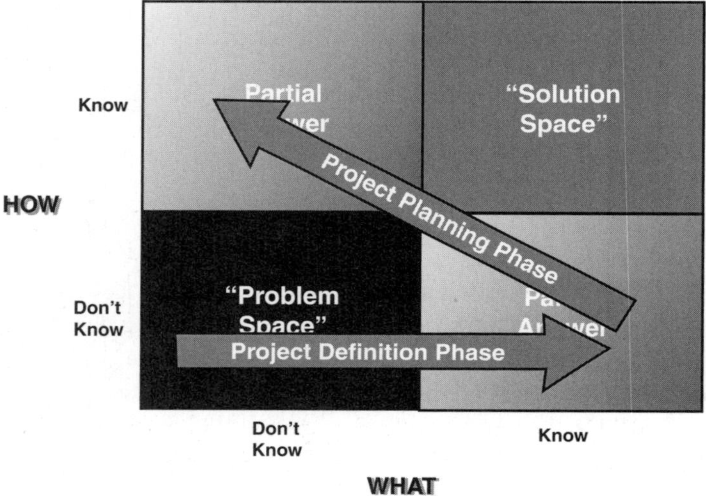

Preparing the Leadership

For any project manager to be successful on a project that will change the way the business will operate, the manager will need to get the leadership of the organization involved. The Project Management Institute has done several studies on the success factors involved in executing a successful project. Nearly all these studies have concluded that management leadership and support are critical success factors. Why? Because people respond to the agenda their "boss" feels is important. And how do they determine what is important to their boss? They notice what he talks about and pays attention to on a day-to-day basis. If you consider your own situation, you probably use this primary technique as well.

How Involved Should the Leadership Be?

While the leadership team will seldom have the time to be "in on the details" concerning the project, the project manager needs to develop specific roles and responsibilities for them. The manager must make clear to the leadership team that at certain times during the project, he or she will call upon them to deliver. Our experience has been that leaders are more than willing to participate if they understand how they can contribute and why. For example, if you need a leader to deliver an important message to the organization, he or she should be willing to do that. However, this will usually mean that you, or someone from the project team, will craft the message the executive will deliver.

Risk Management

In most cases the leader will want to review and edit the message so that it sounds more like the way he would deliver it. There's nothing wrong with that, as long as the basic message stays intact. If he begins to edit it in such a way that it loses the core message, you may need to do a better job of explaining what you are trying to accomplish with the message and educate him on the risks and possible consequences if the message is not delivered as you developed it.

If a communication specialist within the project team developed the message, you may need to get her involved in the conversation as well because she may have a better chance of explaining her words and approach than you do.

Also, many project managers deal with multiple layers of management during the course of planning and executing their projects. Mid-level managers are notoriously difficult to deal with at in times of change. Navigating these political waters may require the help of the senior executives, who can assist as various issues occur during the project.

For example, in one project we worked on, an issue arose about how we would handle a customer's request for special orders. The sales department wanted the order filled quickly and efficiently to meet the customer's need and build goodwill by showing excellent responsiveness to the requests. However, the shipping department insisted the right paperwork be completed within the existing policies before they would authorize and ship the order. Clearly, we needed to resolve this conflict. As we explained to the leadership team, the project team could deliver either solution, but we needed their help to know which way to go. This kind of decision is inappropriate for the project team to make without direction. The leadership team needed to help us resolve this type of situation.

Also Focus on the Project Team

Now that you have some idea of *what* you are going to do, you need to begin to think about *how* you will do it and with *whom*. In other words, you need to start thinking about the people you'll need who can do the work and make Movies-on-Demand a reality. You will need to consider people's technical skills, perhaps the experience they have in the industry or within the company, and determine if you will need resources not available inside the company, such as consultants or contractors. We'll take a closer look at the people involved on projects in Chapters 5 and 6.

The Least You Need to Know

- Since you are working on something that is new and unique, use the project life cycle to get organized.
- Deliverables are part of every project phase and determine whether you can move on to the next phase or not.
- Fully understanding the project and beginning to define it is a critical step to success.
- You will need to know the difference between a project life cycle and a product life cycle to properly define the project.
- Get the leadership team involved at the early stages so they are ready to act when you need them.

Part 2

The Project Definition Phase

You may think it's easy to get a project started, but starting a project off right takes some hard thinking and involves some tough decisions.

First, you need to identify who the players are; these people are the stakeholders who'll help you define the project. Next, you begin the tough process of defining what to include and what not to include in the project you have been assigned. After that, you need to define the specific goals for your project and identify all the risks and constraints that may cause problems for the project once you get it started. You'll then need to create and get approval for a project charter or statement of work, which defines the project you're going to plan and the rules by which you're going to play.

Chapter 6

Identifying Stakeholders and Defining Their Roles

In This Chapter

- Identifying key project stakeholders
- The roles of project stakeholders
- Learning to work together with the stakeholders
- Communicating and managing the expectations of key stakeholders
- A stakeholder questionnaire

Always remember that projects are successful when the stakeholders on the project are satisfied. Thus, identifying a complete list of stakeholders must be the first step in getting your project moving and should be an ongoing responsibility throughout the project. Some stakeholders will be key stakeholders and they will make many of the important decisions during the project. In this chapter, we'll tell you how to identify the key stakeholders—those people who, as you proceed, will have the greatest influence and authority in defining and planning your project.

Start by Identifying the Stakeholders

The first *stakeholders* you need to identify are those who will make a meaningful contribution to a project. Thus, the stakeholder list includes:

- Your project sponsor
- The managers in your company involved with approvals
- The customer
- The project team

def•i•ni•tion

A **stakeholder** is someone who has a vested interest in the success of a project. The Project Management Institute identifies stakeholders as individuals and organizations who are actively involved in the project or whose interests may be positively or negatively affected as a result of project execution or successful project completion.

There may be other stakeholders, as well. For example, when the project involves building a chemical plant, government regulators at the local, state, and national levels are stakeholders. Environmental action groups, community and neighborhood groups, labor unions, and a variety of other groups might also be stakeholders.

Key Stakeholders and Their Contributions

Sponsor (may be a customer representative or functional partnership manager)	Provides authority for project to proceed; guides and monitors the project together with the project manager; key organizational advocate for the project. Typically, the sponsor will approve the project charter.
Core Project Team	Provides skills, expertise, and effort to perform the tasks defined for the project; assists with planning and estimating project tasks.
Customer (may be internal or external)	The individual or organization that will use product created by the project. Establishes the requirements for the project; provides funding; reviews the project as milestones and deliverables are met. Ultimately accepts the finished product.
Functional Managers	Establish company policy; provide people; some will provide review and approval authority.

Organizational Stockholders

Potential stakeholders for any project.

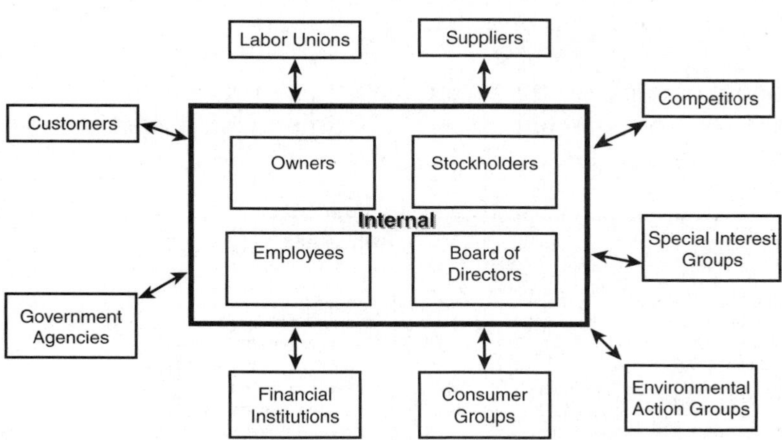

Sometimes the roles of various stakeholders will overlap, such as when an engineering firm provides the financing for a plant it is designing.

Your job is to manage the stakeholders by keeping them informed of any key decisions that are made. You must also communicate with them regularly on the status of the project. As a rule of thumb, stakeholders should never be surprised by any key decisions or project status. However, not every customer representative or manager in the company is or should be considered a stakeholder.

Each stakeholder might have his or her own objectives for the project, and that can often lead to conflicts of interest. For example, the line manager of a department may request a new management information system and want it at the lowest possible cost. However, the vendor of that system is interested in maximizing his profit, and the manager of the information technology department is mainly interested in emphasizing technical compatibility and reliability.

Words from the Wise

He enunciated no rules for success but offered a sure formula for failure: Just try to please everyone.

—E. J. Kahn Jr., developer of Wikipedia, an online encyclopedia

The Customer

The customer is the person or organization who will use the product or service delivered by the project. In some cases the customer may be a department or division of your own company. In other cases, the customer is external. In either case, the customer contributes both funding and project requirements. When defining the customer stakeholders, remember to distinguish between the people with final authority for project approvals and changes and those who you must simply keep informed.

Stakeholder	Roles	Approvals
Project Manager: Joel Baker	Defines, plans, controls, monitors, and leads the project.	Makes recommendations for approval; signature authority for any purchase under $1,500.
Sponsor: Joe Macdonald, Director of Engineering	Authority for most operational project decisions; helps guide the project; assists project manager with planning and approvals by other stakeholders.	Approves personnel requests and hiring decisions; signs off on SOW and project plans before submitting to the customer; signature authority for any purchase under $15,000.
Customer: Managers Sarah Goodwin, Vice President Fred Catwalk, Director of Finance	Helps define the project; authority for all major project plans and changes; budget approvals.	Final approval for SOW and all project plans; initial budget approval; signatures required for any nonplanned purchase of $5,000 or more.
Customer: Experts Allen Strange Jell Elsewhere	Experts who help define the project and develop product specifications.	Works with project manager and team; makes recommendations; not formal signature authorities.

A simple chart like this can help you identify the roles and authorities of the key stakeholders on your project.

The Project Sponsor

The project sponsor is your most important ally in the project; this person shares responsibility for project success and helps everyone on the project team be successful. The sponsor usually has the title of sponsor, but it's important that you identify the person who has this role. If the project is internal to your organization, usually a senior manager within the organization is the sponsor. If the project is for an external customer, the sponsor is usually someone from the customer organization who has authority to make decisions and provide money for the project.

This authority and the person's support are the sponsor's primary contributions to the project. The sponsor supports the project through approving the project charter, advising you as the project manager, assisting you in the development of the scope of the project and the statement of work (see Chapter 7), helping to secure the people needed to complete the project, and consulting on the development of other project documentation.

A good sponsor will also assist you in overcoming organizational and political obstacles. Navigating the political waters within an organization will often require the help of the project sponsor. You will usually need a senior executive to assist in the various issues that will occur during the project and will require someone who can help with the political aspects of a project. Many times the sponsor may be your direct manager, but other times a person from another department or a customer representative with a primary interest and assigned authority for the project will be the sponsor. Developing and maintaining your relationship with the project sponsor is key to making the overall project and its implementation successful; in many ways it's a partnership. The sponsor should always be the first person you confide in when you need help or think you're in trouble.

Risk Management

Always have a process for escalating issues beyond your authority or ability to handle to your project sponsor. Never surprise him! Prepare him by letting him know about potential solutions you are working on. And when you present those potential solutions, explain how they may impact the schedule, cost, or quality of your project.

The project sponsor's role for All-Star Cable, the case study we first looked at in Chapter 5, includes the following:

- Holds the ultimate authority, responsibility, and accountability for the success of the project
- Resolves cross-functional organizational issues
- Promotes innovation to achieve the project goals
- Provides guidance, support, and direction to the project
- Signs project charter and business case
- Signs project plan and statement of work
- Certifies quality of the implementation

- Contributes to and approves the responsibility *matrix*
- Assists in developing project policies and procedures
- Approves project deliverables
- Approves changes to project scope and provides additional funds for those changes as required
- Monitors the progress of the project, the project budget, and schedule
- Works with the steering committee (see the following section)
- Makes business decisions for the project
- Provides user resources to the project as needed
- Shields the project from corporate politics
- Works to resolve conflicts

def•i•ni•tion

It's common for people to devote only a percentage of their time to projects. This is usually identified as a **matrixed** organization, which means someone may work on projects part-time and have dedicated duties in a functional group while she works on your project. In these cases, it's very important that you work with these people's functional managers to ensure their support of the project.

The Steering Committee

The steering committee (sometimes called review and approval team or a project governance board) is the group of stakeholders who must approve and agree on project scope, schedule, budgets, plans, and changes.

Obviously, you will include one or more key customer representatives, either internal or external, in this group, but you will also likely include selected functional managers and executives from your own organization who must approve aspects of the project. The key is to keep this team limited in size to those people who really do need to approve project documents. On a large project you'll need to develop an approval process that describes the people who will have a say in, review, and approve each type of document and project change.

The steering committee for the All-Star Cable project is expected to perform the following roles:

- Advises on the business architecture
- Monitors the project and maintains priority relative to other projects

- Settles priorities between related/competing projects
- Provides organizational support
- Provides timely decisions
- Resolves major issues of significant risk to the enterprise
- Disposes of issues and change requests that impact the organization beyond the commercial area
- Executes formal reviews and management reviews
- Approves changes in budget and/or schedule
- Provides feedback to the project sponsor and the project managers
- Manages environmental factors beyond the control of the project

Functional Management

Company officials with an interest in your project make up functional management, also known as line management. These people may include department supervisors, managers, or vice presidents. With the exception of companies that are organized around projects, these managers are responsible for organizational units within the company, such as engineering, marketing, or finance. Usually, they will supply the people who will be working on your project team, so you must work closely with these people to ensure you get the best people for your project. You also need their commitment to *continue* to support the project with resources. Too often functional managers will cut back the time they allow their people to spend on a project.

Therefore, as the project proceeds, you must keep the relevant functional managers informed of project progress and personnel performance issues. These managers can help you out of personnel jams if you let them; but if you don't keep them informed, they can derail a project from underneath you.

The Working Committee

Now we come to the hard part—getting the business involved. Remember earlier, we realized that a critical success factor will be for the business to "own" the project. You will want to implement a working committee of people from the commercial parts to develop the business case for the project since they will be the ones responsible for delivering business results once the project is completed. These people will need to come from all areas of the business. For All-Star Cable, the project working committee should come from sales, marketing, service, accounting, and so on. However, as you can see from our case study, the impact of the Movies-on-Demand project will be felt by everyone within the organization.

Risk Management

On large projects that may affect many departments within a company, line managers might indicate that their organizations don't need to be involved since they may not see how they will be affected. At first, you can accept this view and proceed with the project, but you should still return to these people periodically, provide them with an update on the project, and invite them to participate again since they may see an impact later on and it will take less time to get them up to speed.

After identifying the obvious functional authorities for your project, you'll need to identify those people who will have informal veto authority on decisions affecting the project. Many of these managers will be involved in approval processes even if they don't have a formal stake (such as required signatures) in the project. For instance, if you have a contract administration function within the organization, they are not really involved in a direct way with the project. However, they control the process you will use to manage procurement activities. It's your job to identify these people and make sure they are included at strategic points in the project initiation, development, and execution.

Key Stakeholders for the All-Star Cable Case Study

For our case study, review the following list of people, the key players in the Movies-on-Demand project. Of course, other stakeholders are not listed, such as the customers and the government regulators. However, people listed here are key to you, the project manager.

The Key Players

Name	Position	Personal Characteristics	Background
Martin Swift	Board of Directors	Male, age 55	First board member. Helped define the strategy that brought the company back on its feet. Doesn't understand or trust technology. Believes the company should stay as basic as possible.
Michael Solis	Board of Directors	Male, age 45	Been on the board 10 years. Has a successful retail business. Is very attuned to sales, customer service, and product delivery. Understands technology to a degree, but is very cost sensitive.
Sarah Mayo	Board of Directors	Female, age 48	Vice president of a large San Antonio bank. Been a friend of the company for many years, providing key financial support during hard times. Been on the board three years. Open to new ideas, and understands the cost of new technology.
David Gonzalez	All-Star President	Male, age 55	Project sponsor. Founded the company. Invested a lot of personal time and money. Fearful of business decline. Started the board to give direction and has given the board approval/veto power. Doesn't totally trust technology, but understands the need for innovation. Concerned about passing the company on to his family in solid condition.

continues

The Key Players (continued)

Name	Position	Personal Characteristics	Background
Micky Nash	VP Marketing	Female, age 37	High-energy, high-influence marketing VP. Not concerned with anything but company growth and profitability. Visionary who sometimes alienates others who take their time with decision making. Has the ear of the president. Has become a friend of Sarah Mayo.
Michael Puerto	IT Director	Male, age 40	Brought on several years ago to provide in-house IT capability to operations and back-office functions. Has developed a very capable staff with a lot of experience specifically in the cable business. Is aggressive and confident. Feels rising IT costs are the cost of doing business. Knows IT is the key to the delivery of products in the future. Has run sideways with the president and the board at times with direction that he felt necessary, but they felt costly.
Southside Citizens Group		Wide variety of people	Vocal force to local businesses. They don't feel like the company has kept their interests in mind. Want to return to a cheap, basic cable service affordable to many. Feel like they have to bear the cost of business expansion and the company doesn't consider their needs anymore. Powerful lobbyists who can change public opinion. Helped the company a lot during its troubled times.

Working Together: The Magic Success Formula

As project manager, you will be responsible for ensuring the stakeholders on the project work together and gain consensus on project decisions. Not only at the beginning of the project but also as it progresses through its phases, the project manager must continue to review who the key stakeholders are and what roles they will play.

Many of the stakeholders, including the sponsor, the functional managers in your company, and the customers, will have more formal authority than you, but even so, you need to lead them. Your leadership will be embodied in the tough questions you ask, the facts you provide, the ideas you inspire, and the enthusiasm you convey for the project (we'll talk more about that in Chapter 18). You'll need to coordinate the stakeholders and guide them through the various project stages. Some experts call this "managing upward." Your ability to do this is at the heart of successful project management.

Stakeholder Questionnaire

As you begin to think about key stakeholders, consider the following questions and how you might answer them. We've provided some lines here for you to jot down your thoughts.

- Who are the key individuals who care about the work affected by the project?

  ____

- What are their responsibilities? ______________________________

  ____

- What do they know about the project already? ____________________

  ____

- Who knows about the project and can help me understand the situation? ______

  ____

- Who doesn't know about the project, and what information will they require?

  ____

- Who created the way the work is currently done? ______________________

  ____

- Who won a promotion as the result of the way the work is currently handled?

  ____

- Who might look bad if things change from the current situation? ___________

  ____

- Who is likely to dislike my ideas for change? ______________________

  ____

- What will they dislike about those changes? ______________________

  ____

- Who will be most affected by the change? How will they be helped or hurt?

  ____

- What information and techniques are most likely to be accepted by these stakeholders? ____

- Could there be any hidden agendas within the key stakeholders? How can we confirm our suspicions? ______________________________________

- Should I consider any other factors, such as age, gender, education level, culture, or heritage? ____

- How will I best manage their expectations for the project? ______________

  ____

The Least You Need to Know

- The identification of key stakeholders on your project is an ongoing process and is key to the implementation, planning, and execution of the project.
- At the very least, the project stakeholders include you (the project manager), the customer, the project sponsor, company functional managers, and the implementation team members.
- Coordinating and communicating with the stakeholders is a primary role of the project manager.
- As a project manager, you'll need to "manage upward," to guide the key stakeholders through the project phases.
- Use the stakeholder questionnaire to help prepare for dealing with key stakeholders.

Chapter 7

Scoping Out Project Success

In This Chapter

- Why specific goals are important to project success
- Six criteria of all good project goals
- Steps for establishing project goals
- Choosing a scope for a project that meets the project goals
- Creating the statement of work (SOW) to establish clear expectations among all project stakeholders

Even a good idea can be a bad idea if its goals (also called objectives by some project managers) and scope are not clearly defined before major resources are committed to it. Smart project goals identify specific, measurable, agreed upon, realistic, and timely results. Different people can interpret fuzzy goals in different ways; thus, stakeholders may never agree on whether you're done or whether you've succeeded or failed. It's not enough to say you're going to build the next version of a software product; you need to establish what the new version will do, how much it will cost to build, and how long it will take to design it, among other goals for the project.

In this chapter, we'll explain why you need to get very specific about what you expect to accomplish on your project. We'll also tell you how to set goals for your project that no one can argue with.

Start with the Business Case

In Chapter 1, we talked about the need to align the project with the business needs and requirements since it's the only reason companies undertake a project in the first place! So you must start with the business case. Most important, it should include the expected savings or revenue increases that will occur once the project is completed.

What Should Be Included in the Business Case

Companies format their business case templates in many ways, but most will include these items:

- Reasons why the company undertook the project—typically the need it is trying to address or the increase in performance it is trying to achieve.
- Options that were considered in addressing the need or performance requirements (there is rarely one way to address the issue).
- Benefits that the company hopes to achieve as the result of the successful project. As we move into the goal section later in the chapter, you will see that these benefits need to be clearly measurable and feasible.
- Analysis of the high-level risks (there will be a much more in-depth discussion of risks in Chapter 8).
- A study of costs and schedule, again at the highest level (upcoming chapters will discuss building the detailed cost estimates and schedule, but this is the basic target).
- The business case for most projects will include a cost/benefit analysis. As a rule of thumb, if a project depends on only one key benefit to justify it, your project is very risky. Why? Because most projects have several benefits so if one is not achieved, others still make the project worthwhile. Generally the assumption for this analysis is to do nothing and then work through the potential options referred to earlier.

Conducting a Feasibility Study

The company may ask you to conduct a *feasibility study* to see if the project makes sense, from an economic or business point of view. The purpose of a feasibility study is to identify any make-or-break issues that might prevent the project from being successful—in other words, to decide whether the project makes good business sense.

The information developed in the feasibility study provides good input into the building of the business case.

Normally, you will develop the business case study that outlines the information we listed earlier so that decision makers can determine whether it makes sense to go forward with the project. This is especially useful if you are not the person who will decide whether to go forward, if, for example, you have a steering committee or governance board that will oversee the project.

def•i•ni•tion

A **feasibility study** is a general estimate used to make a decision about whether to pursue a particular project.

Developing a Feasibility Study for Movies-on-Demand

For All-Star Cable, our case study from Chapter 5, the project manager should be able to answer some very specific questions:

- How do we know that our customers will buy Movies-on-Demand versus going to Blockbuster to get them? How do we know that they will prefer Movies-on-Demand over pay-per-view?
- Why do you believe that we have the capability to deliver movies on demand? Is the technology in place?
- Will you, as project manager, be able to manage the risks associated with this type of project? What risks have you identified so far?
- How much do you estimate it will cost to develop Movies-on-Demand, and what is the payback period? What kind of return will All-Star Cable see on this investment?

Words from the Wise

The project should be stopped if the viability of the Business Case disappears for any reason.

—Managing Successful Projects with PRINCE2

Examples abound of companies that initiated major projects and then flushed millions of dollars down the drain because of poor project planning. The city of Denver spent millions of dollars on a state-of-the-art baggage handling system at its new airport. When the system was finally tested, it not only failed to deliver baggage to the right places, but it shredded and mangled the luggage en route! The project was over a year late and millions of dollars over budget. Pity the poor taxpayers in that city!

Or consider Dell, the large computer manufacturer that spent over $50 million for a computer software program that promised to provide instant access to all the information managers would need to run their business. They tried and tried to make the system work to their customized requirements. Finally, they gave up and abandoned a project in which they had more than $50 million invested!

If you want to avoid similar mistakes, you need to clearly define some points before you commit to a project:

- The goals, including the need for the project and the measurable benefits to the stakeholders and users
- The scope
- The time needed to carry out the project
- A rough estimate of your timeline, resource requirements, and costs

Doing this work up front gives your project more credibility and manageability.

Clear Project Goals Make Sense to Everyone

The Dell story illustrates an important concept about setting appropriate goals for your projects: set realistic goals or you probably will not be able to reach them. Here is additional advice regarding setting project goals:

- Any project you undertake must make sense in terms of an overall goal that benefits people in some way. If a project doesn't have a benefit for someone, why bother? Another way to look at this is to make sure the project goals specify how completing the project will make things better than they would be without the project. You should be able to clearly describe the outcomes and benefits to stakeholders and end users.
- Carefully think out project goals; consider even the most obvious questions to make sure the idea is really as good as people think it is.
- Project goals should provide the criteria you need to evaluate your success in completing a project. These criteria include measures of the time, costs, and resources required to achieve your desired outcomes.
- Review project goals with the core team, and reach consensus before you move into the next phase of the project.

Of course, you can use project management techniques on projects with inappropriate goals and still accomplish something, but you might fail to do anything useful. For example, one of the biggest complaints about information technology (IT) projects is that end users perceive them as a waste of time. Often, the IT department is totally baffled by such claims. In a software application project (as a typical example) they point out, usually quite correctly, that the software works just as advertised. The problem often centers on the fact that people don't know how to use the software to get their job done. As a result, the software rapidly becomes "shelfware" because it never gets off the shelf! Was the project a success? Maybe from a technical point of view, you could argue that it was. However, from a practical point of view, it was a failure. If your key customers don't like the product you have produced for them, then the project is a failure regardless of whether it works or not.

> **Words from the Wise**
>
> It concerns us to know the purpose we seek in life, for then, like archers aiming at a definite mark, we shall be more likely to attain what we want.
>
> —Aristotle

The Primary Goals of Every Project

Every project has three primary goals:

1. To create something (such as a product, procedure, organization, building, or other deliverable)
2. To complete it within a specific budgetary framework
3. To finish it within an agreed-upon schedule

Beyond these goals are other goals that must be specified and that actually define the project. For example, it's not enough to have the goal of building a mid-priced sports car. A more appropriate set of goals would be to build a mid-priced, convertible sports car that will …

- Use both gas and electric power.
- Be of a quality comparable to the Volvo C70.
- Sell for 10 percent less than all comparable cars.
- Offer specific features to meet competitive demand, such as antilock brakes, a geo-navigational system, onboard Internet access, and an electrically powered convertible top.

- Be available for the 2008 sales year.
- Be manufactured by the factory in Japan but designed by the engineers in the United States.

To differentiate primary goals from other project goals, other books often refer to these other goals as "objectives," but "goals" and "objectives" are really just different words for the same thing. Whether you call the ideas goals or objectives, they should meet the criteria outlined in the following section.

Six Criteria for Setting Great Goals

As you and the key project stakeholders begin setting goals, be aware that project goals should meet six general criteria to ensure the project will accomplish something of perceived value.

If you write goals for your projects that always meet these six criteria, you'll be working on projects with a purpose.

The Six Criteria for Good Project Goals

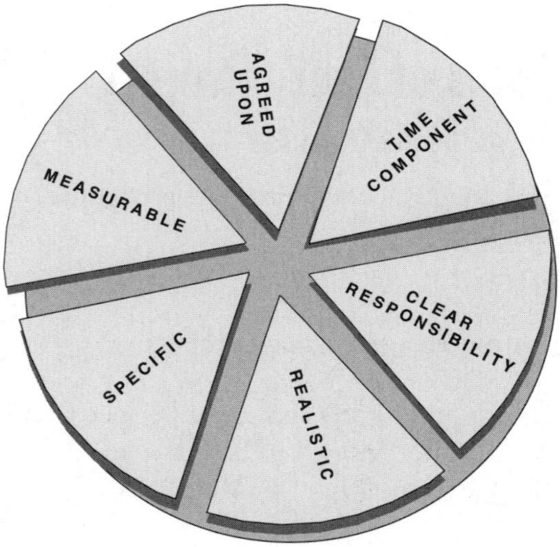

Criterion 1: Goals Must Be Specific

Your goals must be adequately clear so that another, equally competent manager could take over your responsibilities and guide the project to completion. If your goals meet this criterion, you're pointed in the right direction. Ask co-workers to read your goals and determine what has been stated and what the project will look like when it's done. Confused, surprising, or conflicting responses mean they require more refinement.

Criterion 2: Goals Must Be Realistic

Your goals must be possible or at least be within the realm of possibility. For example, if you have a project to implement a software application that costs $5.7 million and you only have $2 million available in cash and credit, you obviously have little chance of getting the project done. In this case, perhaps you should consider a preliminary project to build up your cash reserves before you draw up plans for the installation.

Criterion 3: Goals Must Have a Time Component

Projects must have a definite finish date, or they may never be completed. Projects with no defined end point are in danger of never being finished. And projects with unrealistically short dates blow up like an overloaded circuit breaker. We had an energy company as a client who needed to overhaul the trading software they used to maximize their power generation assets. When we launched the project in January, the original target was for completion in October, a pretty aggressive target, but doable. Suddenly, in February, the deadline was moved up to an April launch! That project was doomed to failure no matter what the project manager and the project team did!

Criterion 4: Goals Must Be Measurable

You must be able to measure your success at meeting your goals. We refer to the clearly defined results, goods, or services produced during the project or at its outcome as *deliverables*. Projects can have interim deliverables that don't reflect the final product. For example, you might need to build a model of the strip mall that you are building (the finished product) early in the project cycle so that more work can be completed later on. The strip mall itself is the final deliverable, but the model may be a deliverable for the design phase of the project.

def•i•ni•tion

Quality is defined by PMI as the "totality of characteristics of (the finished product) that bear on its ability to satisfy stated or implied needs." **Grade** is "a category or rank given (to products) having the same functional use but with different characteristics."

Deliverables, like projects, are evaluated not only by the fact that something is produced but by their quality as well. Don't confuse *quality* with *grade*. Quality is how well the product satisfies the business performance needs of the customer. Grade is the number of features a product may have. For example, consider cell phones. The basic purpose of the cell phone, of course, is to send and receive telephone calls. A cell phone that does what it is supposed to do, send and receive calls with few "drops," is a high-quality cell phone. However, new cell phones have Internet capabilities, and some can handle music like an iPod. The cell phone with all these features is a high-grade cell phone. However, if it drops calls regularly, then it may be high grade, but it is low quality. Low quality will always be a problem. Judging the grade that a customer wants and is willing to pay for, is quite another issue. Determining and then delivering both the quality and grade of the finished product is a key element in defining the scope of your project.

Criterion 5: Goals Must Be Agreed Upon

At the onset of a project, you, as the project manager, and the other initiators of the project (your boss, for example, the customer, or the steering committee in the case of All-Star Cable) must agree upon the goals before you take any further steps toward planning the project. If you don't reach consensus, there's no point in beginning the project; it's doomed from the start because the stakeholders can't agree on the outcomes that will make the project a success. In a large project that crosses many departments or other organizations, gaining consensus can be a long and thankless process. (See the section "Seeing Eye to Eye" later in this chapter.)

Eventually, all the team members as well as the stakeholders must agree to support the project goals if you're going to manage the project effectively. Without consensus on the goals, the project faces a bumpy road to completion. Remember that *consensus* doesn't mean that everyone gets what he wants; it means he will support the goals of the project as defined. Projects started with misunderstood goals often have team members working at cross-purposes or occasionally duplicating each other's efforts.

Criterion 6: Responsibility for Achieving the Goals Must Be Identified

Although you, the project manager, bear the brunt of responsibility for the overall success of the project, others may be responsible for pieces of the goals. Like agreeing on the goals, you must identify the people responsible for the goals, and they must be willing to accept responsibility before the project proceeds further.

Once you identify all the major players who will be making decisions and contributing major pieces to the project, get them to sign on up front. For example, if the All-Star Cable project is going to choose and implement a new piece of software to allow the billing department to input customer requests for changes in services, you need to get an agreement from your accounting group and the information technology group that will support the new software once it is installed.

Establishing Goals Step-by-Step

It's easy to establish goals for your project. In fact, it's so easy that you'll find yourself with more goals than you can handle. (You'll have time to develop goals for specific activities later in the planning cycle.)

Here's how to establish good overall project goals:

1. Make a list of the project's goals. At this point, don't rule anything out. Just make a list, and check it twice.
2. Study the list, and eliminate anything that has no direct bearing on the project.
3. Do away with anything that is really a step in meeting the goals and is not a goal for the end result of the project. Now you should have a "pure" list of project goals, so it's time for the final step in goal setting.
4. Study the list again, and make sure each goal meets all the relevant six criteria. Now determine whether all these goals are doable within one project. Look for goals that really belong to a separate project or are not directly germane to the project at hand. Cross them out. Leaving them in your current project will confuse team members and eat resources you need for this project to succeed.
5. If the items you deleted from the list are important, consider alerting your management to them so they can decide what, if any, action to take. This may require explanation on your part as to why you can't take on the extra work and how each item really deserves a project world of its own.

Time Is Money

Another key to establishing your goals is to consider what the project *will not* do. Often, in setting our goals, we think about what we want the final product to do. However, a valuable exercise will be to list what it will not do, as well.

Successful projects must meet their goals with a minimum of changes and without disturbing the main workflow of the organization. If a project derails for one reason or another, you may have to use additional resources in an attempt to meet dates. This can cause serious organizational problems as other important work is put aside to accommodate the problem project. Your task is to run the project as smoothly as possible with no requirement for additional time, bodies, or money that interferes with other projects or day-to-day operations.

Developing the Statement of Work (SOW)

The project's *statement of work* (commonly nicknamed the rather unflattering SOW) is a critical communication document between the project manager and the customer and/or steering committee. It includes much of the information the project manager has developed during the design phase and sets the stage for all the planning that will follow. The SOW usually includes the following:

def•i•ni•tion

The **statement of work** (SOW) is an integrated set of purposes, goal descriptions, resource requirements, conflicts, assumptions, and authorities that define a project and accompany the evolving master project plan during its development throughout the project.

- The purpose statement that focuses on the business problem that the project seeks to solve
- Project scope, including what the project will *not* include
- The project deliverables
- Goals and objectives the project needs to be successful
- The initial cost and schedule estimates
- Stakeholders for the project and the chain of command
- Benefits and risks in the early evaluations
- Assumptions and constraints the project manager has determined

In Chapter 1, we looked at the link between the business strategy and the performance outcomes the project is tasked to improve. In the SOW, the project manager wants to provide more detail on the business outcomes the project will solve.

Putting It Down in Writing

The audience for a SOW may include all the project stakeholders, but especially the customer. When a project is produced for the company alone (the customer and the project team work for the same company), the SOW is the only project agreement required. When outside customers are involved, both a contract and a SOW are advisable because the SOW specifies project details typically outside the scope of a contract and the contract specifies legal agreements outside the scope of the SOW. In some cases, the contract will refer to a SOW as the official definition of the work to be completed.

The Components of the SOW

A SOW lists and defines the goals, constraints, scope, communication guidelines, and success criteria for a project. The initial SOW, once written, becomes a document subject to negotiation and modification by the stakeholders. When the SOW is finally approved, it becomes the "official rules" for the project.

In size, the SOW can range from a one- or two-page memo on a small project to a 100-page document of understandings for a major technical endeavor.

The usual minimum content of a SOW includes the following:

- **The purpose statement.** Clearly answer the basic question of "Why are we doing this project?" in this section. In addition, reference the business case for the project but don't necessarily detail it. In putting together the SOW for All-Star Cable, the project manager and the project team determined that the purpose of the project was to allow the company to expand its business by entering a new service line that no competitors had, and open that new market.
- **The scope statement.** The scope statement clearly defines what the project will and won't do. Mention the relationship of the project to other priorities or business endeavors here as well, especially when the project is a subproject of a much larger project. For All-Star Cable, the project team decided they would initially target their existing customers as the primary audience for this service. Also, they decided to use a film library from an outside source since they didn't want to maintain a library of movie titles and outsourcing would allow them to change titles more frequently. Also, they decided not to offer "adult" videos as part of the potential titles to the customers since such offerings might offend many of their existing customers.
- **The project deliverables.** This section defines what the project is supposed to produce. This helps focus the team on producing outcomes. List by name the intermediate deliverables as well as the final deliverables. For example, "scale model" is an intermediate deliverable on the way to a final deliverable of "a completely built refinery." Even specify regular status reports, change requests, and other reports as part of the deliverables of the project, along with the frequency and audience for each report. It's important to write the project management deliverables as well as the project deliverables into the SOW; this ensures that the basic communications within the project are clearly understood.

- **The goals and objectives.** This section defines the criteria for success. Not only specify the on-time and within-budget criteria, but also list all the other goals created for the project. For All-Star Cable, the goals were to get 70 percent of their existing customers to order Movies-on-Demand before moving to target new customers. They also targeted a return on investment of 15 percent with a payback of 5 years.
- **The cost and schedule estimates.** This section provides the rough but well-researched estimates of both the cost and the schedule for the project. You'll learn more about cost schedule and cost in Chapters 12 and 13. For our case study of All-Star Cable, the president of the company has asked the project team to complete the project within 12 months with a budget of $2 million. More complete planning will be required to see if both of these targets are realistic.
- **The list of stakeholders.** In this section introduce all the key project influencers, managers, and sponsors. At a minimum, identify names and roles of the steering committee, project manager, key project team members, sponsor, working committee, managers with an interest in the project, and customer contacts. (See the list of stakeholders from Chapter 6.)
- **The chain of command.** This section defines who reports to whom on this project. A project organization chart is required here. Another useful tool is the written responsibility matrix (that you will see more about in Chapter 29), the table that defines the project's important roles and responsibilities. This section of the SOW is particularly important because projects often cross organizational boundaries; thus projects have their own reporting structure that is outside the functional reporting structure of the overall organization. If project roles and reporting requirements aren't defined and agreed to in the SOW, conflicts about decision-making roles and authority may derail a project midcourse. A good example might be decisions the working committee is authorized to make versus those that must be passed by the sponsor.
- **Benefits and risks in the early evaluations.** Here the initial benefits and risks to the project are identified. They will probably be vague at this stage and must be filled out more completely later. For All-Star Cable, the benefits and risks are clearly linked. For example, the benefit of moving into this new area before the competition is providing the service might allow the company to grow their customer base. However, a clear risk is that a competitor will enter the market before them and they will lose their competitive advantage.

- **Assumptions and constraints.** Detail any assumptions that limit the project or agreements that form the basis of interactions here. Don't leave anything out that could affect the future management of the project. If you want the project to be considered a success, all "side" or "off-line" agreements must be agreed to in the SOW. Document them in this section. As for assumptions for All-Star Cable, the project team assumed they could use the existing cable system to deliver the movies and that it would not require a complete retooling of the system.
- **The communication plan.** This section details the basic reports that will be produced and any meetings that will be held during the detailed planning phase of the project. At this point, specify the frequency and audience of the status reports and basic meetings for the project planning phase. On large projects, you will likely produce a more detailed communication plan later in the planning cycle or during the project implementation phase(s). These later communication plans will add more information about the author, content, and frequency of reports to be produced and meetings to be held during the later phases of the project. On small projects, these more detailed communication plans probably won't be required if the SOW is sufficiently detailed. We'll look at the communications plan in more detail in Chapter 21. In the communication plan for All-Star Cable, the project manager wanted to pay particular attention to their customers and the Southside Civic Association.

Risk Management

Too many goals and objectives are like too many cooks in the kitchen; they spoil the broth. When considering a project, look for tasks or sets of tasks that should really remain as separate projects and split them off as such. Management may attempt to add objectives to your project that don't belong there in order to meet other political agendas. Work to make sure this doesn't happen, if at all possible, by keeping the scope of the project clear and achievable.

Seeing Eye to Eye

Gaining consensus is the all-important process of getting honest buy-in from the people involved that all aspects of the project are understood and agreed upon. Further, consensus implies that people chosen for certain roles will accept them and that the goals are smart (meaning they're specific, measurable, agreed upon, realistic, and timely). Before you proceed with the project, consensus must be reached on the

SOW. Give the stakeholders plenty of time to give their input. It may take multiple meetings and multiple iterations of the SOW to get it right.

Once the SOW is agreed upon by all the key stakeholders, the final step in initial consensus is getting signed agreement on the SOW from the stakeholders. The signatures provide evidence that everyone agreed to the project as defined in the SOW. At this point, the SOW establishes the baseline for the detailed planning activities and establishes a detailed schedule and budget for the project.

As time goes on in the project, the SOW will likely need to be amended and agreed to again. Making changes to the SOW becomes an important way to manage stakeholders throughout the project life cycle. The SOW at the end of a large project might be quite different from the SOW you agree to at the beginning of the endeavor. But the difference is not important. The only things that matter are that everyone has been informed and all changes have been agreed to by key stakeholders and always put into writing. Thus, consensus building will be an ongoing activity during the project, especially when project changes are necessary.

The Least You Need to Know

- Goals (also called objectives) consist of specific, measurable, agreed-upon, realistic, and timely aims.
- Your goals for a project should include completing it on time, within budget and using available resources, and achieving the desired quality of end product or result.
- Goals require clear, concise writing so that project participants understand each one.
- When planning a project, stakeholders must specify and agree upon its size (scope).
- Write and approve the statement of work (SOW) to document the goals, scope, deliverables, cost and schedule estimates, stakeholder roles, chain of command, assumptions, risks, and communication guidelines for a project.
- The SOW becomes the basis for the rest of the formal, detailed project plan and is a tool for managing stakeholders throughout the project.

Chapter 8

Managing Risks and Constraints

In This Chapter

- Understanding that risk involves uncertainty and loss
- Handling risks of all kinds
- Maintaining a risk log
- Constraints that bind you

A good project manager measures risks in advance. Even with clear goals, you need to establish the probability that something will go wrong and will keep you from completing the project successfully. On a small project, this step may only take a few moments to ponder, but on a larger project, risk assessment can be a complete project in its own right. The goal of the risk and constraint analysis is to establish the feasibility of the project within the economy, politics, laws, and organizational structure that limit your business. These risks and constraints should also be documented in the statement of work (SOW).

A project that moves beyond the initiation phase without taking risks and constraints, including the organizational and business risks into account, will be buffeted by the surrounding internal and external forces and will be more likely to fail. Bad weather? A delay. Your main supplier goes bankrupt? A delay. A strike? A delay. Waffling among senior management? A delay—and maybe even project termination! Maybe even your job … well, I won't say it. You get the idea.

The Three Types of Risk

As you might assume, the kinds of risks you'll encounter vary with the project. Team members may fail at their tasks, sunspots may blow away your satellite uplink in the middle of an important transmission, and the concrete rebar used in your new corporate headquarters may turn to rust about one month after installation.

Ultimately, all the risks in a project boil down to these:

- **The known risks.** These are risks you can identify after reviewing the project definition within the context of the business and/or technical environment. You must draw on your experience and that of the stakeholders in defining risks of this nature.
- **The predictable risks.** These risks may occur. They are also anticipated risks based on work with similar projects. They have to do with things such as staff turnover or economic changes that can have an anticipated impact. Instinct, rather than concrete evidence, tells us to be wary of these risks.
- **The unpredictable risks.** These are the things that go bump in the night or the "stuff that just happens" beyond the control of the project manager or team. You simply can't predict everything! As one example, we were just finishing a project at Hobby Airport in Houston that included the handling of baggage. Just one week before the project was scheduled to finish, the 9/11 attacks occurred. Suddenly there were many additional requirements for baggage handling that we had no way of predicting!

Risk Areas

We can further break down risks into areas that may impact delivery of the defined product or service. The primary risks among these include:

- **Funding:** You may not get the full amount of capital that your project needs.
- **Time:** You may find that things are taking longer than originally planned. Thus, you risk running out of time.
- **Staffing:** As work on the project begins, you might realize that you can't find the right staff in the marketplace or don't have the requisite experience or skill set available in the company to meet objectives.
- **Customer relations:** If your customer doesn't have time to work with the project team and assist in defining the attributes of the solution to project problems, you risk having a dissatisfied customer as the project proceeds.
- **Project size and/or complexity:** The project is so large or so complex that it taxes your ability to complete it on time or within budget. There are just too many factors to attempt to control, especially given the time or budget restrictions.
- **Overall structure:** As a result of political decisions, competing work groups or organizations fracture responsibility.
- **Organizational resistance:** The project makes business sense, but key groups are resisting the changes the project deliverables require.
- **External factors:** External risk factors hover outside your control, such as new government regulations or shifting technologies.

Don't Forget Business Risks

Business risks may also have an impact on the acceptance of a product or service. These risks include the following:

- **Market acceptance:** The product is a good one, but customers don't want to buy it.
- **Time-to-market:** It will be a good product, and customers will want it, but only if you can deliver it six months earlier than projected.
- **Incompatible product fit:** It will be a good product, and customers will want it, but due to the cost of producing it, customers won't be able to afford it.
- **Difficult-to-sell:** It's a great product, but who's going to sell it? It will be too expensive for retail outlets but won't cost enough to provide dealers with incentives for selling it.

- **Loss of political support:** If a project loses support from executive management, the whole project could be jeopardized. This might happen when a new manager is brought on board or loss of financial support occurs.

The Ultimate Risk: Acts of God

As humans, we can do little to prevent acts of God from affecting projects, but we can take steps to avoid the most likely problems. Don't build precision models in San Francisco under concrete freeway ramps, for example, and avoid vibration-sensitive experiments near the runways of the Dallas-Fort Worth airport.

Otherwise, with this in mind, insure your project. It's the best insurance against hurricanes, floods, earthquakes, and other unpredictable acts of God. (Check the policy to verify it covers such events and does not prohibit any exclusively, as is common in most commercial policies.)

Taking Risks Stage by Stage

Risk can occur during any phase of a project's life cycle, but you should be aware of some common ones at each stage. Let's take a look at them.

Risks During the Project Definition Phase:

- Unavailable subject matter experts
- Poor definition of problem
- No feasibility study
- Unclear objectives
- No buy-in from the organization

Risks During the Project Planning Phase:

- No risk management plan
- Spotty planning
- Underdeveloped requirements and specifications
- Unclear statement of work
- No management support
- Poor role definition
- Inexperienced team

Risks During the Project Execution Phase:

- Changes in scope
- Changes in schedule
- Lack of control systems
- Unskilled labor
- Material availability
- Strikes
- Weather
- Regulatory requirements

Risks During the Project Close-Out Phase:

- Unacceptable to customer
- Poor requirements fit
- As-built changes
- Budget problems

So how can you address these potential pitfalls? Try these ideas:

- Identify potential problems early in the planning cycle (the proactive approach) and provide input into management decisions regarding resource allocation.
- Involve personnel at all levels of the project, focus their attention on a shared project (or product) vision, and provide a mechanism for achieving it.
- Avoid the problem by eliminating the cause of the threat. For example, if you feel the loss of a key team member during the project might be a significant risk, you could avoid the problem by simply finding someone else to fill that role.
- Use a mitigation strategy to reduce the impact of the risk by reducing the probability of the risk occurring. Using the same example above, you might add another person to your team who has similar knowledge and experience so that if you end up losing a key team member, you have someone who is capable of stepping in to fill the role.
- Use a retention strategy. This simply means that you accept the risk as possible and develop a plan for dealing with it if it occurs. This usually happens for risks you and the project team think are relatively unlikely to occur.

Risk Tolerance

Before you begin to make decisions about how to plan for risks, you need to consider the amount of risk (the risk appetite) you and your project sponsor (or your steering committee) are willing to tolerate. You might be willing to accept more tolerance for risks in some areas and less in other aspects. For example, in our All-Star Cable case study, the project schedule is very important, as the management team wants to beat the competition into the marketplace. Therefore, the project manager and the steering committee might be less tolerant of risks that would impact the schedule. However, they might be far more tolerant in accepting risks to the budget.

You may want to plot your risks on a chart like this one and determine, with your project team, where the risk tolerance line is. Any risks that fall above the line (wherever you establish it) require planning in case they occur.

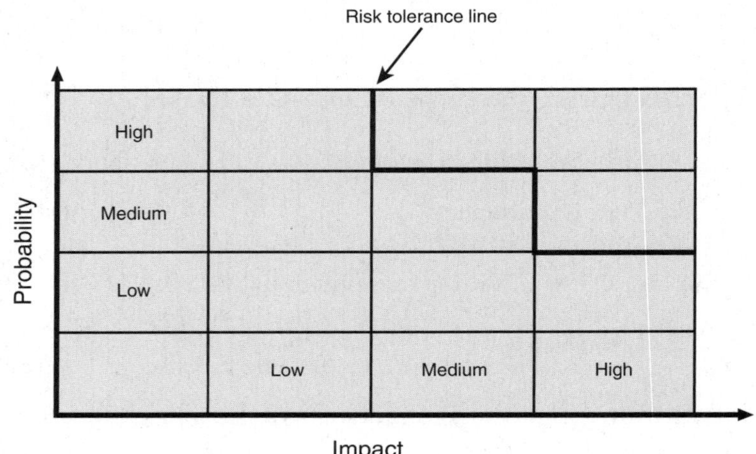

The Basics of Risk Management

You can reduce the risks on your project through *risk management.* Some folks even refer to project management as "the practice of risk management." Here are the steps we suggest you follow on your projects:

def•i•ni•tion

In basic **risk management**, you plan for the possibility that a problem will occur by estimating the probability of the problem arising during the project, evaluating the impact if the problem does arise, and preparing solutions in advance to keep the risks at an acceptable level.

1. **Identify the risks by listing them and describing their potential impact on the project.** Identifying risks involves careful analysis. Assume that anything can go wrong. Learn from past projects. The failures of the past are often the best source of risk-control information. You can also anticipate problems by looking at critical relationships or resources in the project and anticipating what could occur if these change. To look at deliverables from different points of view—including those of the staff, subcontractors, vendors, suppliers, service providers,

management, and customers—also helps. Also evaluate the environment, labor practices, and the availability of raw materials or technologies.

2. **Analyze the probability that the risk will occur and the potential impact of the risk.** When you consider the impact, also consider whether the risk will impact your schedule, budget, quality, or people. Then, assign a number on a scale from 1 (lowest impact) to 5 (highest impact) to quantify the potential impact of the risk to your project. Next, determine how likely you think this event will occur and use the same 1 to 5 scale.
3. **Determine the overall severity or importance of the risk.** We do this by multiplying the probability number by the impact number (each on a scale of 1 to 5) to come up with a measure of severity.
4. **Determine which risks are most important for further action.** We usually establish a "risk threshold" that makes sure all those that are high in both impact and likelihood get the most attention (a 25). Risks with less severity are considered for further analysis. You can use whatever number seems appropriate for your situation and risk tolerance; the key is to come up with a risk threshold that establishes the risks that require further attention throughout the project.
5. **Document a response plan for the risks.** The project sponsor should approve this plan as part of the SOW or project plan. You have four basic options for dealing with the risks on your list:

   - Accept the risk. This means you intend to do nothing special at this point. If and when the risk emerges, the team will deal with it. This is an appropriate strategy when the consequences for the risk are cheaper than a program to eliminate or reduce the risk.
   - Avoid the risk. This means you'll delete the part of the project that contains the risk or break the project into smaller subprojects that reduce the overall risk. Be aware that reducing or avoiding the risk in this way may also change the business case for the project. Sometimes you'll want to take on more risk to earn more return. This option is similar to the sentiment of "no pain, no gain" in the athletic world.
   - Monitor the risk and develop a contingency plan in case the risk becomes imminent. If the best offense is a good defense, then when you encounter problems, having a contingency plan in place is vital to ensuring continued success of the project. Developing contingency plans for key risks is one of

the most important aspects of risk management. These contingencies are alternative plans and strategies to be put into place when necessary, often referred to as "Plan B." The whole concept of contingency planning is based on the assumption that you can develop more effective and efficient scenarios if you do so proactively—before things happen—rather than reactively when you are under the stress of a slipping schedule or a cash shortage.

- Transfer the risk. Insurance is the most obvious, although often expensive, way of transferring risk. Risks including theft, fire, and floods are effectively transferred to the insurance company. Another way of transferring risk involves hiring someone else to implement a part of the project. For example, in a fixed-price contract with a vendor, you transfer the risk of cost increases to the vendor. Of course, fixed-price contracts aren't always possible, but when they are, they can reduce a substantial amount of a project's budgetary risk.

Use a form like this one to analyze and respond to the risks in your projects.

Risk Management Worksheet

Type of Risk	Jeopardy	Description of the Risk	Expectation of the Risk (1 to 5)	Impact of the Risk (1 to 5)	Severity of the Risk (Expectation X Impact)	Contingencies Plan of Action
Critical resource delay	Budget, schedule	Crane not available due to other project	3	5	15	Increase funding for lease from another vendor
Permit delay	Schedule	Building permit not approved	2	4	8	Focus on the task, not additional contingency required
Project staffing	Schedule, resources	Can't hire enough carpenters	1	3	3	Not necessary to monitor; low risk

Remember that risk management and response planning are ongoing processes. You must regularly reevaluate. Every project encounters problems neither planned for nor desired that require some type of resolution or action before the project can continue. Depending on the size and type of problem, various resources may be required to solve it. Note that, in some cases, no action is required! Project managers get to live long, productive lives by properly recognizing which is which.

There is always a balance between the costs associated with mitigating risks and the impact and likelihood they will happen. For example, you could actually order extra equipment for a construction project to make sure you have enough when you need it. However, there would be a considerable increase in your costs. You would need to weigh those increased costs against the impact and likelihood of not having enough equipment when you need it.

Time Is Money

Ultimately, the key to managing risk is to be aware of everything that can negatively affect the project. Be suspicious. Look for problems. Persistence in analysis reveals risk, and new risks bring new plans for dealing with them. Although risk management starts at the beginning of the project by identifying the problems and constraints that are known, it will continue as you identify and contend with the unanticipated sources of risk that inevitably emerge until the project is finished. If you were a project manager running a project in New Orleans in Fall 2005, think of the impact Hurricane Katrina would have had on the completion of your project!

Track Risks with a Risk Log

Maintaining a risk log allows you to track information about the risks to the project, their analysis, their status, and the plans to deal with them if they occur. Many project managers track risks in an Excel spreadsheet; others use a database, depending on the size of the project. Some project management software programs also have risk logs as part of their features.

Always review and update your risk log regularly. Some risks will disappear as the project progresses, and others will appear. For example, in our All-Star Cable case study, one risk might be the development of a new remote control device to control the television. However, once the prototype is developed and tested to ensure that it works technically, that risk disappears. However, a new risk, the ease of training the home user to use the remote to order movies might now appear as a risk to be tracked and planned for.

It's also important to identify who owns the various risks, both from a monitoring and tracking perspective, but also for developing plans for handling them. If someone is not specifically assigned to a particular risk, don't be surprised if no one handles it!

During the project close-out phase discussed in Part 6, we will talk about reporting on the lessons learned during the project. For now it's important to recognize that your risk log will be an important tool as you develop your lessons learned at the end of the project.

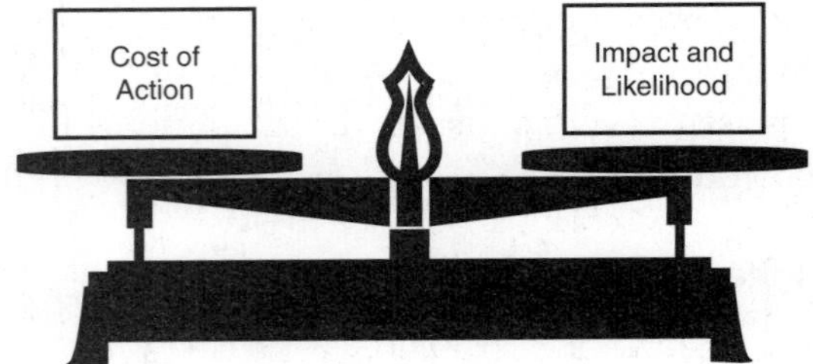

Managing risks is a balancing act between the costs associated with planning and managing risks and the likelihood and impact of a risk occurring.

(Adapted from PRINCE2)

Constraints vs. Risks

Unlike risks, *constraints* can be identified in advance. Constraints are the real-world limits on the possibilities for your projects. A typical constraint is budget. You will only receive a certain amount of money to finish the project, and to get more you'll likely have to lobby long and hard. If you ignore the constraints defining your project, it will fail in some way. Your job as project manager is to make sure you understand the constraints of your project and work within their limits.

Constraints to Consider

Project constraints, along with risks, are a major factor when establishing the project plan and getting the project underway. You may want to add a roof to the new baseball stadium you are building, but you may be constrained to assembling little more than a simple field with two sets of bleachers. The constraints that bring a grandiose project down to Earth include answers to questions like these:

> **def•i•ni•tion**
>
> A **constraint** is any restriction that will affect the performance of the project or any factor that can affect when an activity is scheduled.

- How much money is really available and when?
- By what date must the project be completed?
- What inside resources are required?
- What outside resources are required, and can you afford them?
- Can you get consensus among project members, executives, and stakeholders that the project is important and deserves your time and effort?
- What are you willing to settle for that will still meet your needs?
- Is there a way to do it using fewer or less expensive resources? (If there is, your problem may be solved.)

The process of answering these questions permanently grounds some projects as the real world intrudes on what's really little more than an energetic pipe dream. Constraints are a modicum of reality. Use them as a tool to fine-tune a project, as well as to brush off grandiose suggestions.

Words from the Wise

Laws and regulations can be constraints, sometimes acting in strange ways. For example, a project might be planned to implement a new accounting procedure to meet new laws or regulations (for example, the Sarbannes-Oxley Law). In that case, the constraint is that, if the project is not completed by a certain date, the organization might be either breaking the law or face a fine. So perhaps the scope might be pared back in other ways: for example, deciding to implement a manual procedure first and then later integrate it into computerized systems.

—James MacIntyre, project management expert

Project constraints are quite broad. Similar to the restrictions every manager faces when confronted with any task, you must identify constraints, like risks, beforehand or an expensive project may hit the skids (along with its manager) after being bogged down in an avoidable quagmire.

Constraint 1: The Budget

The budget is both a constraint and a risk. Most projects suck up money faster than you may realize. Whether you're opening a new sales office or developing a new product, the budget will constrain your efforts. Most organizations will also charge your project budget for the employees you borrow and any company-provided services you may require. Depending on the charge-back service, you may find it less expensive to bring in outsiders because you can choose exactly the skill set you require without dealing with the corporate baggage that comes with insiders from some organizations. Be aware of the danger of agreeing to a budget to please the boss, management, or the customer when you know in advance the funds will be inadequate. See Chapter 13 for more information on project budgeting.

Constraint 2: The Schedule

Time waits for no one, especially not the manager of a faltering project built around impossible dates. In addition to being a risk for failure, the schedule is always a constraint, even if a project's due date is not that critical. If it rambles on after the predicted end date, the budget will expand, and team members may be pulled off to handle other responsibilities. Missing an end date may cause serious marketing consequences. A new but late-to-market product may arrive at the market window only to find it closed and firmly locked.

Constraint 3: The People

We'll explain how to deal with people issues as you build your project team in Chapter 14. For now, keep in mind that people's skills, as well as their conflicts, are always a project manager's most pressing concern. You can argue for more money and time, but the people really make the project. If the right ones aren't available or are unaffordable, you will have to make do with the team that's available, no matter how inexperienced. The availability of the right people is both a risk to anticipate and a constraint that you must deal with as the project proceeds.

Constraint 4: The Real World

Once a project is underway, reality has an ugly habit of settling in. One of the biggest reasons projects run into difficulty is that too often people underestimate the amount of time and effort it takes to complete all the work undertaken in a project.

Constraint 5: Facilities and Equipment

Every project assumes that required equipment will be available within the project's time. Whether it's a 20-ton grader, an electron microscope, or a simple freight elevator, the right tools must be available for their period in the spotlight. Just like people, equipment resources are key to completion. If a project slips its dates, that critical piece of equipment might be tied up on another project somewhere else.

The constraints for your project should be well-documented in the SOW as part of the scope statement (see Chapter 7 for more on the SOW). These constraints limit what you can do in the project.

Risky Business

Identifying risks and constraints beforehand provides you with time to mitigate those you can fix or to notify the stakeholders (both verbally and in writing) that the project may be in jeopardy before it even begins. A critical analysis of the project is crucial to get it off to an acceptable and workable start.

Going into a project with a "We can do anything" attitude may support team spirit at the onset, but when things come unglued and reality sets in, your team will become frustrated; management will complain; and you will kick yourself for not identifying the potential problems up front.

The Least You Need to Know

- Project risks and constraints are known roadblocks you need to account for before the project is underway.
- Remember that you won't be able to predict everything that might happen. However, that does not absolve you of your responsibility to analyze and plan for risks.
- The impossible remains impossible no matter how enthusiastic your team is.
- Focus on the most likely risks and plan for dealing with them in advance. The best defense against "losing your head" is to have a plan for dealing with it!
- The risk management process can help you identify, quantify, and ultimately reduce the risks (problems) that may affect your project.

Part 3

The Project Planning Phase

You've made it through the definition steps, reviewed the project for potential risks, and identified how success will be defined for your project. Now you can start planning the key elements for successful projects: the activities, schedule, and budget. The plan is a roadmap for your project that helps you guide the work from start to finish. Not only does it detail the work that will be done, but it also serves as a tool for communicating with both stakeholders and the project team.

In addition to the goals and objectives for your project and the risks and constraints, most project plans contain three standard components: the work breakdown structure (WBS), the schedule, and the budget. In this part, you'll learn how to put these elements together as a complete plan for projects both large and small.

Finally, you will learn how to find the people with the knowledge and skills you need by matching them with the right work so you can ensure success!

Chapter 9

The Breakdown of Tasks: What Really Needs to Be Done?

In This Chapter

- Understanding the work breakdown structure (WBS)
- Reasons you should break a project into work packages
- Subprojects as milestones and milestones as groups of tasks
- The right WBS levels for your project
- Measuring the quality of task completion

Project managers use a tool called a work breakdown structure (WBS) to break larger activities, sometimes referred to as milestones, into individual components.

Breaking Your Project into Bite-Sized Pieces

Often taking the form of a tree diagram or an outline, a WBS is a hierarchical chart used to organize the project's required activities into related areas. You can also use the completed WBS for budgeting and personnel-selection purposes as well as scheduling and network diagramming.

Organization is crucial in the work breakdown structure. On a large project, organizing related areas into milestones or subprojects makes it easier to visualize the overall project without getting into the details.

def•i•ni•tion

A **work package** represents the lowest level of project activity that has both time and cost associated with it. A work package should have a unique deliverable associated with it.

In a WBS, a project breaks down into the following levels:

- The total project
- Subprojects if the project is a complicated one
- Milestones that summarize the completion of an important set of *work packages* or the completion of an important event in a project such as a subproject (which is just a smaller portion of the overall project)
- Major activities (also called summary tasks)
- Work packages (also sometimes called tasks, activities, or work elements)

You can have as many subprojects, milestones, major activities, and work packages in your WBS as you need. As a project manager, the levels in your WBS will help you control work at each level. An appropriately organized WBS can help identify the right time to ask and answer resource and staffing questions.

The Work Breakdown Structure and Your Project

The WBS document organizes and summarizes the work necessary to complete the project. Every WBS starts with a summary of high-level project areas and milestones. In our All-Star Cable case study, those areas are storage, related systems, interfaces, applications, and reports. For most larger projects, however, organize the activities you list into some kind of hierarchy (which you'll learn about in a moment) and then translate them into a network diagram (explained in Chapter 10). The complete WBS ultimately will include a schedule (see Chapters 13 and 14) and a list of resources required to complete each task (see Chapter 11).

Your WBS should be able to help you do all of the following:

- Identify the major parts of the project so that all the work needing to be done is clearly indicated.
- Organize the work in the most logical sequence so the work packages can be efficiently scheduled.
- Identify work packages you need to assign to various team members.
- Identify the resources necessary to complete each work package so you can develop a budget.
- Communicate the work to be done in a clear-cut way so team members understand their assigned jobs and responsibilities for completing the project.
- Organize related work packages using logical milestones.

Time Is Money

When you believe you have a credible draft of a WBS, put it away for a while and then revisit it. This gives you a chance to get an objective view of the various parts. You might see something you forgot to consider, or you might notice a better way to organize the work.

Your WBS is the underpinning of a successful project because the need for resources and the schedule come from the WBS and the way you sequence activity. On larger projects, the WBS will likely undergo several revisions before you get it right. If you are new to project management, you should have the core team members or other key stakeholders review the completed WBS and sequences to ensure they include all the work necessary to get things done.

Take a look at the following outline-style WBS for All-Star Cable. The outline method works best for projects that have too many layers to conveniently lay out in the tree format. We also include a tree diagram for another project just to give you an idea of what one looks like.

All-Star Cable Company MOD Project

Start project

Storage

- Design data model
- Load data
- Write stored procedures

Related systems

- Analyze system
- Design new related system
- Construct new billing system
- Test new system
- Accept billing system test
- Implement new billing system

Interfaces

- Customer graphical user interface
    - Design new customer graphical user interface
    - Test customer graphical user interface with application
    - Obtain customer graphical user interface approvals
    - Approve customer graphical user interface
    - Build prototype
    - Move customer graphical user interface into production
- Employee interface
    - Design employee interface
    - Build employee interface
    - Build employee interface prototype
    - Test employee interface with users

Obtain user acceptance

Move employee interface into production

Applications

Design full application requirements

Submit request for proposal for off-the-shelf software

Evaluate software

Decide to make or build

Make make/build decision

Purchase software

Install software

Test software (unit)

Test software (system)

Accept software

Move software into production

Reports

Analyze information needs

Design reports

Modify existing reports database

Test with test files

Produce full-scale systems testing

Complete full-scale deployment test

Project management

Planning

Communication

Project tracking and reporting

Closeout activities

Finished project

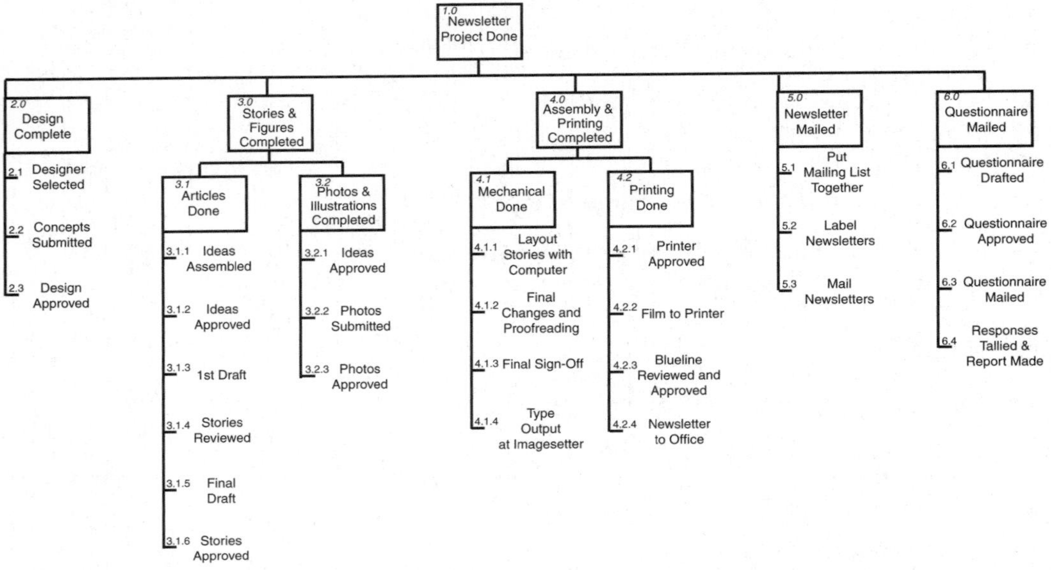

A sample tree diagram for a project.

You can choose to focus on whatever level of the project is germane to your current management needs. However, the smallest unit in your WBS should be the smallest unit of work you must track in your project; this is the work package. Only the work package level is actually assigned a time estimate and a cost; everything else in the WBS is simply an organizational tool for summarizing how the work packages combine to complete components of the project.

Don't allow the lowest level in your WBS to reach the level of absurdity, but do track everything that could affect something else in the plan. While doing this, you must remember that not everything in life can be planned down to the minute; if it could, nothing would ever go wrong. You'll need to make your best guess about the detail and sequence of most project tasks.

Organizing the WBS

There's no magic formula for organizing a WBS. In the All-Star Cable example, the WBS is based on the category of tasks. (In project management, *task* is a generic term for work that is the lowest level of effort in any project.) Although I'm sure you can think of other ways as well, you could base your organization on any of the following:

- **Functional or technological disciplines.** Decide what is required in each phase of the project. Schedule the machine tool operators separately from the marketing specialists.
- **Organizational structure.** In a clearly divided organization or a cooperating set of separate organizations, establish the WBS according to reporting structure. If outside vendors are involved, they can be included in this kind of planning.
- **Physical location.** If you are working with separate facilities, build the WBS based on the geographical locations instead of the people.
- **Systems and subsystems.** If there is clear demarcation between several aspects of a project, assemble the WBS to reflect this.

You can use the "wrap-up" approach as well. In a wrap-up, you start at the bottom, listing each element, and work up. As you move up, each layer contains a wrap-up of all the elements of the layer underneath it.

You might want to consider these few other suggestions when creating a WBS. They are especially important for assembling a complex WBS:

def•i•ni•tion

An **element of work** is an activity required to complete a project that's too small to be elevated to the rank of work package. Elements of work are the steps to complete a work package.

- Each *element of work* (also known as an activity) should be assigned to only one level of effort. Never repeat an element in another part of the tree or outline.
- A narrative must accompany the WBS. You may want to label each box or line with a number that references a page in an overview narrative document to provide more detail than "Get CEO approval for expansion plan." Software tools such as Microsoft Project will allow you to attach "notes" to as many tasks as you would like.
- Clearly identify related work packages in the WBS. A great way to show the linkage is by color-coding tasks.
- At all levels, the WBS should provide measurable deliverables for each aspect of the project. There are deliverables for the project itself, such as the cable box for All-Star Cable, and there are deliverables for work packages, such as building the drop-down screen menu the customer will see on his or her TV set.

- Assemble the WBS in a format that allows changes if and when the project shifts slightly in direction. Computers are ideal, but a carefully protected whiteboard (wrap it loosely with plastic wrap) can fit the bill for a simple project. Use lots of sticky notes as well so things are easy to move around as you make changes.

Along the Critical Path

When maintaining a WBS for a large project, you need version control in place. This means that each version, no matter how preliminary or final, should be date- and time-stamped. That way, older plans can be relegated to the file, and everyone works with the most current document. Even if you work on a computer and don't print all versions of the WBS, save each iteration separately by date so you can be sure you're using the latest and greatest plan. Also, save the older versions in an archive file, either in hard copy or electronically, so you can use them to track project history and to serve as a learning tool to evaluate what (if anything) went wrong.

Five Steps to the Work Breakdown Structure

You must complete five steps to develop a WBS that meets all of its goals:

1. Break the work into independent work packages that you can sequence, assign, schedule, and monitor.
2. Define the work packages at a level of detail appropriate for the length and complexity of the project.
3. Integrate the work packages into a total system with a beginning and an end. This may involve combining tasks and then creating milestones.
4. Present the work packages in a format you can easily communicate to people assigned to complete them during the project. Remember that each work package should have a deliverable and a time for completing that deliverable.
5. Verify that completion of the work packages will result in attainment of all the project goals and objectives.

For most large projects, assembling and organizing a WBS takes time, but a carefully assembled WBS goes a long way toward streamlining a project after the work begins.

Criteria for Ensuring Quality Work

As you develop the WBS, you need to have some way of determining whether a task is done and is done correctly. You can do this through establishing measurable quality levels based on the standards in your industry. You can also do this by establishing standard quality checklists and formal testing procedures, which are often done on engineering projects. You can also use peer reviews or stakeholder acceptance reviews to ensure quality. In a peer review, you ask colleagues who are not a part of the project to examine the project plan and the deliverables produced to date and provide you and the project team with suggestions for improvement.

One way to document these criteria is to develop an outline of the WBS with the quality criteria and review process noted next to each appropriate work package or milestone. Completion and evaluation criteria improve the clarity of the WBS and will ultimately improve the quality of the project plan. This is important because it's a lot cheaper to fix a problem or task description during the planning stage than during implementation.

Work packages are important elements for ensuring quality and are useful in the following ways:

- Work packages are a way of modularizing the project into manageable segments. Thus, tracking the progress of work packages is a way to assess and control the work done.
- By breaking work into work packages, you can determine the skills you need to complete the work and can quantify how many people will be required to do the work.
- Work packages allow you to communicate the work that needs to be done to other team members without going into too much detail.
- Breaking the work into work packages ensures that all the work sequences are identified and understood.

The bottom line is this: Work packages help you organize the hundreds of small work activities, or tasks, that go into completing a project. Without work packages, the amount of work to track would make your head spin because you would have no way to keep track of things or prioritize work.

Time Is Money

Don't forget to put the project management tasks into the WBS. These tasks take time, too. You might group these tasks under a summary task called "managing the project," which would include time for developing reports, holding meetings, and gaining approvals from stakeholders.

A work package for our All-Star Cable case study might be the development of a high-level diagram of the proposed architecture for delivering Movies-on-Demand. As project manager, if that diagram is due to you in two weeks, you will know if the work is completed or not. That's what we mean by a unique deliverable.

Including too many elements in the WBS amounts to micromanaging in the extreme, which will probably miff your staff; they might think you're attempting to manage their lives as well as the project, an impossible and thankless task.

Give Yourself Plenty of Time

Building a WBS for a complex project takes time. The WBS is a way to take the requirements the stakeholder gave us (from Chapter 6) and turn them into the work that will need to be completed for the project to be delivered. List work so you can assess the overall amount of work and sequence it in the most logical fashion. A list of activities can be short and simple or long and detailed, depending on the size and goals of the project. Don't try to sequence the tasks or estimate time and budget during WBS definition. Those steps come later (see Chapters 11 through 15). Finally, don't try to do it all yourself, unless you are working on the project all by yourself. Enlist the members of your project team to help you think through all the required work.

The WBS makes communication among core project team members easier. And, as we've emphasized throughout this book, forgetting to list an important task can have a very negative effect on the project's bottom line and schedule. Therefore, it's a good idea to have the members of your project team help you in developing the WBS. Generally, you have chosen them for their knowledge and experience, so rely on that expertise to build the WBS. As project manager, you may take the high-level pass at the various activities, but rely on people who are more experienced in particular areas to finish it. You will be glad you did. The WBS should account for the production of every deliverable on the statement of work (SOW) that was approved for the project. Use the goals and deliverables in the SOW as a starting point for developing the tasks.

Risk Management

In dealing with vendors, allow more time in the WBS for them to deliver than you may need. Vendors have a nasty habit of over-promising and under-delivering.

Defining Your Deliverables

Developing work-sense (something like horse-sense) takes time. "Do I lump all these procedures into one work package? Or are they actually two, five, or nine separate ones?" Correctly defining the level of effort in a project provides an easier way to control the project and keep it in the groove.

Most project managers use the 8/80 rule as a guideline for determining whether an activity qualifies as a work package. The rule states that any work package that takes less than one day to complete (8 hours) is probably too small, and you should consider combining it with something else. On the other end of the spectrum, if a work package takes longer than two weeks (80 hours), it is probably too large, and you should consider breaking it into smaller work packages. Of course, the span between one day and two weeks may depend on the overall size of the project. If the project will take 18 to 24 months to complete, you might consider work packages that are longer, say one month. For you as the project manager, the important principle is that you need to know if a work package is being completed on time. If it is not, you want to have enough time to recover and keep the project on schedule. If you wait too long, you may not have the flexibility to put some extra people on the package to get it finished in time to save the schedule.

Another way to judge the lowest-level task you should accommodate in your WBS is to consider budget or time criteria. The lowest-level task should require at least .25 to 2 percent of the total budget or project time. You also can use segments, such as half or full days, to define the smallest task levels. These approaches may appear initially imprecise, but they establish a general guideline for the lowest-level tasks in your project.

A third option is to use the reporting period rule to determine the work packages. This rules states that no work package should be longer than a standard reporting period. Thus, if you make weekly status reports, no work package should be longer than a week in length. This helps eliminate work package statuses that are 73 percent or 38 percent done; work packages will only be reported as started (50 percent done), not started, or complete (100 percent). If a work package using this rule is started and is on the not-complete list for more than two reporting periods, you have a problem to solve.

When you start building the WBS, you will need to consider all of the required deliverables, including any drawings, designs, documents, and schematics, for example. Here are some other tips regarding your project's deliverables:

- **A deliverable should be clearly stated.** The "design the button layout on the hand-held remote control" task is much clearer than the "design the TV control system" task, which may be really five to ten separate work packages. The latter is so unclear that you can't schedule it because there are too many elements; team members won't know where one work package starts or stops. ("Do we complete the remote control and the TV's receiver side of the system as well as the power controls? Or do we just do the remote control?") But the "design the TV control system" task could be a milestone—one that includes tasks for the remote control, primary power system, and television receiver.

Time Is Money

Remember, work packages are tracked in the plan, but elements and activities are not; elements and activities still need to be accounted for, however, in the overall time allocated for the work packages.

- **All work in the same work package should occur within a sequential or parallel time frame without gaps for possible other work in between.** Thus, "framing and plumbing the bathroom" is not a well-formed work package in your bathroom remodeling project because plumbing the bathroom is not necessarily related to framing the bathroom, and other tasks, such as adding insulation, could come after the framing task. It's better to define the tasks as separate work packages, "framing" and "plumbing," in the project plan rather than to risk confusion about the sequence or priority of events. Also, don't confuse work packages with milestones, which are a significant event within the project such as the completion of a major deliverable.
- **A work package should only include related work elements.** When washing your car, for example, the work package "get soapy water" wouldn't fit with "polish the car" because there's no relationship between the procedures, and they occur at different times in the project cycle. (At least they do when I wash my car!) Therefore, a work package called "get soapy water and polish the car" is not a well-formed work package because it involves unlike steps.

Sometimes it is easier to write a list of the work packages that you may need to do and then work on rolling them up into the WBS. Use a brainstorming technique to capture all the information, and then develop a more detailed diagram, as shown in Chapter 10, to see how they will relate to each other.

Refining the WBS

As you progress through the project, you will gather more information and learn more, which should allow you to refine your plan to greater accuracy and predictability. Project managers refer to this refinement as *progressive elaboration*. It is one of the key reasons for keeping your project plan accurate and current.

So that's a wrap! Now you know how the work breaks down in your project. You've taken all the project goals developed in the SOW and broken them into specific work packages. But that's just one important step in planning. Now, let's take a look at sequencing the work in a network diagram.

def•i•ni•tion

Progressive elaboration is defined as continuously improving the plan as more information becomes available in the progression of the project.

The Least You Need to Know

- A single task is a cohesive work package with a unique, measurable deliverable you can monitor and track.
- A work breakdown structure (WBS) organizes the tasks of a project into hierarchies and milestones.
- Milestones divide the project into logical, measurable segments. When you complete all the milestones, the project should be done.
- Once you create a complete task list and WBS, you can plan the schedule and resources for the project.
- Build criteria for measuring the quality and completion of tasks into the WBS and the project plan.

Chapter 10

The Network Diagram: A Map for Your Project

In This Chapter

- The network diagram: your project's roadmap
- Why use a network diagram?
- The concepts of precedence and concurrent (or parallel) activities
- Symbols and conventions in network diagramming
- Understanding complex time relationships for critical projects
- Major network diagramming systems

You may be thinking this is going to be the chapter in which you get to use networks and computers to plan and control your project from the depths of the Internet. Sorry! Even though you could put information about your project plans and status on the Net to keep team members up-to-date, when most project managers talk about the network, they're not talking about a schematic that creates a picture of your project.

The network, in project management terms, is a proven way to organize and sequence the activities of a project. Anything but the simplest project should have a network diagram. In fact, you don't even need a computer to create a network diagram (but it sure helps on big projects).

In this chapter, we'll explain the value of a network diagram. In Chapter 30, we talk a lot more about the computer tools you can use to quickly build the network diagram. It's important that you understand how to create your own network diagram so you will know what your computer program is doing for you.

What's a Network Diagram?

The *network diagram* (also called the project schedule network diagram) shows the path of the project, lists starting and completion dates, and names the responsible party for each task. For people not already familiar with your project, such as management and new team members, the network diagram explains the project using a pictorial representation to show how the work on the project fits together. Remember the peer or stakeholder reviews we talked about in the last chapter? Network diagrams can help there, too!

> **def•i•ni•tion**
>
> A **network diagram** is the logical representation of scheduled project activities and defines the sequence of work in a project. It is always drawn from left to right and reflects the chronological order of the activities.

If properly sequenced, a network diagram will …

- Show the sequences and relationships between activities necessary to complete a project.
- Identify relationships among milestones in the project that can be used for monitoring progress and completion.
- Show the interrelationships of activities in different parts of the work breakdown structure (WBS) hierarchy.
- Establish a vehicle for scheduling activities (see Chapters 11 and 12).
- Help reduce uncertainty in the project by breaking it into many small phases that have been analyzed and sequenced in advance of starting the work.

If you put the network diagram on a wall where the whole project team can see it (especially your boss), you can then reprint it regularly and use a bright color to mark off the activities as they are completed. The network diagram can be a powerful way to communicate what has been done on the project and what remains to be accomplished. Of course, if the project gets stalled and the activities don't get done, it also can be a sure way to let people know you're in trouble. (Hopefully, this won't happen to you!)

Why Do You Need a Network Diagram?

If your project involves more than one person or more than a handful of activities, the sequence of activities is probably not a simple matter of working on one activity after another. Project work often happens in parallel because people may be working on different activities at the same time. To make things more complicated, the activities may be related to other activities that come later and are dependent on the earlier activities being finished. All these relationships and interdependencies can be tough to figure out in your head and impossible to understand from a list of activities that must be completed. This is why you need a network diagram: to help you understand how the work should really go together. Only then can you develop a somewhat reliable schedule for your project.

The WBS and the Network Diagram

A WBS is a great first step in identifying the work packages in a project. However, WBS representations don't graphically display the sequencing relationships between various parts of the project. A WBS only shows the hierarchical relationships between work on the project; you can't schedule a hierarchy as easily as a sequence. Therefore, you cannot use it to create a schedule or to coordinate work done by different people or resources unless all the activities in a project are sequential, which they rarely are.

Complex *Gantt charts* can display relationships among the activities, and these are best produced by computer programs. (See Chapter 11 for more on Gantt charts.) Network diagrams are an easier way to identify and plan sequences.

Network diagrams reveal the workflow, not just the work. Networks are always drawn from left to right with lines drawn between activities to indicate the precedence among activities. Arrowheads are placed on the lines to indicate the direction of the workflow through time.

Although it is possible to create a network diagram for a small project without first developing a WBS, some limitations to network diagramming make this undesirable. Network diagrams simply sequence the work

def•i•ni•tion

Named after Henry Gantt, who developed them in the early 1900s, a **Gantt chart** is a special bar chart that lists activities on the left side of the chart; dates are listed across the top, and activity duration is shown as a date-based horizontal bar running across the page.

activities and identify their relationships in time. Networks are not as good as a WBS at demonstrating hierarchical relationships (milestones) in a project, but you can use them to demonstrate the sequence of activities and relationships among activities in different milestones in the WBS. So it's customary to complete your network diagrams after the WBS.

In addition, a network diagram is awkward for managing budgets and personnel assignments. A WBS is awkward for scheduling. Thus, the use of both a WBS and a network diagram provide a powerful combination for managing and controlling your project.

You must understand two central concepts before you can create a network diagram for a project: the concept of precedence and the concept of concurrent (or parallel) activities. Let's take a closer look at each.

Precedence Relationships in a Project Network

Precedence defines the sequencing order and how activities, called work elements, are related to one another in the plan. If one activity must be completed before the next activity can be started, the first one has precedence over the second. In the All-Star Cable project, for example, the development of the graphic user interface (GUI) must be completed before it can be tested. In a network diagram, this precedence is illustrated by drawing one activity to the left of the other. Other precedence occurs in the project as well. For instance, we must build the employee interface prototype before we can test it with the user groups.

> **def•i•ni•tion**
>
> When one activity in the project must be completed before another activity can be started, the first activity is said to have **precedence** over the other.

Concurrent (Parallel) Activities

Although some activities must precede others, many activities can be started at the same time as other activities. This leads to the other important diagramming concept: parallel activities. Many project activities can be worked on in parallel as long as suitable resources are available. For example, it is possible to begin working on the data storage model for All-Star Cable at the same time that others are working on the interfaces and application development activities within the project. However, both of these take precedence over the reporting activities within the project. In a network diagram, it is possible to identify parallel activities by drawing them in parallel to each other in the same plane. These activities may also be called simultaneous or concurrent activities.

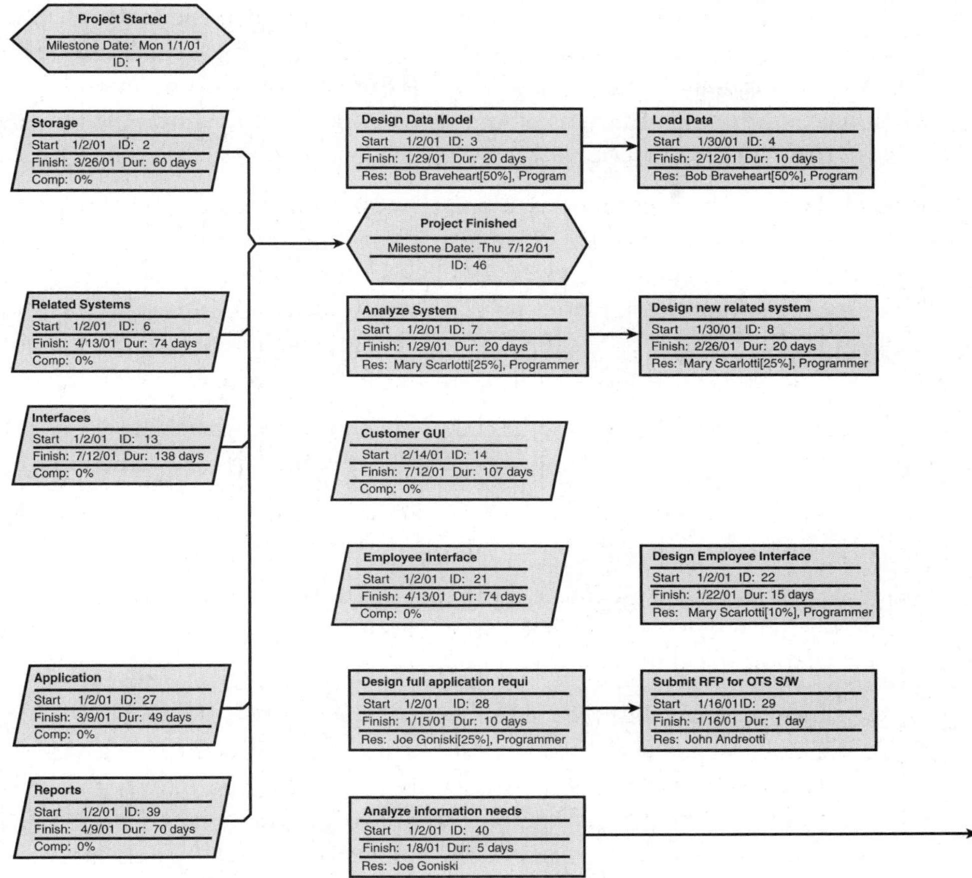

This is just a small portion of the network diagram for All-Star Cable's Movies-on-Demand project.

The concepts of precedence and parallel activities are important because the relationships between activities ultimately will establish the basis for scheduling a project. (You will learn about this in Chapters 11 and 12.) That's why we often call network diagrams precedence diagrams. Adjusting the parallel activities and the precedence alters the time and resources required to complete a project. The goal in developing the network diagram is to identify activities that can occur in a parallel manner and to specify the precedence that exists among the activities. This leads to the development of an optimum sequence of activities for scheduling purposes.

It can also help to determine if "crashing" or "fast tracking" the project makes sense. Crashing is a term project managers use when they want to compress the time to catch up on the project schedule by adding more people if the budget will allow it. Fast tracking is when a project manager determines that activities can be done in parallel without compromising the project. In each of these instances, the activities may not have been planned that way, but the network diagram allows the project manager to see that crashing or fast tracking is an option.

Boxes hold the description of each task. Lines connect the activities to one another. Network diagrams are really a simple matter of linking activities in boxes with lines. The activities are laid out horizontally from left to right to coincide with the time sequence in which the activities will be completed. Groups of activities that lead to specific deliverables are identified by parallelograms. These may mark the milestones in the chart (such as project finished in the All-Star Cable example).

So everyone who uses network diagrams can figure out what's going on, a number of basic conventions (rules) in reading activities in a network diagram exist:

- The defined sequences of activities are represented by placing activities in horizontal order from left to right in the network.
- Activities that can happen at the same time are shown in columns. We call these parallel activities because the work can happen at the same time as other work in different rows.
- The precedence between activities and milestones is shown by drawing lines from activity to activity, indicating that the activity on the left must be completed before the activity on the right can begin. The activity that must be completed first is called the precedent task. The activity that starts after the precedent activity is called the dependent task. That's why the network diagram reveals the dependencies among activities. (Think this is getting pretty technical? Don't worry. This is as hard as it gets.)
- Lines among activities can cross rows to show how activities in the various sequences relate to each other.

Most project management software will ask you about the relationships among activities so that they can be understood in a network diagram. Here are some of them:

- One activity may depend on the completion of multiple activities or milestones. You must enter the precedence for all of these activities into the software by understanding which are the precedent activities to the dependent task.
- An activity may start independently of some activities but still be dependent on others. Software packages will only draw lines between activities with dependency.

- An activity without a precedent activity or milestone can logically be started at any time after the initial "Start Project" activity because it has no other dependent relationships. Such an activity will have its own row.

The sequences of activities you put in your network are not absolute. Experienced project managers often revise and adjust the activities until they are optimized. When people begin thinking through precedence, they often find that activities have been left out of the WBS. If you discover this problem, add these new activities and make sure to note them in the appropriate places in the WBS. The network and the WBS should always match. In reverse, if you find that some activities are redundant, remove them from both documents.

If an activity defined in the WBS doesn't seem to fit in the network diagram, this usually means it's out of place. The activity could be too small to include in the network diagram or too large and require further breakdown into more elemental activities. If you change an activity's status, make the change in your WBS so it and the network diagram match.

Be careful not to sequence activities in an arbitrary order. Just because you've always done something a certain way does not mean it's the best way to do it. Try to look at the activities from a new point of view; find better ways to get the work done. A network diagram provides a great opportunity to do this. Can you sequence the activities differently for better use of resources? Can you split some activities into two or more activities to make the organization of work more flexible? It's usually a good idea to have objective outsiders review the sequences, in addition to the project team, to avoid bias in the sequence of work. Sometimes a person outside the politics of a project can identify a better way to complete the work.

Complex Time Relationships for Critical Projects

The optimum way to represent precedence in projects isn't always a simple matter of completing one activity and then starting another (called a finish-to-start precedence). Your precedence diagrams can also specify complex timing relationships between activities. By overlapping activities in the diagram and using arrows to represent specific timing, you can show relationships in which activities must be started at a certain point after another activity is started. This is especially important in complex projects. For example, using precedence diagramming techniques, you can show the following complex task-sequencing requirements:

- **An activity that should start at the same time as another activity because they're logically related.** For example, in All-Star Cable, the project team could be gathering reporting requirements for Movies-on-Demand at the same time they are taking an inventory of the existing reports that All-Star used in Pay-for-View. Overlapping activities like this reduces the total project duration.
- **An activity that must be completed at least five days before another can begin.** For example, the pouring of foundation for a house must be done five days before the walls are framed to allow the cement to cure.
- **An activity that must be finished before another activity can be finished.** For example, the planning of a product can start before the design approvals are started, but the planning cannot be completed until the design approvals are done.

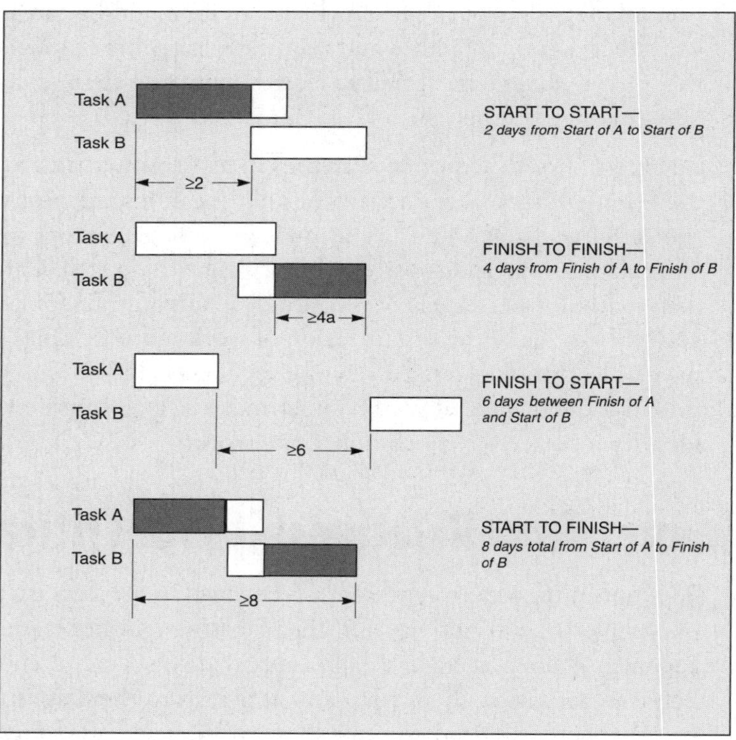

Complex precedence diagramming conventions for showing lead and lag times between activities.

For most simple business projects, it isn't necessary to define these types of complex *lead* and *lag* times at the activity level. Simple precedence relationships (finish-to-start relationships) are adequate for all but the most complex projects. The terms are mentioned here, however, because they are often referred to in computerized project management software or in other project management literature. You should know what the terms mean even if you don't use them. As a project manager, it's a matter of pride and being well-informed. These advanced techniques can also come in handy when you need to adjust activities to meet a deadline.

def•i•ni•tion

Lead is the amount of time that precedes the start of work on another activity. **Lag** is the amount of time after one activity is started or finished before the next activity can be started or finished.

When Is Enough Enough?

In Chapters 7 and 8, you learned how goals and constraints establish the scope for your project. In creating a network, as in creating the WBS, the project goals and scope establish the level of detail for defining the work that must be completed. Even so, the question arises in developing every network as to how many activities should be included. No hard and fast rules exist, but we would suggest that you identify work down to the work package level. However, the best advice is to use your good judgment.

Three Major Network Methods and Others You May Encounter

We've discussed the basic precedence diagram because we think it is the easiest, most effective networking diagram for most small to mid-size projects, the projects most people manage in everyday business. But even if it's just to impress your boss by using nifty acronyms, you should know that related systems of network diagramming and scheduling techniques are used in industry today.

The two most common forms of networking systems are the Performance Evaluation and Review Technique (PERT) and the Critical Path Method (CPM). The techniques are similar in principal to what we've already presented. The differences lie in how the projects display information and deal with scheduling uncertainties. And given that these techniques were developed by engineers for engineering projects, a lot more symbols are used to represent the relationships between activities in a network.

Until PERT/CPM techniques were developed, simple Gantt charts or other bar charts were the best tools available to represent project sequences. Gantt charts show a graphic representation of work on a time scale. You will learn more about Gantt charts as a useful way to represent the overall project schedule in Chapter 11. These charts are really just timelines that show activities in parallel. The complex versions produced by today's project management software usually show the dependencies between activities represented in networks, work in progress, and comparisons between the current status and the planned status (baseline) of the project.

CPM is often cited as better for construction-type projects. It is argued that PERT is more appropriate for software-oriented projects. For that reason, the project manager for Movies-on-Demand has decided to use the PERT method for establishing the schedule.

The primary reason for this is the different approaches the two systems use for scheduling, not because of the networks, which are largely the same in terms of sequencing possibilities. In CPM, one time estimate is used for creating the schedule; PERT uses a more complex system based on three time estimates that are used to determine the most probable time for completion.

Along the Critical Path

One of the pioneering efforts to show the interrelationships among activities on a project was undertaken by the science management team of Morgan R. Walker and James E. Kelly in the mid-1950s at the E. I. Du Pont Company. Their joint efforts resulted in the Kelly-Walker network technique. However, in later publications of their work, they referred to the method as the Critical Path Method. Du Pont tested the CPM method in the construction of a major chemical plant and in several maintenance projects that were completed by the middle of 1958. It is claimed that Du Pont credited more than $1 million in savings to this technique in the first year it was used. (And remember, that was in 1958 dollars!)

During the same period, the management scientists of the Special Projects Office of the U.S. Navy, along with the firms of Lockheed and Booz, Allen, and Hamilton, developed a similar network system called PERT, which stands for Program Evaluation and Review Technique. The system was developed to help coordinate more than 3,000 people involved in the development of the Polaris missile. The use of PERT is credited with reducing the time required to complete the project by two years.

This more complex time-estimating approach is deemed by some to be more appropriate for research projects with high degrees of uncertainty and risk. For most general business projects, these differences are not critical, and some people call all network systems by the name PERT/CPM because of their similarities.

Circles or Boxes? Who Cares?

Okay, this next section is for people who just want to know more about the PERT/CPM differences. It might get a bit technical, so you can opt out now if you just want to get your project plan done. See you in the next chapter.

Traditionally, PERT/CPM networks use circles and arrows to describe work in a project. The two systems use the same basic diagramming conventions you've already learned as a way to link activities, except they refer to milestones as "events." These two concepts, activities and events, are central to the traditional PERT/CPM diagrams. An activity is a specific project activity that requires resources and time to complete. An event is a specific end state for one or more activities that occur at a specific point in time. An event occurs as a result of completing one or more activities.

AOA and AON

There are two methods of representing activities and events in PERT/CPM networks: activity on arrow (AOA), also called activity on arc, and activity on node (AON). The method used is largely a matter of preference. In AOA, the arrows are the activities, and the circles (called "nodes" in PERT/CPM) are the events. In the AON method, the activities are the circles, and the lines demonstrate the precedence between activities. We show some of the traditional ways of diagramming activities in a PERT/CPM chart in the following diagram.

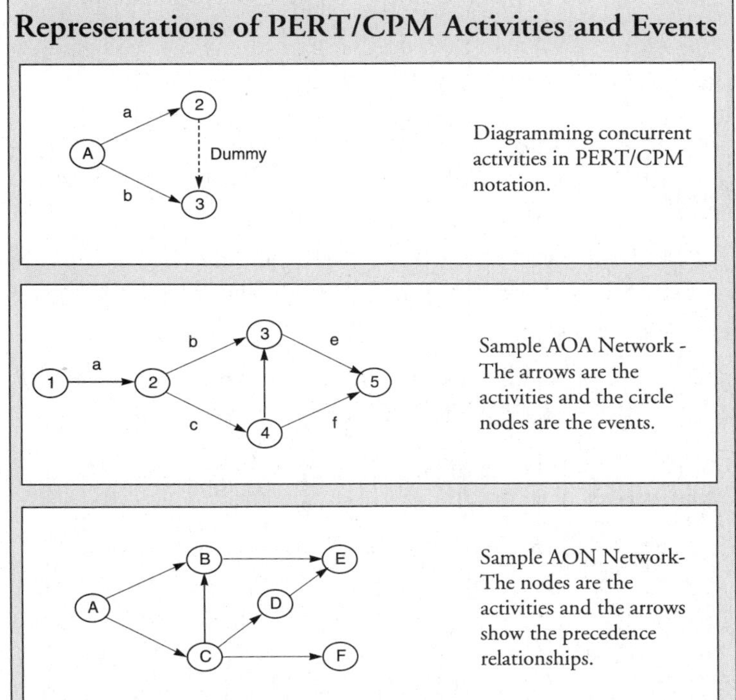

PERT/CPM activities.

Simple precedence networks using boxes, as shown here, are really just another version of an AON PERT/CPM network. We think the boxes are a lot easier to use. (Bet you do, too, at this point.) We've found that most mid-size business projects are easier to describe and understand using the boxes than by creating complex number, circle, and arc networks. In fact, most computerized project management programs now offer boxes to replace the circle/arc format.

We're glad you made it through all this because it's important for an informed project manager like you to be familiar with some of the other diagramming options in project management. As you get more experience, you might want to experiment with these other diagramming techniques for your networks. (We suggest you get a comprehensive book on PERT/CPM techniques before you do.)

Tried and True Networks

Over the years, with the advances in computer software, some of the representational techniques in PERT/CPM and precedence diagramming have been improved or modified and expanded. Still, the simplicity of the original system has withstood the tests of time and application, and no truly substantive changes have been made in the original methods.

In Chapters 11 and 12, you'll learn how to turn your network diagram into a schedule you can be proud (and confident) to present to management for approval.

The Least You Need to Know

- The network diagram isn't always necessary for small projects, but it's a good tool for most projects to establish the order of steps and the relationships among the various activities in a project.
- As a project manager, you predict the future. The tough part is making the future match your predictions! A network diagram can help.
- Most project management software supports the task-in-box diagramming method, which is relatively easy to use.
- A network diagram provides you with a great roadmap for completing your project on time.

Chapter 11

Project Start to Finish: Establishing the Time to Get Things Done

In This Chapter

- Scheduling based on the work to be completed
- Building reliable estimates using experienced people with a variety of perspectives
- Using Gantt charts to manage the schedule
- Building your confidence in scheduling by using one of four ways to create an estimate

As you would assume from reading earlier chapters in this book, the schedule is intertwined with the work breakdown structure (WBS), the network diagram, the risk assessment, and eventually the budget. Change one and you invariably influence the others. We have separated the schedule and the budget in the next few chapters, but in reality, you need to work on both at the same time. The schedule and the budget work together to float a project or sink it.

The Schedule or the Budget: Which Is First?

Some new project managers are inclined to start with the budget first, but we don't recommend it. Because time is money, the schedule will affect the final budget in many ways. That's why we discuss scheduling first. The best project managers establish the schedule before finalizing the budget, even if everyone doesn't always understand the logic. It's best to try to determine how much time is really required to complete a project before you start worrying about the budget.

The experienced project manager can assess an activity, understand what's required, and provide a reasonably realistic estimate of the time requirement as if pulling the number from the air. You will get to that point someday with the help of this book and with a few projects under your belt. But until you get that experience, you can establish a reasonable schedule using this and the subsequent chapter's advice as a process guide. And maybe more important, in the following pages, you also will learn how to deal with external pressures (such as bosses and customers) that demand unrealistic dates. No matter what your manager says, you can't build Rome in a day.

Building a schedule also verifies the project's viability. If, when assembling the schedule, time is not on your side, you may need to work out an extension with management or an increase in resources. Working on the schedule might also reveal missing activities. Remember, everything is interrelated, so expect to adjust the network diagram, WBS, and budget as you adapt the schedule.

The Schedule Synchronizes the Project

Accurate, realistic, and workable scheduling is what makes a project tick. The schedule shows who is doing what and when they are supposed to be doing it. Scheduling involves converting the well-organized and sequenced tasks in your WBS and network diagram, as well as the list of resources and vendors you will develop in Chapters 15, into an achievable timetable with start dates, finish dates, and assigned responsibilities for each activity.

Carry out the steps in creating a schedule sequentially, as follows:

1. **Establish the scheduling assumptions.** From earlier chapters, you already know why it's important to clarify goals and objectives before the project plan reaches its final stages. For the same reasons, it's important to specify scheduling assumptions before the schedule is completed. Answering the following questions should help in this process. We've also included a simple worksheet (see Chapter 12) that will assist you in determining the assumptions germane to your project.

- Are there a fixed number of resources (remember that resources mean people, time, technology, and money) you can use on the project? Or can you add them to meet the schedule priorities?
- Is there an absolute date by which the project must be completed so that it doesn't become worthless? (An example would be designing a new trade show booth for the big July show. If the booth is a no-show, then the time and money used to design and build it as well as the cost of the trade show floor space is lost.)
- Can you negotiate the completion date based on a realistic schedule of when all the deliverables (goals) can be met?
- Will people work standard workdays or will overtime be allowed or expected? Watch for holidays and expect to pay extra for having people work on Christmas Day!
- Are all resources currently trained and available? Or will your project require hiring additional people and acquiring new equipment? If training or hiring is required, schedule it.

Here are some examples of assumptions for our All-Star Cable example: a network expert from the organization will be available from August through October; new cable boxes for Movies-on-Demand will be operational as planned by January 25; no major changes in procedures for billing will occur within the next six months. Assumptions protect the project from being severely impacted by planned change in other parts of the organization, change the project manager may not be aware of. Assumptions can also reveal risks and limitations and enable you to build contingencies for them into your plan.

Time Is Money

Even though it takes a woman nine months to have a baby, two women can't have a baby in half that time!

Large projects require you to document your assumptions in writing. That way, you are less likely to forget something. Also, when you review those plans with your project sponsor or the project steering committee, they may alert you to incorrect assumptions you are making. Simple projects don't always require documentation of the assumptions, but you should have a verbal agreement on them among your team and outside resources.

2. **Estimate the number of resources, the activity *effort*, and the work package *duration* based on the resources you have on hand or can afford.** Remember that these estimates are all constrained by your personnel and equipment resources. In most cases the more resources, the less time required. Here you need to estimate the duration of an activity over a number of days.

   def•i•ni•tion

   Effort (also called labor estimates) is the time it takes, usually in hours or days, to work on an activity or work package. **Duration** is the time, usually in days, that it takes to complete the activity within the WBS. It is sometimes confused with elapsed time.

   Sometimes duration and effort are the same. If it takes seven hours of effort for a secretary to stuff envelopes during the course of one day, then the effort is one workday and the duration of the work package is one workday. Sometimes duration and effort are very different. It may take only four hours of meeting time to get the building inspector's approval of a building's wiring, but these meetings happen over a period of two weeks. Thus, the effort for getting the wiring approved is four hours, but the duration of the work package is two weeks.

   To create both an accurate schedule and a detailed budget for a project, it is important to know both the effort and the duration required to complete a work package. It's also important to know that you can often, but not always, shorten the duration of an activity by adding more people to complete the labor. Thus, estimating the number of people and resources that will perform an activity is an important consideration when estimating duration.

   Duration stands out in project management terms because the accumulated duration of activities along the critical path in the project plan directly affects all the subsequent activities in the project. (We'll explain the critical path in Chapter 12.) It is the duration of the activities that, when added together, establish the time required to complete the project.

3. **Determine calendar dates for each activity and create a master schedule.** For a complex project network, you will also need to determine the critical path and float for each activity on the project. (You'll learn how to do this in Chapter 12.)

4. **Adjust the individual resource assignments as necessary to optimize the schedule.** This is called the resource-leveling phase. (You'll also learn about this in Chapter 12.)

5. **Chart the final schedule.** In most cases, a computer program makes all of these scheduling steps easier unless the project is very small.

Estimating Time: Your Best Guess at Effort and Duration

Of all the steps in scheduling, estimating the duration of tasks is the most important. Unfortunately, this is like trying to predict the future. You can only guess, but there are better ways to guess than others. Without accurate activity duration estimates, the entire plan and project might crumble around you.

When estimating the duration of activities, you can use these five options to make the estimates (guesses) as good as possible:

- Ask the people who will actually do the work, but have them estimate the work they'll be doing, not the duration. For example, in our all All-Star Cable case study, the project manager has asked his team to estimate the time it will take to interview the potential vendors for the equipment needed, and they told him they would need about two hours per vendor. However, he knows that it will take a good deal of time to schedule the interviews and evaluate information gleaned during them. So with three vendors, the interviews might take one or two days (level of effort), but the activity will likely take nearly two weeks to complete (the duration). You'll have to extrapolate the durations based on the workload, other commitments, and the project member's experience with similar activities.
- Get an objective expert's opinion (for example, from someone who isn't working on the project).
- Find a similar task in a completed project plan to see how long it took to get done. This is called an analogous estimate.
- When you know the relationship between a certain activity and time, use that estimate. For example, most programmers can tell you how many lines of code they can develop per hour or per day. This we call a parametric estimate.
- Make your best educated guess. This is the last resort when you're under pressure, so make sure the guess is more educated than it is arbitrary. If possible, instead of guessing, try the preceding options.

Who Should You Ask?

To get reliable estimates on the duration of tasks and the effort required, you will likely need to ask other people about the time it will take them to get things done. The following sections present some of the people you can ask to help determine the task duration and the effort estimates for your schedule.

Representative Team Members for Each Part of the Project

Seek out the most experienced team members who will be completing work on your project. (We give you ideas for choosing your project team in Chapter 14.) If they have worked on similar projects in the past, they can use what are called historical estimates, or how much time it took them last time. Again, we typically ask them for the level of effort, not the duration. Some team members will pad their estimates a little or a lot, and some will be overconfident about their abilities to accomplish miracles. You must adjust the duration in the final plan to account for these idiosyncrasies if you want to come up with the optimum schedule.

To sit down with all the key team members to estimate activity durations is often useful. Even if nothing useful (to you) comes out of the sessions, they still serve to build team relationships and to give you a better understanding of the project from the team members' points of view. It's also an excellent technique for assembling a rough-cut schedule in a hurry.

Outside Vendors and Service Agencies

You must get estimates directly from any outside service providers and consultants who will work on your project. Never estimate their time for them. You can negotiate their estimates, but if you dictate a vendor's schedule without his input, you'll never get the schedule you demand. You should politely request a written estimate that fixes the cost and commits him to a schedule (unless the project runs off the rails or changes in scope, of course). Shop price and time!

Experienced Managers or Experts

People in your organization who have handled similar projects can provide excellent advice and can study cost estimates for problems. They also might be able to provide exact estimates if they worked on a project that had elements common to yours. Or they may be much more experienced project managers and be willing to help. If no such experts exist within your company, you could get advice from a consultant or a colleague in another company who can help verify your work and duration estimates.

Management and Other Project Stakeholders

If you want your managers and stakeholders (such as the steering committee members) to buy into your schedule, you need to give them an opportunity to help plan the schedule or at least review it before you submit the project plan for approval. By bringing stakeholders into the process, they'll see that you will efficiently use your time and wisely spend their money. Their involvement will assist you in getting the final plan approved because they'll already have a grasp on the realities of the schedule.

Weighing the Risk

After getting information on the labor requirements and activity durations from various sources, you'll need to use your judgment to determine the duration you'll actually assign to the schedule. Each of these durations will have a risk associated with it. It's often useful to come up with a best-case schedule and a worst-case schedule based on these risks. For example, the project manager for Movies-on-Demand may estimate it will take the team one month to design and build the various reports the company will require after Movies-on-Demand is implemented. However, if the project manager only has one person with the skills to complete the design, there is risk. What if the developer gets sick? Or gets into an automobile accident and is hospitalized for a while? The project manager must always plan for these kinds of risks.

A Compromise Between Best and Worst Case

In estimating every activity, assume that the actual time required will fall somewhere between flawless execution and major disaster. The best approach is to establish a compromise between the two. Some project management methodologies, such as PERT (see Chapter 10), provide the mechanics for estimating all three. These include …

- **The optimistic estimate.** Everything goes like clockwork and without problems.
- **The most likely estimate.** A few problems crop up, and normal delays compromise the optimistic estimate.
- **The pessimistic estimate.** Allowances are made for many elements to go wrong, substantially delaying or jeopardizing the activity. The pessimistic estimate assumes the project is going ahead.

Ultimately, you will use these three estimates in combination with each other to come up with a "most likely" schedule based on your confidence in the estimates. Sometimes people just go with the pessimistic estimate; at other times, the most likely estimate wins out. If you use the optimistic estimate, you're just looking for trouble.

Many managers of large, high-risk, big-money projects use these estimates and feed them into a formula to determine the most likely duration. The approach that's best for you will depend on the project, your experience with similar work, and your organization's culture.

Along the Critical Path

In the standard PERT methodology, the accepted formula for coming up with the "most likely" estimate of a task's duration is:

Expected duration = [OD + 4(MLD) + PD] ÷ 6

OD = Optimistic duration

MLD = Most likely duration

PD = Pessimistic duration

The Confidence Factor

Just how reliable are your estimates? You might be comfortable with the timetable for delivery of a photocopier and other office equipment to a new company headquarters but be unsure how long it will take to complete the electrical wiring for the building. You're even more uncertain about the task to design a new logo, which takes lots of creativity and political approvals.

For the duration of each activity on your list, you'll have varying degrees of confidence. The tasks with the highest degree of confidence are usually those you've performed previously or those you'll do yourself. The tasks you aren't sure of usually are those with which you have either no direct experience or very little control.

The degree of confidence is also influenced by the complexity (or simplicity) of the task and how much the task is dependent on the completion of preceding (and possibly complex) tasks.

Remember that if you do the estimates alone, your team members may not buy into them. You might create and sell a schedule to management that team members cannot or will not support or deliver on. Remember to involve key team members in task estimating.

If many of the estimates have low confidence associated with them, move your schedule dates toward the worst-case scenario. If most of the estimates are high confidence, a schedule closer to the best-case estimate is the best choice. The more complex and interdependent the tasks, the more you might want to lean toward a worst-case scenario.

Risk Management

Don't pad the schedule just to cover your uncertainties. Too much padding is as bad as agreeing to complete the impossible in no time at all. A little padding (called contingency planning) is standard practice in all project plans because no one can foresee the future, but padding adds expenses and time to your project. Most experienced project managers will include a 10 to 15 percent contingency in the budget to cover unexpected delays to the schedule.

Scheduling a large project to the hour from the beginning of the project would produce silly schedules and mounds of useless paper. On the other hand, inadequate schedule detail at the beginning of a small project might leave team members thinking they have more time to get things done than they really have. It takes practice, but you'll get the hang of it.

As you develop your schedule, remember to evaluate the dependencies your project has on other projects for success. For example, if the project manager for All-Star Cable knows the information systems department is developing and rolling out a high accessibility network and that the Movies-on-Demand system will require that network in order to work, then there is a risk the IS people will not complete their project on time or that it might not work as advertised. The MOD project manager will need to build some contingency into the project plan to cover that risk.

If you do add a little protection to your schedule for risky tasks, never make your padded time estimates too obvious because this tactic won't win you any popularity contests with management. Such obvious protection schemes will have management sniffing through the entire project for inflationary tactics at all levels, including in the budget. Ultimately, you'll not only lose credibility, but also the real resources and time you need to get things done.

If your schedule starts looking like it will take too long to get things done, try adding more people or resources to the plan. This impacts the budget, however, and sometimes tasks suffer because just too many people are working on the same activities. Just having more people doesn't always mean you'll get things done faster. Adding people always has unforeseen costs in management time and coordination, so make sure this idea is really a good solution to adjusting the schedule before you do it.

Details, Details ...

After estimating the task duration and making a judgment on the estimates, you must decide on the level of detail you want to put in the initial schedule. Usually, the scheduling level should relate to the levels in your WBS or network diagram. For example, you can probably schedule a small project down to the day on the first go-around, but you won't be able to schedule a megaproject any finer than by the month or week.

For planning purposes, you may produce the schedule at the weekly or monthly level. As work on the project proceeds, you can schedule the work at finer levels (remember progressive elaboration in Chapter 9?). Many large projects are scheduled phase by phase instead of scheduled entirely from the beginning.

Applying Calendars to a Resource

Every resource will have dates and times when it will be available for use on your project. These dates and times are called the "calendar" for that resource. For people resources, create calendars that include their work hours, workdays, holidays, and vacation days. Remember the details!

Risk Management

Don't forget holidays and vacation time when scheduling project duration. One project manager thought he was going to get a lot accomplished between December 10th and the end of the year. Unfortunately, several people on the customer side of his project team had vacation time coming and took the last three weeks of the year off! Also, if you are working on a project with an international team, remember to check on the dates of holidays in those countries and schedule accordingly.

You also need to specify how many overtime hours will be allowed, if any. Sometimes you may want to assign a different person to a task based on his or her calendar availability instead of paying overtime.

For equipment resources, you need to indicate any special restrictions on availability. For example, if you have only one electron microscope available and three different research projects are using it, you'll need to specify when this resource will be available for your project. (Or vice versa, you'll need to tell the other projects when you'll need it if your project has priority.) As you develop the schedule for tasks, you'll need to take the calendar into consideration as you write out the dates.

On a complex project, dealing with the calendars of all the resources can get very complex. Thank heaven for computerized project management programs that enable you to define calendars for all the resources including workdays, hours, and nonworking periods such as holidays and vacations. The computer can then do the complex scheduling for you.

Risk Management

Computer programs will allow you to establish the workday and the work week. However, on some global projects that is not so simple to define. For example, one project we worked on had people in Australia, the UK, and the Middle East. The work week is Saturday through Thursday in the Middle East! As you can imagine, that complicated things, even with a computer program!

Putting It Down on Paper

Once you nail down the assumptions for the schedule (that is, the number of people and the activity sequences) and the activity effort, you can begin assembling a reasonable schedule. For a simple project with few dependencies, you can simply list activity effort. For more complex projects, use the WBS and the network diagram to schedule your project.

Scheduling with a network diagram is conceptually simple. Plug in the estimated activity effort for each activity on the network, and then add their efforts to get the total time required to complete the project. Just lay the days out on a calendar, and voilà!—you have a schedule. To show you how it's done, we've provided the following example of a network diagram with task duration and dates added.

Of course, nothing is ever as simple as it sounds. You need to take into account workdays, holidays, vacations, parallel tasks, and other special circumstances. That's why scheduling a large project is easier with a software program designed for the job. (See Chapter 30 for more information about project management computer programs.) You'll also need to level the resource utilization on a large project if you're overworking some of the resources (or underworking others). You'll learn more about making these schedule adjustments in the next chapter.

Schedule Charting Pros and Cons

You should be aware of several schedule-charting formats. The trick is choosing the format that best suits your project. Here are some of your options:

- **Calendar charts.** Annotated calendars can be extremely useful for keeping track of schedules for many small projects. You can enter multiple projects or different team member tasks in various colors. Calendars are a good communication tool when displayed in a central location where many team members can see the dates. Large display calendars with reusable, washable surfaces are available at many business supply stores for this purpose.

- **Gantt charts.** You can best use Gantt charts as a visual overview of project timelines; however, don't necessarily think of them as a substitute for a network diagram or master schedule listing. Gantt charts can be very useful in initial schedule planning, for simple projects, or for individual timelines on a complex project involving many people. These charts are also good for comparing project progress to the original schedule.
- **Milestone schedules.** Milestones can be assigned to summarize major paths on a network (we covered milestones in Chapter 10). You can also use milestones to chart an overall project schedule. A milestone schedule doesn't have enough information to help you manage a project, but it can be useful for communicating an overall schedule on a large project to upper management or other people who need an overview of the project without task details.

More on Gantt Charts

Simple Gantt charts, sometimes referred to as project timelines, are the most commonly used scheduling charts in business because they're easy to produce and easy to understand. A line on the Gantt chart shows the date each task begins and ends based on its precedence and duration.

The time periods you use on the top of your Gantt charts will determine the level of scheduling detail you display: daily, weekly, monthly, or whatever is appropriate for your project. If a project takes a year or more to complete, you may want to use a monthly or weekly Gantt chart. If your project takes 30 days or fewer, a daily Gantt chart will provide more useful information. Gantt charts are most effective if you can present the whole chart on one document such as on 8½" × 14" or 11" × 17" paper.

In a Gantt chart like the one included here, you can see the activities and their numbers to the left of the activities. The small icons let the project manager know that additional notes are attached to those activities. To the right of the activity, you will see the names of the people who will be working on that activity. The percentages indicate the percentage of time they will devote to that activity. This is also a time-scaled diagram. This combines the timeline approach of the traditional Gantt chart with the precedence relationships of the network diagram. For example, if you look on the chart for the activity three, *Design Data Model*, you will notice an arrow coming out and down to the next activity, *Load Data*. That arrow illustrates the precedent relationship between the two activities.

This chart comes from Microsoft Project and illustrates All-Star Cable Movies-on-Demand.

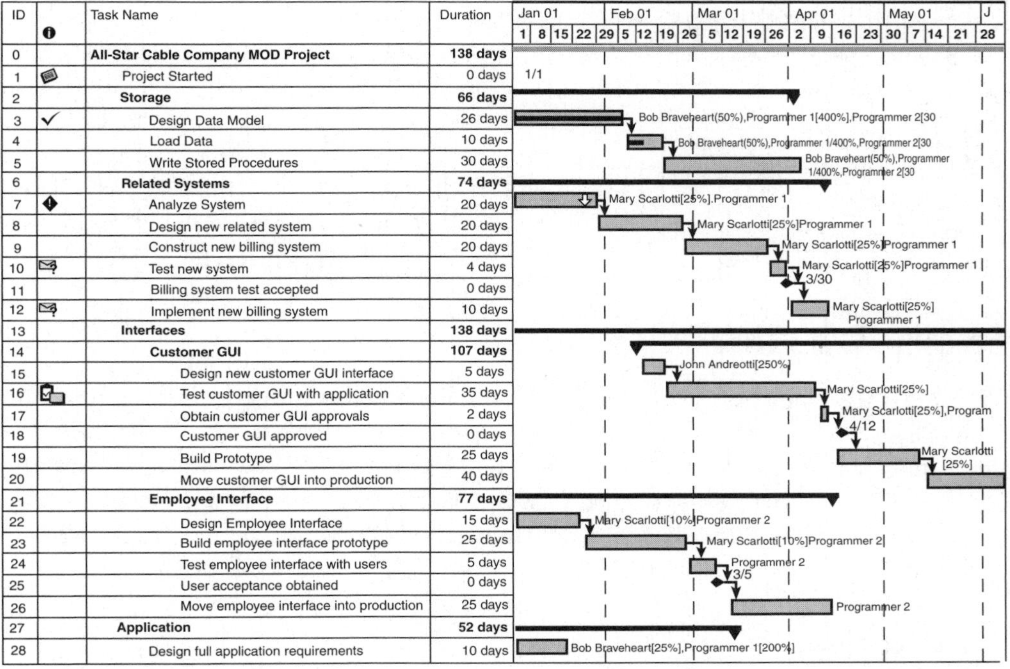

ID	Task Name	Duration
0	**All-Star Cable Company MOD Project**	**138 days**
1	Project Started	0 days
2	**Storage**	**66 days**
3	Design Data Model	26 days
4	Load Data	10 days
5	Write Stored Procedures	30 days
6	**Related Systems**	**74 days**
7	Analyze System	20 days
8	Design new related system	20 days
9	Construct new billing system	20 days
10	Test new system	4 days
11	Billing system test accepted	0 days
12	Implement new billing system	10 days
13	**Interfaces**	**138 days**
14	**Customer GUI**	**107 days**
15	Design new customer GUI interface	5 days
16	Test customer GUI with application	35 days
17	Obtain customer GUI approvals	2 days
18	Customer GUI approved	0 days
19	Build Prototype	25 days
20	Move customer GUI into production	40 days
21	**Employee Interface**	**77 days**
22	Design Employee Interface	15 days
23	Build employee interface prototype	25 days
24	Test employee interface with users	5 days
25	User acceptance obtained	0 days
26	Move employee interface into production	25 days
27	**Application**	**52 days**
28	Design full application requirements	10 days

Gantt charts are useful for envisioning the entire project through time.

Simple Gantt charts don't show the interrelationships among tasks. You need a network diagram for this or a project management program that produces complex Gantt charts that indicate summary activities and relationships between them. Also, a Gantt chart alone may not provide enough detail to communicate schedules to individual team members in a complex project. For this, you'll want a project list that includes work package assignments and schedule dates.

Other Considerations as You Build the Schedule

As you work through building your schedule, there are some additional things we think you need to consider. While some of them might seem obvious, you would be surprised at how often people sometimes overlook the obvious!

Risk Management

If you must share your preliminary drafts of the plan with management, make sure "DRAFT" or "INCOMPLETE" appears on each page. That way, you won't be held to an unfinished plan by senior managers who assume that an early version of the project plan is the final one.

Revisions and the Schedule

Assume that your schedule (and every other aspect of your plan) will require several revisions. Be sure you save each version with a unique identifier (such as the date) so you don't accidentally refer to an earlier version at some point in time. As feedback arrives from both team members and outside resources, you might redraft the task estimates and dates several times until you come up with a workable, approvable timeline (schedule) for the project.

Learning Takes Time

Even in the most routine jobs, some time is required for learning the procedures in the company and adapting to the new work environment. This is especially true of some consultants who must become familiar with your company's way of doing business before they can get down to work. When you schedule a project, allow for these various training and development requirements. You might even want to identify training activities as specific tasks in your WBS or network.

The Heat Is On

Every project is a rush. With that in mind, how do you, as project manager, avoid succumbing to unrealistic expectations and un-realistic goals? Assuming the people commissioning the project are somewhat rational human beings, your best tool is the schedule. Think of it as a game. Management will constantly challenge costs, time, and resources. You must make them believe, through a well-documented schedule and plan, that your estimates are realistic and not unduly padded.

Team Member Estimate Errors

Chances are, you're counting on the core team members and experts to provide the best and most accurate scheduling estimates possible. But rather than carefully thinking through the process for which they are responsible, some members of the team might simply choose a number and feed that into your plan. If it's unrealistic, you're stuck with it.

To avoid this problem, insist that your project team use a method like PERT (that includes "best case," "worst case," and "most likely") to reach their estimate. And be sure you know which method they are using and challenge them to defend their methods. You must be comfortable that the estimate is reasonably accurate and defensible.

Make sure the estimators consider elapsed time in the duration estimates. For example, if their task is to evaluate a new software package, they need to build in time to order it, install it, test it, and go through some conversations with support staff. What looks like four days of effort (32 hours) could result in a 12-day duration when all the "dead" time between activities is accounted for. Have the team estimate both numbers—the effort and the duration. If they don't understand the difference, have a training session with them before they complete the estimates.

The Just-in-Time Strategy for Scheduling Resources

The just-in-time strategy for getting materials and supplies is credited to the Japanese, but the technique is now common practice worldwide. Just-in-time delivery depends on accurate scheduling and project coordination. With an accurate schedule in place, you can order just what you need and get it delivered exactly when you need it. This means that supplies, equipment, and even people arrive only when the project is ready for them.

By having goods delivered (or people hired) exactly when they're needed, you save money for storage, reduce upfront costs for ordering materials, and are assured that you don't have extra stuff on hand that is costing you extra money.

The key to making this approach work is, you guessed it, communication. A temp agency hiring 20 people for your project will want enough time to hire the needed people, but you should notify them as soon as you know the project might be delayed. The window for just-in-time delivery must be agreed upon in advance; otherwise, the whole schedule falls apart.

Having a contract with suppliers that lets you adjust dates is the essence of just-in-time delivery. That way, you don't have to warehouse items from the supplier. You need to make just-in-time delivery a mandatory contract clause: no delivery until a written request is made and guaranteed delivery within a set number of days or hours after you put the order in. This type of requirement is necessary when you are working with a project that uses a large amount of physical materials, such as construction projects.

What Happens When They Want to Rush Me?

At some time, you'll be asked (or maybe told) to shorten the schedule, even though you know it's nearly impossible to get the work done any faster. Before you cave in to dictate, sit down with everyone pressuring you and go over the schedule, day by day, if necessary. Be friendly and cooperative and explain each task and the assumptions about your time estimates represented in the schedule.

Your goal for this process is to communicate why the project requires a certain amount of time. In a truly impossible situation, you might need someone senior to you (usually the project sponsor) to go to bat when others attempt to force an unworkable adjustment to the plan on your shoulders.

Now you're ready to learn about how to fine-tune a schedule to meet your stakeholders' objectives.

The Least You Need to Know

- Scheduling involves estimating the task durations for the project and plotting the dates on a calendar. You need to account for holidays, special events, and unknown circumstances.
- No schedule is ever perfect, but the goal is to make the best estimate possible. Use your own judgment and the experience of others to help you make your estimates.
- A Gantt chart is an excellent tool for studying overall schedules, but it doesn't show the interdependencies among tasks shown on the network diagram. Thus, using both in a project plan is a good idea.
- Base time estimates on best-case/worst-case scenarios. Your degree of confidence in the accuracy of these estimates should dictate the ultimate schedule, which should be a compromise somewhere between the two extremes.

Chapter 12

Determining the Critical Path and Its Impact on the Schedule

In This Chapter

- Understanding the critical path
- All about float and slack in a project
- Important adjustments in complex project schedules
- Leveling the resource utilization
- Ways to adapt a project to meet a schedule

In Chapter 11, you learned the good news: scheduling is a simple matter of estimating durations for tasks and then plotting the dates on a calendar. Now here's the bad news: even using computer-based project management software, scheduling a complex project is, well, complex. Because an accurate schedule is essential to managing projects of all sizes, don't cut corners. You need to consider some of the complexities of scheduling before you finalize your project plan. That's what this chapter is all about—the complexities of project scheduling.

Use a worksheet like this one to help detail the assumptions about the schedule for your project. Don't forget to refer to the statement of work (SOW) for additional scheduling criteria and constraints.

Scheduling Assumptions Worksheet

Project Name: San Francisco Office Project   Date: May 22

1. Are all the resources currently available for this project?
   - If no, list the resources required that are not available:
   - *People* Leasing Agent Needs to Be Found
   - *Equipment*
   - ☐ YES ☒ NO
2. Is there a due date when the project absolutely must be complete?
   - *If yes, enter date:*
   - *Reason:*
   - ☐ YES ☒ NO
3. Will overtime be allowed?
   - *If yes, how much?*
   - ☐ YES ☒ NO
4. Are there any holidays or other breaks during this project?
   - *If yes, list dates:* July 4
   - ☒ YES ☐ NO
5. Have additional resources and people been approved for this project?
   - ☒ YES ☐ NO
6. Have the work schedules and availabilities of all resources been documented?
   - ☒ YES ☐ NO

Notes: Follow the Philidelphia Office Plan as Reference

For complex projects, computers have a significant advantage over manual scheduling. Yes, you'll learn how to calculate the critical path and float in this chapter, but you should get a computer program to help on projects of more than 25 or 30 tasks (see Chapter 30). Then you can easily change and revise the schedule as you work through the issues and changes in a project.

How to Determine the Critical Path on Any Project

When you have determined task durations and are confident in your estimates, it's time to assemble a schedule using real dates. On a large/complex project, however, one more step remains in the way of assembling a working schedule. For projects with multiple parallel tasks and subprojects, you must determine a *critical path* to identify the time required to complete the project. (Most small projects with few tasks can skip this step.)

The *critical path* is a sequence of tasks that forms the longest duration of the project. Think of the critical path as the activities within your project where you have the least amount of flexibility to complete them. If a task is delayed on the critical path, the project is delayed. For example, for All-Star Cable, if the cable boxes for the customers are delayed, the entire project will fall behind schedule.

Tasks not lying on the critical path are more flexible. You can delay printing the instructions for using the cable boxes as long as they arrive at the same time as the boxes themselves.

Adding together the duration of tasks on the critical path determines the total time the project will take. Because each task on the critical path must follow its predecessor in order, all tasks following a late task will be late. Yes, the delay will hold up the entire project. That's why the critical path is, well, critical.

Not Just Floating Around

Tasks not on the critical path also must be completed. You can't build a house and ask someone to move in before the water and sewer are connected, but such tasks can occur later in the project's time frame without substantially delaying other tasks downstream. This gives them a flexible start and finish date, which in project management lingo is called *float*.

def•i•ni•tion

The amount of time that an activity may be delayed from its earliest possible start date without delaying the project finish date is called **float**. Float is also known as slack or slack time. The equation

Latest possible finish date – earliest possible start – duration = total float

calculates the latest date you can start, given the duration that an activity will take and still finish on time for the next activity to start. If the total float for a task equals zero, then that task is on the critical path. The amount of float is the amount of flexibility for starting a task.

The Different Views of Critical in Project Management

The term critical chain is used to describe a concept quite different from the schedule-based definition of tasks on the critical path. The concept of the critical chain is one of the ideas preferred by Dr. Eliyahu M. Goldratt's Theory of Constraints (TOC). The TOC states that any system has at least one constraint. Otherwise, it would be generating an infinite amount of output. Bearing this in mind, the TOC in project management is explained through use of the chain analogy: "A chain is only as strong as its weakest link."

If you look at your project as a chain in which each department, activity, or resource is a link, what constrains your project from achieving its goals? Only through identifying and focusing on the weakest link, the critical link in the chain, can you make substantial improvements. In other words, if the weakest link dictates the pace of an organization's ability to achieve its goal, it makes sense that attending to this critical link will allow the organization to achieve a substantial rate of throughput faster.

To illustrate how you can apply the TOC without getting into too much theoretical detail, the critical chain concept illustrates that you can improve project control and scheduling through identifying the critical links in a project's chain and then focusing creatively on reducing these problems. The objective is to develop solutions of compromise based on fresh thinking that can help you continuously improve project performance through time. The performance is improved continuously because, as you fix one weakest link in the chain, a new weakest link emerges. Since project performance is never perfect, you will always have a weakest link to work on.

If you're interested in the application of the critical chain concept and the Theory of Constraints on project management, visit the Avraham Y. Goldratt Institute on the web at www.goldratt.com. An adequate presentation of TOC is beyond the scope of our book, but for people interested in continuous quality improvement, there's a lot of substance in Goldratt's work.

Establishing the Critical Path

The critical path is easy to determine in a project documented with a good network diagram. Simply add each parallel path's tasks together, and the path requiring the most time to complete is the critical path. In the case of All-Star Cable, the building of the interfaces takes 138 days. That makes it the critical path. Critical tasks, those on this path, not completed on time, will delay the project unless you can make up the time further down the critical path or an on-the-path task finishes ahead of schedule. (Remember we mentioned "crashing" the project in Chapter 10?)

Risk Management

When its tasks go late, the critical path becomes the roadblock to project completion. That's why you should put extra effort into estimating these tasks. If you lack confidence in the task schedule or resource availability, delay the project until everything fits into place. When the project is already underway, put your best people on the tasks on the critical path and focus your energies on monitoring them. You can use the Critical Path Worksheet a little later in this chapter to calculate the critical path and float for the tasks on your projector, or you can look into getting a computer program that can do it for you.

Myth or Reality?

The concept behind critical path is simple: if you delay a task on the critical path, you delay the project. This seems to make perfect sense to most people new to project management. The path on the project has to go from beginning to end.

Unfortunately, as in all things involving people and plans, complexities occur. First, some tasks on the critical path may be less important than others. Some tasks may be there for mathematical reasons (which you'll learn about in a bit), not managerial priorities. Because of this situation, many managers also create a priority task list, a list of the most important tasks on the project. You can use this managerial list of priority tasks, along with the mathematical list of tasks on the critical path, to focus attention on the important work of the project.

Always remember that regardless of the mathematics of it or the managerial importance, when you change task dependencies, duration estimates, and other network details, you need to reevaluate the critical path and reassess the schedule. There's no way around it. You can't change the sequences without impacting the schedule.

Use the Critical Path Worksheet to Calculate Path and Float

If you're new to project management, the calculation of the critical path initially sounds complicated. It's really simple, however, assuming you've done your homework by correctly listing, estimating duration, and assigning precedence to each task. If you're using a computer-based program, it will probably identify the critical path automatically. Otherwise, follow these steps:

Let's look at All-Star Cable and see how we can calculate the float in their project:

1. List the tasks and estimated activity durations on the worksheet. So for the sixth task, "Construct new billing system," let's say that the activity duration is 20 days.
2. Calculate the earliest starting date for each activity. In the case study, the earliest start for "Construct new billing system" becomes July 10. We know that because we have referenced the network diagram and we can see all the activity durations that immediately precede the beginning of that activity on the network diagram.
3. Calculate the earliest finish number for each task. In this case, we know that the earliest finish date is August 6.
4. Calculate the latest finish number for each task, which is often called the backward pass through the project schedule. The latest finish is the last day a task can be performed without changing the end date of the project. For this activity, notice that we cannot finish after November 4 without pushing the entire project past the deadline. You will need to know the activities that must precede this activity.
5. Determine the total float for each task. Total float is determined by the following calculation:

   Total float = date of the latest finish – date of the earliest start – duration

   In this case, that calculation is November 4 minus July 10 minus the duration of the activity, which is 20 days. When we make that calculation, we discover that we have 64 days of float for this activity. (Note that we are referring to business days, not calendar days.)

   The tasks with zero float are on the critical path. If you look at the activity labeled "Move customer interface into production," you will notice that the earliest start and the latest start are exactly the same as are the earliest finish and the latest finish. That means that this activity has no float available and has a zero in the float column. This activity must be done between those dates, or the entire project schedule will be off.

Even if you use a computer to help you with your network diagrams and critical path calculations, it's important that you understand the basic scheduling principles presented here. If you don't understand the basic principles of float, start dates, finish dates, and critical path, you won't understand how the computer derives the schedules it produces. And if you don't understand these concepts, you won't be able to appropriately modify the schedules to suit your project's priorities, especially if they change later.

Critical Path Worksheet
Project Name: All-Star Cable Movies-on-Demand

Task	Duration	Earliest Start	Earliest Finish	Latest Start	Latest Finish	Total Float
Design data model	26 days	5/15	6/19	8/25	9/29	72
Load data	10 days	6/20	7/3	9/30	10/13	72
Write stored procedures	30 days	7/4	8/14	10/14	11/24	72
Analyze system	20 days	5/15	6/11	8/13	9/9	64
Design new related system	20 days	6/12	7/9	9/10	10/7	64
Construct new billing system	20 days	7/10	8/6	10/8	11/4	64
Test new system	4 days	8/7	8/12	11/5	11/10	64
Implement new billing system	10 days	8/13	8/26	11/11	11/24	64
Design new customer interface	5 days	6/27	7/3	6/27	7/3	0
Test new customer interface with application	35 days	7/4	8/21	7/4	8/21	0
Obtain customer interface approvals	2 days	8/22	8/25	8/22	8/25	0
Build prototype	25 days	8/26	9/29	8/26	9/29	0
Move customer interface into production	40 days	9/30	11/24	9/30	11/24	0
Design employee interface	15 days	5/15	6/4	6/19	7/9	25
Build employee interface prototype	25 days	6/5	7/9	9/9	10/13	68
Test employee interface with users	5 days	7/10	7/16	10/14	10/20	68
Move employee interface into production	25 days	7/28	8/29	10/21	11/24	61
Design full application requirements	10 days	5/15	5/28	5/15	5/28	0
Send Request For Proposal for Off The Shelf Software	1 day	5/29	5/29	5/29	5/29	0
Evaluate software	10 days	5/30	6/12	5/30	6/12	0
Decide to make or build	3 days	6/13	6/17	6/13	6/17	0
Purchase software	2 days	6/18	6/19	6/18	6/19	0
Install software	5 days	6/20	6/26	6/20	6/26	0
Test software (unit)	5 days	6/27	7/3	9/22	9/26	61
Test software (system)	5 days	7/4	7/10	9/29	10/3	61
Move software into production	11 days	7/11	7/25	10/6	10/20	61
Analyze information needs	5 days	5/15	5/21	7/3	7/9	35
Design reports	25 days	5/15	6/18	6/5	7/9	15
Modify existing reports database	5 days	6/19	6/25	11/5	11/11	99
Test with test files	5 days	6/26	7/2	11/12	11/18	99
Test full scale system in production	4 days	7/3	7/8	11/19	11/24	99

Normalizing the Schedule

You must review the schedule to determine whether the resources you assigned are actually available within each task's schedule window. Obviously, you need to start with the activities on the critical path, those that have very little float, and work the rest of the schedule from there. Move things around based on the float available to ensure that you don't overload someone and that others are fully utilized. After individual assignments are finalized and reviewed by the team, you must adjust the schedule to accommodate any other necessary changes. Senior management needs to review and approve it as well, as part of the project plan.

When you use the critical path in a project, you can schedule the tasks not on the path (called noncritical) in a number of ways to accommodate various needs of the organization. Three strategies are as follows:

Time Is Money

If one unique resource commands the premier place in the project, you must wrap your schedule around its availability. For example, you may be able to find plenty of Java programmers, and you can rent a piece of equipment to test circuits from a vendor, but locating a qualified engineer who can handle fiber optic cables may limit your scheduling options.

- Schedule all noncritical tasks at the earliest date possible. This offers a way to free up resources earlier for other projects or the later critical tasks.
- Schedule all noncritical tasks as late as possible. This shows how much work you can delay without causing the critical tasks (and thus the project schedule) to slip.
- Schedule a subset of noncritical tasks. As you meet milestones, complete the rest of the schedule. This gives the manager scheduling flexibility and a way to assign resources to critical activities without causing political problems.

When assigning people, the rules are simple:

- Make sure you know the specific availability of all the people (as much as humanly possible).
- Assign the best-suited available people to each task, particularly those on the critical path.
- Use equipment and people efficiently to ensure the smallest gaps in working schedules.
- Redo the schedule over and over until you get it balanced. (Get help from experts if it takes more than three tries.)

Time Is Money

Another key reason for understanding the float you have for activities is so you can recover if needed. In other words, if you have an activity that is getting behind, you can shift a person (or more) to help get the activity back on schedule before it is too late. You will only know who you have available if you know what float you have for each activity. And you must do it with enough time to make your corrective action effective.

Loading Up and Leveling Out

Many ideal schedules forget to deal with conflicting availability of equipment, potential overuse of key people, and the needs of other projects and priorities. For example, the ideal employee to design the new employee interface may be unavailable the week you need him or her because of their "day job." If you can't reschedule the task to accommodate his or her schedule, you may have to choose someone else.

After working on your schedule, you will likely find that some team members have too much work—more than they can accomplish in a standard workweek. Others may not have enough. The amount of work each team member or piece of equipment is assigned is called resource loading. As you would expect, it's easy to overwhelm your best people with an impossible workload while underutilizing others.

To compensate for overloaded workers, redistribute scheduled work from people with too much responsibility to those folks not fully booked. This is called resource leveling. As you level resources, you must consider skills and availability. If Bob Braveheart, your computer network expert, has an unreasonable 64 hours of work scheduled per week, you can't redistribute the extra workload to three or four other team members who lack experience with computer networks. Instead, you need to acquire additional experienced resources and adjust the schedule and ultimately the budget to accommodate the necessary changes.

The Reallocation Questions

Before you reallocate and level the resource commitments, you need to ask yourself these questions:

- **How many hours per day is each person or piece of equipment available?** Can we expect employees to work 8 hours a day? They probably do, but all that time is not necessarily applied to the project. After all, they do have to go to the bathroom, take phone calls (some personal, most legitimate business calls), get coffee, talk to other project team members informally (sometimes personal, but more often it's discussion about work on the project), and talk to other employees in the company (sometimes personal, but frequently it's important networking with other team members or peers). As a manager, you should completely support these activities. Comfortable employees who feel they have control over their work life are that much more productive. As a manager, however, you probably recognize that a workday usually consists of only about 6½ hours of productive work time as a result.

- **Is an assigned piece of equipment allocated to multiple projects for multiple project managers?** Depending on shared resources is not an optimum state for a project manager, but frequently we have limited control over the resources we get on a project and have to take other priorities into consideration. Too many times in the past, we have had teams composed of individuals who have a minimal time allocation to another project. ("No more than a couple of hours a week, I promise.") Then, during project execution, we don't see him or her for a couple of weeks due to legitimate problems on the other project. ("Sorry, Sally is the only one who understands payroll, and we lost the ability to create payroll checks; we need her to help us figure out the problem.") Have a contingency plan built in for these people.
- **Have you factored in time lost to anticipated interruptions?** You can expect downtime due to weather, holidays, vacation and sick time, doctor's visits, and other personal requirements.
- **Have you factored in sufficient time for administrative overhead?** This means allowing time for attending company meetings, allowing for company travel time, completing time reports, completing weekly status reports, and conducting project team meetings. This may also include reviewing team deliverables as well as internal reviews of prototypes or documents.
- **Are you using people with specialized skill sets appropriately?** Are team member assignments accurate in terms of matching skills and task requirements? Should you reallocate these people or reassign work? Have you considered the productivity of the people as well as their relative skills?
- **Are you scheduling people without appropriate skill sets?** Frequently, we send team members out to be trained on a new skill and expect them to come back fully proficient in that skill. Depending on the skill, you should assume reduced productivity for a certain period of time to allow that person to become

fully proficient after applying the new skills in the project environment. The period of time should be directly related to the complexity of the new skills.

- **Have you planned for the time required to acquire additional people?** Depending on the environment you work in, getting the authorization to bring in additional staff regardless of whether they are full-time employees or temporary contract staff will be more or less difficult. In some organizations, that may take as little as a week or as long as two months. Our experience suggests you plan on an average of four to six weeks. Once you have the authorization, time is required for getting applicants, interviewing them, checking references, making an offer, and waiting for the prospective employees to finish commitments at their current place of employment. Then, once they do come on board, they will require time to get up to speed on the project's purpose, it's goals, and their job. If you're the project manager for All-Star Cable and you only have six months to finish the project, you can see why taking six weeks to bring on a new project team member is a problem. During all of this time, remember that your project is supposedly making progress.

Ready for Leveling Out

After making adjustments in response to all the preceding questions regarding people's schedules, you're ready to do the final leveling of resource commitments. One of the tools to help you do this is the resource histogram, a visual tool that allows you to chart resource task allocation for each period through the project. In the example, notice how the histograms chart the availability of the resource and the effort of that resource through the life of the project. Most computer programs will calculate this for you.

In weeks 1 and 6, the resource is overallocated but is underallocated in weeks 2 through 5. In this example, you would want to smooth out the peaks and valleys as best you can by moving work packages out of period 1 into period 2 or 3 as time is available. You can move the activity within the available float for that activity (remember critical path?). You can extend the duration of an activity because you have available float. You also could reassign some or all of the work to underallocated people if they have the right skills for the job. But you'll have to refer to your skills inventory to do that.

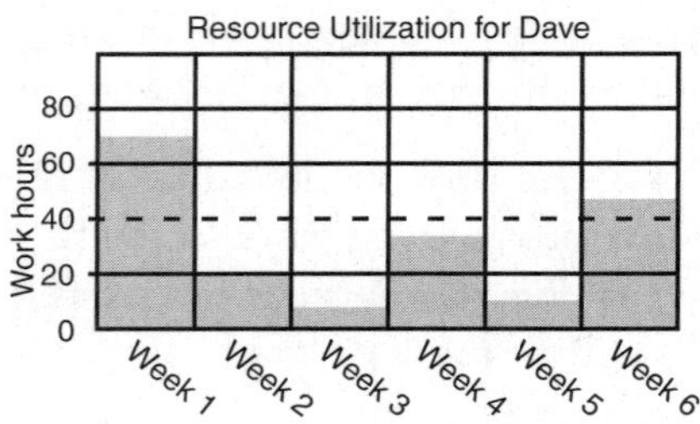

The resource bar graph can help you visualize resource utilization during phases of a project. Here you see that Dave is overallocated during weeks 1 and 6.

Options for Adjusting the Schedule

In total, here are your options for reworking a schedule when you realize that no matter what you do, people will be overworked:

- Reduce the scope of the project or keep the current scope and add people, keeping in mind that more people and equipment will impact the budget. Obviously, you have to do this with approval of the steering committee.
- Give a work package more time, or split it into two or more work packages, modifying who is responsible for completing them to make the process work. You can also adjust the basic finish-to-start precedence relationships (but only when appropriate) by adding lead or lag time to tasks that enable some of the work to occur in parallel. (Refer to Chapter 10 if you've forgotten how this works.)
- Move a task to a time when more people or equipment are free. This will mean calculating the entire schedule again to make sure the moved activity doesn't impact the critical path.
- Outsource the work. Remember that outsourcing work, while reducing work done by the implementation team, also adds new tasks for vendor management. Outsourcing also assumes that the vendor people have the right expertise and are available and uncommitted.
- Negotiate for additional time in the schedule with a later completion date and a budget increase. You'll need stakeholder agreement to do this. Don't negotiate the time required to complete the activities (these should be good numbers if you've done your estimating correctly). Instead, negotiate the balance among the time, resources, and results (goals) of the project.
- Deliver components of the project in a phased approach, thereby extending the total project schedule but still giving the customer acceptable products or services.

- Find more productive (better-trained, more experienced) people. This choice may increase the budget, but you might get most of the added employee expense back in terms of increased productivity, if you choose wisely.

Adjusting a Schedule to Meet a Forced Deadline

Many projects have a forced or dictated deadline because a customer may need a project completed by a specific date. In our All-Star Cable case study, the reason the president may need the project completed by the end of the year is because he knows a competitor is working on this same type of project and he wants to be the first into the marketplace with it. If this happens and you realize you can't make it, you have three options:

- Reduce the scope of the project.
- Add additional resources.
- Work out some way to extend the completion date (not always possible).

Chart the Final Schedule and See If It Works

When the final schedule is in place and approved (along with the rest of the project plan), distribute it to all team members and post it in a common area so that team members can measure progress. This helps you maintain a healthy competitive attitude as the various team members rush to meet or exceed their scheduled delivery dates. At that point, you cease to be a project planner and take on your role as project manager. Of course, you still need a budget before you have an approved plan. With the schedule in hand, the budget will be the next piece to tackle.

The Least You Need to Know

- Understanding the concept of critical path is important in keeping a project schedule on track.
- When assembling a project schedule, you must be able to determine how much float you have to work with.
- Normalizing the schedule is important as you consider the people who will do the work.
- Put your best people on the tasks within the critical path, because these are the tasks with the least available float.

Chapter 13

Budgeting and Cost Control Options for Your Project

In This Chapter

- Four classic budgeting mistakes and ways to avoid them
- Factoring in direct and indirect costs
- Budgeting methods
- Fine-tuning the budget
- Control of the purse strings
- Calculating the time value of money

"Hey, how long do you think it will take to design the new GUI (Graphical User Interface) for Movies-on-Demand?"

"If you mean how long before we can have the GUI into production, I'd guess about six months."

"What do you mean, you guess? I need an estimate for the budget."

"Okay, I estimate it will take six months to put the GUI into production."

Words from the Wise

The conceptual budget process is: People + Resources + Time = Budget.

Unfortunately, this kind of dialogue goes on all the time as project managers work to build their budgets. Based on this type of estimate, it's no wonder so many projects run into trouble. However, there is a better way, and that's what this chapter is all about. All budgets start with estimates, so that is where we want to begin.

How to Avoid the Classic Budgeting Mistakes

It's important to understand that, once you establish a budget, it becomes sacrosanct. You're stuck with it. Changing an entrenched project budget is like trying to modify the Ten Commandments, if you could find the original stones and do a little chisel work. The following classic mistakes are ones that you (or a project manager friend) have probably made. The idea is to not make them again.

- **Classic mistake 1:** A senior manager stops you in the hallway and asks for the estimated budget for the project you have just been assigned. Maybe it's his authority or maybe he just caught you off-guard, but you feel compelled to answer. You blurt out some numbers and immediately realize that was probably a mistake. The reason? The manager is on his way to a meeting and will use that number to talk about the budget. The problem here is that by speaking off the top of your head, you may misinterpret the scope of the project or the statement of work. You can avoid this predicament by looking concerned and replying, "I wouldn't want to give you an inaccurate number, so I don't want to offer a guess right now. But I'm currently working on it. How soon do you need it?"
- **Classic mistake 2:** Some project managers try to develop a budget without completing the work breakdown structure to get the effort that will be required to complete the project. The problem here is that you have a poorly defined project and are likely to be overly optimistic about what you can accomplish. It's best to wait until you complete your WBS, sometimes even down to the work package level, before you begin the budget process. Without understanding the time it will take and the people who will need to complete the work, estimating a budget is just pulling numbers out of thin air.
- **Classic mistake 3:** Sometimes project managers fail to account for the risks in completing the project. They failed to complete the thorough risk assessment we covered in Chapter 8. As a result, they don't have enough flexibility in the budget (or the schedule) to handle the risks effectively.

- **Classic mistake 4:** The project manager did not apply the proper experience and skill levels of the people available to the project work that needed to be done. By not properly matching the work and the skills and experience of the people, it took longer to complete the work than they expected. As a result, the quality of the project suffers, and it usually misses on both budget and schedule.

Three Levels of Accuracy for Estimating

You have three levels of accuracy to use in establishing your budget, which are applicable at different phases of the project:

- **Ballpark estimate.** During the project definition phase, the ballpark estimate is only useful if you are experienced enough to have a true "gut-level" feel for what the entire project might cost while you are still defining it. For All-Star Cable's project manager, a ballpark estimate on the budget would only be a guess since he had never tried this type of project before.
- **Rough order of magnitude.** During the project definition phase, you might recognize aspects of the project that are similar to a project you worked on before. If so, you can often complete this type of estimate in a matter of days using your previous experience. If our project manager for All-Star Cable had worked on the pay-per-view system when the company put it in several years ago, for instance, he would know what that project cost and be able to calculate a rough order of magnitude for this project. You may hear some managers use the term *parametric estimates* for this type of estimate.
- **Detailed estimate.** This level of budgeting would occur in the project planning phase when the project team is developing all the plans for the work they will need to complete. The project manager then rolls up all the estimated costs and develops a budget. For that reason, project managers often call this technique a "bottom-up" estimate. This type of estimate can take months on a large project.

Other Sources of Data for Building the Budget

Of course, the work the project team is doing comprises a significant amount of the money that will be spent on the project. However, you will need to estimate other costs, too:

- Project managers often leave out or miscalculate internal labor costs. For All-Star Cable, the project manager is using company staff from accounting, IT, market research, marketing, and so on. All these people must be accounted for in the budget to really know what the project will cost. Even though many of these people will be on salary, don't think of them as free. That would only be true if they had infinite hours to work, which of course they might object to. You must calculate their labor, and most project managers use either daily or monthly rates and generally calculate that rate including benefits.
- Internal equipment costs may also be considered—items like computers, photocopiers, and printers are just a few examples. Depending on how the company wants the budget drawn up, you may also need to consider office space even if you are not renting it separately. For example, in our All-Star Cable case study, the project team is taking over space normally used by the accounting department. So the accounting manager wants additional budget money for space for her employees who will be relocated. That money must come from the MOD project.
- You may also need to include cost of external labor and equipment in the data you collect. For example, if the All-Star Cable team will rent specialized equipment to test cable boxes that vendors are supplying, these costs will need to be folded into the estimates. Likewise, you must also factor into your estimates any contractors needed to supplement the team.
- Material costs are an important consideration. Office supplies are a perfect example. People will need paper, pens, and a variety of other materials over the course of the project.
- If project team members will need to travel to various sites for any number of reasons, don't forget to estimate the cost of those trips, including airlines, hotels, meals, and so on.

Direct and Indirect Costs

Before you put any numbers to paper, you must know the difference between direct and indirect costs on a project. Your budget must account for both of these types of costs, although how this is done will vary from organization to organization.

Direct costs are those costs specifically required by the project. Indirect costs are those costs not specific to the project because their value can be shared among many projects. You'll need to find out (usually from the finance officer for your project or from the accounting department) how your company allocates indirect costs for projects. Then you'll need to establish the appropriate line items for indirect costs as part of the overall budget.

Direct costs include the following:

- **Labor:** The cost of the people working on the project. Benefits for the employees may be charged as direct costs or as a percentage of all overhead for housing the employee (which might include the cost of facilities, benefits, and so on).
- **Supplies and raw materials:** The cost of materials consumed by the project.
- **Equipment:** The cost of tools and machinery.
- **Travel:** The cost of travel associated with the project.
- **Legal fees:** Direct legal expenses charged specifically for work on your project.
- **Training:** Training for project team members and for the project end users and customers during project installation or implementation.
- **Marketing/advertising:** The costs of project introductions, announcements, promotions, and public relations; these costs can be quite large on a project that introduces a new product.

Indirect costs include the following:

- **Facilities:** The physical location required for the project participants and shared resources, such as the company intranet or communications network. The exception is when facilities are purchased or leased specifically and exclusively for the use of the project.
- **Site-specific requirements:** State- or county-specific charges for business operations.
- **Management and administrative overhead:** The cost of paying for the managers and support staff (such as human resources people) used by your project but who don't directly report to you.

Indirect costs may be allocated on a percentage basis from some central accounting or management organization such as a corporate office or the department responsible for the project. Don't forget to include these costs, because they could doom your project to budget overruns before it even starts.

You will need to gather other possible sources of data to accurately put together your estimates. Talk with your project team and your project sponsor to identify anything you may have forgotten.

Building a Budget

How do you establish a budget? You take it task by task, step by step. Doing the budget for a small project, such as establishing an internal copy center, might take an afternoon. For large projects such as All-Star Cable's MOD system, a team might take a couple of months to bring expenses into line and to remember forgotten tasks.

The budget should help the project manager control the project; however, it's common for the project manager to find the budget controlling him. A realistic budget is central to keeping control of the project. It's okay to have one that's a little too conservative, but you can't turn lead into gold.

The budgeting process can be intimidating to project managers. How much will it really cost? What if the price of pork bellies doubles on the Chicago Mercantile Exchange? How can I control an important staff member who demands a salary increase? What if I make a mistake? (If you see someone at the office with the shakes, it's probably because he or she either has recently given up coffee or is assembling a project budget for the first time.)

Risk Management

"Money talks" is one of life's truisms. (We'll skip the second part; you already know the sentiment.) You'll find that this is especially true when you control a project budget of which outside providers want a share. Don't take money, gifts, or vacations of any kind on a vendor's tab. This keeps the bids on the level and the lawyers out of your life.

The process of building a budget should be an orderly one; otherwise, it's impossible to get reasonable numbers. You must thoroughly understand the components of each activity and then use the bottom-up method to cost out each one. Yes, you might make an error, underestimate, overestimate, or blow it completely, but all you can do is try, using your best estimating capabilities. Even so, business conditions might change, the project might get bumped into a new direction, or a task might fail. So what you are making in your astute budgeting is a set of assumptions that may change. Wish for luck while remembering the following:

- Costs are tied to project goals. For All-Star Cable, the company is betting on Movies-on-Demand to be the next big growth engine for its revenues. It is literally betting the future on this project.

- Costs are tied to time frames and schedules, and doing things faster usually costs more money. The estimates you developed in your work breakdown structure, coupled with the schedule you developed to complete the project, are critical to this. If the steering committee wants the project done faster, this will undoubtedly cost more money. It's your job to estimate, to the best of your ability, how much more they are looking at.

Get Expert Opinions

When establishing detailed estimates, the costs require expert input. With specific activities developed in the WBS and a schedule at the ready, ask the people who will be doing the work about their charges for time and materials (refer to Chapter 14). It's important for each contributor to understand exactly what you want. For example, if you want an estimate for doing systems testing on the new MOD billing system, get written estimates and make sure they match your requirements. If you are using vendors, use the *answer-back process* to make sure you have a valid and complete estimate.

- **Other project managers or experts.** People in your organization who have handled projects can provide excellent advice and study cost estimates for problems. They also might be able to provide exact estimates if a project they have worked on had elements common to yours. Or they might be much more experienced project managers and be willing to help out. Expert project managers estimate budgets accurately not because they have years of experience, but because they look at the budget and final costs of similar tasks on related projects. You can do it, too. If you completed a similar project in your company in the past, review the project close-out files and lessons learned to discover how that project was budgeted and how close it came to meeting that budget.
- **Your management team.** Although sometimes unhappy about a project's cost, your management might be able to provide advice from their own years of managing projects. Plus, by bringing them in early, they'll see that you're carefully covering your bases and are spending their money in an equitable manner. That observation will assist you in getting the final budget approved because management already will have a strong grasp on the realities of the project and its budget requirements, not to mention faith in you and your abilities. This concept is referred to as pre-selling the project budget.
- **Purchasing department staff.** The purchasing department might or might not save you money, because this department might help you in your quest for success or might stand in your way at every turn (we'll cover this in more detail in

Chapter 15). Use them if they've proven helpful in a timely manner in the past. Avoid or work around them if they are difficult to deal with. You might need permission from senior management to avoid working with them. This tactic is a slap in the face to the purchasing people, so don't expect to win any popularity contests with them next time you order a box of number-two pencils.

- **Standard pricing guides.** Many government-regulated organizations and some private companies offer standard pricing in printed-guide format. Do you need to know how much Federal Express charges to move an elephant from Zoo A to Zoo B? Just look it up in the free user guide, assuming you have the current version!

Once you have gleaned and carefully listed these cost estimates along with the names of the contributors, it's time to do a task budget roundup. In this process, you take all the estimates for Task A and combine them. Use a worksheet (probably in a spreadsheet) or enter the numbers in your project management software. After you wrap up costs for all the tasks separately, you can add the total of the entire plan to ascertain the project's total cost. Costs that are not available because Joanna in research is out of town must be guesstimated with a large highlighter used to indicate that the total is possibly fictitious. With a computer, most unknown/unverified estimates can be indicated separately. Your manager and most stakeholders will want to see the budget in two formats, by cost center and by month, to assess cash flow and cost allocations. Some project managers will also want to present the budget by project milestones, WBS summary levels, or project phases.

Time Is Money

Make an extra copy of a draft network diagram and write the budget for each task next to its box. In a glance, you will see where most of the money is being spent. Next, make sure that's where you should be spending the money.

Types of Budgeting Methods

There are two established methods for budgeting: top-down and bottom-up. Which is best for your project depends on your organization's standard approach to decision making. Does management dictate most mandates? Or is the staff expected to produce ideas and decisions that percolate up to management for final analysis? Your answer to this question will determine the most likely budgeting approach for the project.

Bottom-Up Budgeting

In bottom-up budgeting, staff members get together and attempt to hammer out a budget from the task-level detail. As a group, they can speak frankly. One member might have a solution that's superior to another. It's also a good way to avoid missing a subtask. If one group member forgets it, another (hopefully) will remember it. This helps avoid budget-gobbling tasks appearing mid-project and throwing everything off down the line.

Top-Down Budgeting

More difficult than bottom-up management, the top-down approach has senior managers estimating budgets from their experience and then allocating funds to lower-level managers for execution. Top-down budgeting works if managers carefully allocate costs and possess significant project management experience.

Many progressive organizations use a combination of top-down and bottom-up budgeting to ensure the top-down numbers (which establish general expectations) are grounded in the reality of the workers' experience.

Risk Management

Are you assembling a budget using a spreadsheet program such as Excel? Don't accept the final numbers without calculating them separately using a calculator. Otherwise, an error in an underlying formula might be invisible.

Phased Budgeting

Phased budgeting, like phased scheduling, can use either top-down or bottom-up estimates or both, but it estimates only one phase of the project at a time. Costs are divided into those associated with the project definition phase, the project planning phase, the project execution phase, and the project close-out phase. At each transition from one phase to the next, the project manager revises the budget and the steering committee approves it. On very large projects, this is a commonly employed methodology because it limits risk and uncertainty in the approved operational budget.

Refining the Budget

When the budget numbers are in, although subject to correction, the next step is to fine-tune the numbers. You might have to go through this process several times as new estimates arrive and are revised or as tasks enter the project that were forgotten or ignored in the initial estimating pass.

You need to follow all these required steps as you refine your estimates:

1. **A rough cut.** This is a number pulled out of a hat, and it might have little to do with the final number. You may ask people to give you a number based on their experience. However, it's just a guess!

   Rough cuts should never become the actual budget numbers. This will kill a project manager and project faster than anything because rough cuts are often remembered as real budget quotations. Run like hell if you're asked to stop budgeting at this step.

2. **A second cut.** Carefully review the resources required for each task estimate. These include the cost of labor, supplies and materials, equipment, overhead, and fix-priced bids from vendors (which account for all the vendor costs). This estimating process might demand the use of outside providers or might require more than one take as a complex subset of work is reliably broken down. You should also look at historical project costs to help guide your estimates. All estimating should involve the relevant stakeholders.

3. **Getting it right.** The third pass is the one in which you (and the team, of course) do the fine-tuning. For example, you need to make sure you know whether you'll need to budget the cost of company employees working on the project or whether that will be considered a sunk cost. The answer will affect your budget numbers. Again, the relevant stakeholders need to be involved in these refined estimates.

4. **Wrapping it up.** If the budget appears to be workable, that is, affordable, it gets wrapped into the project plan while simultaneously heading for the steering committee for approval.

5. **Presentation for approval.** At this point the budget should not be a surprise to anyone on the approval cycle, because you have presold the budget throughout the development process. Your complete draft for the budget is now ready for approval. Even though people have seen it before, they may still ask you to find ways to cut it, to modify the project, or to scrap the project as not worth the money (more common than you might think). If you're lucky, it gets approved right there. If not, continue to revise and present until you get consensus and signatures on the bottom line.

Adding a Little Insurance Money

Are you uncertain of the level of risk in a project? Want to provide a buffer of extra money? Most project managers will add about 10 to 15 percent to the budget to ensure completion and treat it like an insurance policy. *Contingency reserve* is a standard procedure in managing any project. There's no way you can be fully calculate or anticipate every risk.

Instead of overpadding the budget, negotiate for the money you really need, or, as suggested previously, adjust the project scope and objectives to be less expensive. Or use a technique like PERT, which we covered earlier in Chapter 10, that includes some of that padding as part of the calculation. Remember, it takes three estimates for effort, best case, worst case, and most likely, and calculates the effort using a formula. Formulas work wonders in establishing credibility.

At the same time, remember it's often easier to get required money at the beginning of the project than to keep coming back for more because your estimates were bad.

def•i•ni•tion

Contingency reserve means adding extra money to a budget in case overruns occur. This is a standard project management tactic (also known as a contingency plan) used to mitigate unexpected cost overruns.

Master Budget Control

Who holds the purse strings? You? Your management? A combination of both? Whatever the arrangement, you want as easy access to the money as possible. Work with your management to get signature authority for the project. That way, you can pay bills and purchase supplies in a timely manner. In another typical arrangement, you theoretically own the budget but must get multiple signatures from senior management each time you need to spend a chunk of it. This slows projects to a crawl because some members of the executive suite might be out of town and unable to sign. Besides, executives often let authorizations requiring their signatures sit in their inboxes because they're too busy with their own projects.

The Time Value of Money

Everyone knows that what a dollar buys today will be less a year from now. For that reason, it is prudent to calculate the time value of money invested in a project. These four techniques will help you validate the budget you have constructed. And take this element into consideration as you sell your project budget: they go from fairly simple to very sophisticated.

- Cash flow
- Payback
- Net Present Value (NPV)
- Internal Rate of Return (IRR)

For the purposes of illustrating each of these approaches, let's take a look at two projects and consider how they would be analyzed using each of these techniques. We're going to keep it simple, so let's imagine two projects where the initial investment is $100 and the cash received over three years flows as shown in the following chart.

	Year 0	Year 1	Year 2	Year 3
Project A	($100)	$25	$40	$60
Project B	($100)	$60	$40	$25

Cash Flow Analysis

If you look at the chart, at the end of Year 3 both projects would show an equal amount of money ($125), and therefore, from a cash flow perspective, they are equal. This is fairly easy to compute.

Payback

If we look at the payback on the two projects, things change in our analysis. Because Project B receives money faster, we can see that it takes only 2 years to recover the initial investment. In Project A, it will take the business 2.6 years to receive the payback from the investment in this project. From this analysis, Project B begins to look better.

Net Present Value (NPV)

The Net Present Value method is a sophisticated capital budgeting technique that equates the discounted cash flows against the initial investment. Mathematically it looks like this:

$$NPV = \sum_{t=1}^{n} \left[\frac{FV_t}{(I + k)^t} \right] - II$$

Calculating Net Present Value.

Where FV is the future value of the cash inflows, II represents the initial investment, and k is the discount rate equal to the firm's cost of capital. If we assume that the cost of capital is 7 percent, then we can calculate the NPV for the two projects and come to the following answers:

- NPV for Project A = $7
- NPV for Project B = $11

Now we begin to see a fairly significant difference in the return on the investment the company would make in the two projects. It would tell the management of the company that there is more money to be made on Project B, particularly if capital is scarce.

Internal Rate of Return (IRR)

Using the following formula to calculate Internal Rate of Return, we also see a significant difference between the two projects. When we calculate the IRR for Project A, we find a return of 10 percent. When we calculate the IRR for Project B, we find we have a return of 14 percent. Again, this can help management understand the money to be made in betting on the two projects.

$$IRR = \sum_{t=1}^{n} \left[\frac{FV_t}{(I + IIR^t)} \right] - II = 0$$

Calculating Internal Rate of Return.

The reason for the better return for Project B is the fact that the money flows in earlier. While that may seem obvious in a simple example like this one, it will be far less obvious in large, complicated projects.

Obviously, these methods, particularly the more sophisticated ones, rely on a set of assumptions that in reality will probably turn out to be wrong. Who can really predict the future? So a project manager might run 2 or 3 scenarios where he changes the assumptions to see what happens. As an example, let's suppose the projects were dependent on the price of oil (as of this writing, the price of oil is beginning to skyrocket). The project manager might run scenarios with oil at $50 per barrel, $60 per barrel, and $70 per barrel to see what happens. (He would not generally calculate a scenario for a cost of $10 per barrel or $200 per barrel, as they are highly unlikely.) As you can imagine, using these different scenarios would cause the results to change.

What you are doing in this type of analysis is helping management decide where to place the bet on projects, and you hope that your project will be the winner. It also feeds into your risk assessment where your scenarios would run from "best case" to "worst case" and "most likely."

For small projects, you probably can use the simpler methods. However, the project manager for All-Star Cable would probably want to run the more sophisticated NPV and IRR calculations in building a responsible budget. And remember to go back and review the risk assessment once the calculations are complete.

All in all, if you estimate carefully and document your assumptions thoroughly, you'll get a good budget approved, one that gives you enough money to get things done on time.

The Least You Need to Know

- Establishing a reliable budget is likely the most difficult task a project manager faces. Don't get caught in one of the classic estimating traps.
- Be sure to factor in direct costs (such as labor and equipment) and indirect costs (such as facilities and site-specific requirements).
- For the best accuracy, always complete the budget after you complete the WBS and the schedule.
- For larger projects, take the time to calculate the Net Present Value and Internal Rate of Return for your project before you complete the budgeting process.

Chapter 14

Building a Winning Project Team

In This Chapter

- The importance of a well-chosen core project team
- Determining exactly who you need on your implementation team
- Matching required skills to available talent
- Places to find people for your project
- Assigning people to the team
- When you can't choose your team members

As you build the project team, you will need to carefully consider the knowledge and skills of each individual and what he or she can contribute. You'll also need to think about which phase(s) of the project life cycle they will be involved in. You will require the largest number of people during the execution phase, and smaller numbers in the definition and planning phases. However, the people you choose for those phases should usually be the key thinkers and innovators. They must help you plan the project, and their technical knowledge will be very valuable.

This chapter explains how to scope out required skills, assess current talent, and develop a list of people required to complete each phase on your project. We also offer guidelines for filling the gap in people skills when adequately trained resources are not readily available.

The First Step

The first step in building your organization and human resource plan is to determine what kinds of people you will need. As you consider the kind of background your team will need, ask yourself these questions to help you think through your requirements:

- What kinds of experience do they have/need?
- What is their availability?
- What knowledge and skills will they need?
- Do they have a personal interest in the outcome of the project?
- Will they work well in a team environment?

You will probably think of other questions, but this list should help you begin to sort through the possible candidates and select the appropriate ones.

One of the key considerations in building the project team should be that except for some of the very technical people, each key team member needs to have an understanding of the business. You can have great technical people, but you cannot give them the in-depth knowledge or experience of the business. Having business analysts who can stand toe-to-toe with organizational people and talk about the business, ask the right questions, and question the answers they receive is the only way to build real credibility with the organization. Staff your project with strong business analysts who can challenge the ever-present parochial view that "we're different here."

You'll actually be doing most of your hiring after the plan is approved and you move into the project execution phase (that starts with Chapter 17), but you need to verify personnel costs and resource availability before you put the plan into effect.

Building the Core Project Team

Choosing the core team could be the single most important decision you make as a project manager. Strong team leaders effectively combined with knowledgeable experts (where necessary) build the momentum required for successful project planning. And good planning is paramount to a successful implementation of the project.

The core project team usually consists of the most important players, those who will be associated with the project from start to finish. The core team will be involved in the project design phase and the planning phase and then will bring others on board for the implementation phase. While the core team doesn't usually have signature authority for the project, they are directly responsible for the overall success of the project's planning and implementation phases.

Rank is not always a consideration in forming the core project team; for a larger project, skill or experience might be more important factors. On small projects, the core project team might be only you and another key person with whom you will be working on the project.

The membership of the core team may change slightly as you move out of one phase of the project and begin the next phase. For example, Ed may be the team leader for the testing plan during the planning phase, but Diane may take the lead for testing during the execution phase of the project. Throughout the project, however, your core project team should consist of your most trusted employees and central advisors.

For complex projects, to have a tool to help you determine your personnel needs and match those needs with qualified individuals is useful. One such tool is the responsibility assignment matrix (RAM), as shown in the following table. In addition to helping you match individuals to tasks, you can use it to help figure out who you need to consult on particular decisions or issues and who will actually be responsible for carrying out certain duties. Signature authority is usually reserved for managers who control critical aspects of the organization the project will depend on. They are key stakeholders, and you will not be able to use their facilities or people without their approval. Bob is a case in point in the following matrix.

Responsibility Assignment Matrix (RAM)

Phase	Ali	Bob	Callie	Diane	Ed	Frieda
Requirements	A		P		I	R
Design		S		P		A
Development	A	I	P	A	I	
Testing	A	S	A	A	P	A
Training	P	I				A

P = Primary A = Assigned R = Review Required I = Input Required S = Signature Required

In the matrix, we have given the primary responsibility for certain tasks to those who have the knowledge or experience we need. Often, project managers will give them a title such as team leader. For example, Callie is an experienced developer who has worked on projects similar to the development needs that we anticipate will be important for All-Star Cable's MOD. Therefore, Callie becomes the team lead for development. Ali, on the other hand, is less experienced and will need someone like Callie to help direct her work, or assign work for her, at times. And Bob is the manager for infrastructure at All-Star Cable, so he will need to be consulted or be asked to sign off on certain aspects of the project.

Time Is Money

As you build your core team, look for people who can work within an ordered system of checks and balances. Avoid people who might impose their own agenda on the project or the classic "prima donna" types. If you have a choice in the matter, choose individuals who will accept your role as project manager without resentment or hostility.

You may also decide to use the RAM as a tool to help you bring new people onto the team or as a way to determine who to recruit if you happen to lose people along the way, which almost always happens!

Only when you have the tasks and the work breakdown structure (WBS) in hand can you identify all the resources required to complete the project. The project sponsor and the core project team may help you do this; however, it isn't until after the project plan is approved and the execution phase begins that you'll actually start working as a fully functioning project organization. (We'll cover how to organize the project team during the execution phases in Chapter 19.)

The Complete Implementation Team: Where Most of the Work on the Project Is Done

The project implementation team includes the core team and other people who will actually do the work to develop the project deliverables. On almost any project, this team is made up of people with differing personalities, skills, ability, knowledge, and temperament. Your mission is to evaluate the project prior to choosing implementation personnel and to build an implementation team that takes advantage of each team member's skills without taxing his or her weaknesses.

Unfortunately, this isn't as easy as it sounds. Building the team and keeping it together are two of the most difficult tasks for any project manager. Whether through neglect or confusion, it's easy to let the team spirit slip away, and a spiritless project comes in with a bang and leaves with a whimper. Don't let this happen to you and your project! Even though we have spent a lot of time talking about activities, budgets, and schedules, your most important job will be managing the project team. Read this chapter, and learn how to find the right people for your project to reap implementation success.

Words from the Wise

Some of us will do our jobs well and some will not, but we will all be judged by only one thing—the result.

—Vince Lombardi, Hall of Fame football coach

Matching Skills to Tasks on the WBS

You can answer with confidence the questions about the people skills you need for your project by using a structured approach that starts with the project's WBS. For each task in the project, answer questions similar to the following:

- Is there a specific technical skill or combination of skills required to complete this task?
- How much experience should the person or people have to complete this activity? Does a person need to have specific experience doing this activity or can general experience be applied? If so, what general experience is required?
- Does this person have the knowledge or education required to fulfill the role that you need filled?
- In addition to technical skills, are any specific interpersonal skills required to complete this task effectively, such as good written or verbal communication skills, diplomacy or negotiating skills, or management ability?
- How many of these skilled people will you need for each task and how will you organize them by job title and job function?

List the skills and experience next to each WBS level, or use a worksheet like the example shown for the All-Star Cable Movies-on-Demand project. With a form like the example shown here, often called a skills requirement worksheet or skills matrix, you can list the actual skills you'll need to complete your project on a task-by-task or milestone basis. Use this type of worksheet to determine the skills, and then decide whether you can find these people internally or whether you will be forced to find them elsewhere.

Skills Requirement Worksheet
Project: All-Star Cable Movies-on-Demand
Produced by: H. Lieberum Date: 05/01/06

WBS	Tasks	Skills Required	Experience
2.0	Storage	Data management Data modeling	Oracle DB
6.0	Billing system	Accounting System development	Financial systems
13.0	Interfaces	Development and testing User interface with drop-down menus	Retail environment

In addition to completing the skills requirement worksheet, to decide on the team members you need, consider questions like these:

- If you could choose anyone you wanted for your team, who would you choose and why? (Hint: Your answers should involve both skills and personality for each person you choose.)
- Given the team that you actually get to work with, what levels of supervision will be required? You must be brutally honest here, especially if you're evaluating the skills of people who also happen to be friends or colleagues. Regardless of the talent involved, there's no sense in pretending your team members will be self-sufficient if they won't be. Some people simply need more direction than others, and these people will need some of your time.
- Where will the people come from? Do you have the talent in your own department (assuming these people have the time to be assigned to your project) or must you hire outsiders or raid another department for talent? (We'll tell you where to obtain people in the following section.) The source of the people will affect their cost and availability and maybe even the quality of their output. All these things will affect the schedule and budget you have yet to create and get approved.

Answering these questions will allow you to compare the talent required for the project to the people actually available. Are the people you need ready, willing, and able? If so, are they affordable? Will your project demand that already overburdened coworkers take on yet another responsibility? How much will outside resources, such as consultants, experts, and temporary labor, really cost?

> **Along the Critical Path**
>
> Free help! If you have a college or university within a reasonable distance of your company or facility, check to see if they have classes in project management at the graduate (usually) level. You can often get students who are smart and motivated to work as interns on your project. Professors are often anxious to give their students practical experience (and students are often just as anxious) on a real project. You will need to consider the risks of untried resources and work with the professor on how the students will be evaluated, but their participation might be well worth it!

Wow! This whole thing is sure interrelated. That's why you need to put on your thinking cap while you're planning. The better you understand your choices, the better chance you'll have to make good ones. It's also a good reason to involve others like your team leads in the discussion.

Where Will the People Come From?

Staffing a project can be difficult because co-workers are already buried in their own work and hiring outsiders is expensive. Typically, your options are limited by people's availability and their cost. But an organization that wants or needs to complete a project must make staff available even if it means pulling people off other projects or bringing in outside help. Staffing options include the following:

- Using your own staff and other people from your department
- Using staff from other departments
- Contracting with consultants, outside vendors, or temporary agencies
- Hiring and training new staff

As with business options, each of these choices has an upside and a downside. Just working with unfamiliar faces can mean a few surprises. You might have to adjust the project to accommodate each personality and productivity level while keeping a wary eye on the project dollars and timing.

Your Own Staff and Other People from Your Department

If staff members with appropriate skills work in your department and aren't already (fully) committed to other projects, using them is the easiest alternative. You have

> **Words from the Wise**
>
> Motivation is a fire from within. If someone else tries to light that fire under you, chances are it will burn very briefly.
>
> —From *The 7 Habits of Highly Effective People* by Stephen R. Covey (Free Press, 2004)

easy access to these people; you have a working knowledge of their strengths and weaknesses; and depending on your rank, you may have control over them.

However, don't kid yourself. If you use internal people, you will need to change their performance contracts to include the project goals. Think about it: if they have to choose between two competing tasks, they will choose the one they are getting paid for, their day job! If you want them to commit to the project in addition to their regular jobs, the project must show up on the performance evaluation and have a positive (or negative) impact on their year-end bonus. Otherwise, you will always lose this battle.

You may also want to set up two organization charts, one that shows them in their regular job and a second one that shows them in the project organization. Visually, this sends a strong message. By that we mean that in the functional organization, for example Information Technology, we would see Bob Braveheart as a manager of infrastructure with seven people reporting to him. In the second organization chart for All-Star Cable, we see Bob as the team leader for infrastructure development that includes five people, ranging from developers to database administrators. The people in IT know they need to listen to Bob because he is their boss. On the project team, the org chart shows Bob as the boss of the infrastructure development team.

If your project requires outside expertise (either from inside or outside your organization), this will require time and money. Projects with high visibility can be problematic politically, too. If other departments see you utilizing vast amounts of resources on a single project, you may have to justify your resource use as other projects slip. Further, you may be considered hard to work with because you use only people from your own group when more experienced talent is known to exist elsewhere in the company or organization.

Staff from Other Departments

Working with others in your organization makes for good communication and camaraderie among those involved. In a large organization, this might get you the technical or specialized staff you need, or it might allow you to bring in competent people whom you watch with awe as they keep the team moving efficiently and effectively. For example, you might need a financial wizard from the finance department to track your budget and streamline purchase orders.

On the downside, the main difficulty you will encounter is convincing someone's manager to allow her to join your project. If possible, get her seconded to the project full-time. Otherwise, you might discover that your outside staff member is late on her tasks because her boss agreed to let her join your project without reducing her current workload. This is a common problem in projects. People are told that 40 percent of their time is on the project, but no commensurate reduction has occurred on their day job. Negotiate carefully with line managers in advance to set the expectations as much as possible. Don't assume anything here. Don't forget to consider aspects of the job. For example, to get time with the accounting people will be hard when they are closing the books on a month or a quarter. Factor that into your plan and your schedule!

Contracting with Consultants and Temporary Agencies

Outsiders are always available—for a price. With careful selection, you can fully man a project with exactly the right mix of people. Hire them when you need them, and let them go when they're done. This is a flexible arrangement in that you have no responsibility (other than paying the bill) to keep them on or even to provide office space, because all but some temp agency employees will already have space of their own. The biggest risk here is that you will lose them if they find a permanent job. You will need to work out how that situation will be handled in advance with the agency.

Also, consultants can be expensive. The key to using outside consultants is to schedule their work carefully. The cost for a highly trained consultant priced at $150 per hour by his firm is mitigated if, with careful scheduling, he comes in, works using his own well-developed methodology, and leaves in five hours. But should the work fall behind, he may spend several hours, or even days, cooling his heels while the clock is running. In this situation, he will become an expensive liability, regardless of his admirable skills and experience.

Along the Critical Path

Be careful of using the word "headcount" when you talk about additions to your project team. Headcount is the term used to describe the fixed number of internal employees approved to work in an organization or on a project. Hiring a new person "increases headcount." On many projects, using an outside consultant or other temporary worker only increases costs. Sometimes it's easier to increase costs than to raise headcount because headcount enlargement shifts the permanent overhead costs. You must account for expenses for office space, furniture, tools, benefits, and even additional management time. Thus, if you need a person for a project and you don't have a job for that person after the project is done, it's usually easier, and in the long run less expensive, to propose an outside team member than to propose additional headcount.

Good consultants are masters at selling themselves; otherwise, they would be out of business. Remember, just because someone proclaims herself an expert doesn't necessarily mean she has a track record to back up the claim. Make sure the vendors you choose have been around the block a couple of times. Also, watch out for the "bait and switch." That is when a consulting group shows you resumés for experienced professionals for your project, but when the day comes to actually start, a group of newly minted MBAs shows up. You will spend time training them and constantly worry if they can keep up.

Even hiring low-level labor must be handled carefully. The temporary agency's polished salesperson may overwhelm you with smooth promises and glossy brochures, but eventually you'll just need hardworking developers to write that code. Remember, the gloss and polish you pay extra for probably won't make any difference if you just need good code developers.

You'll want to work with the procurement professionals in your company. They are experienced in writing contracts with incentives for good work and penalties for poor performance.

Hiring and Training New Staff

If the project is a long-term commitment or is ongoing with a finish date far enough out, you might find adding to the headcount is the most expedient method for bringing in the manpower and expertise required. For example, in our case study for All-Star Cable, you know you will need people to support Movies-on-Demand once the project is finished. It might make sense to hire them so they are familiar with the deliverables and the history of the project. Of course, you noted the word "training" in the title of this section. You must be fully prepared with time and money to train your new bodies in everything from their task requirements to the culture of your organization. But adding new workers often brings a fresh point of view, takes some pressure off other staff members, and is an easy way to add a much needed skill set not available elsewhere in the company.

Time Is Money

If your skills analysis reveals you need to employ more people, the company will likely have detailed hiring guidelines that include job description formats, pay scales, interviewing procedures, and reference requirements. Learn about these now before you have to start recruiting people. And don't forget to establish a good relationship with your human resources manager. This person can be a lifesaver when you need to get people on board quickly.

Keep in mind that not everyone you hire will like being a part of the team or will make a good team player. Individual contributors with specialized creative skills, such as engineers, designers, and writers, may sometimes appear to you and other team members as difficult to work with. That's okay if their expertise is a must-have for the project. Although you should avoid mercurial personalities with no people skills whatsoever, a genius with a compelling vision might make the difference between a mediocre project and a great one. Just keep him out of supervisory roles wherever possible. Another approach is to assign him to tasks with little dependence on others. That way he won't need to interact too often. Or you may want to use him as a subject matter expert that you only bring in at certain times to take advantage of his genius, but you don't have to supervise him.

You must structure the project team to work like a clock. Appropriate matches of worker to co-worker, manager to worker, and manager to manager are crucial. One good project manager we know even thought through the seating assignments. He wanted certain people to be close to each other so they could collaborate easily.

In a long project, this team assembly becomes more important. Someone who gets along with a colleague for a five-week project may grate on the person's nerves during a project spanning a longer period of time. Conflicts are inevitable, but do your best to assemble a team that's prone to cooperation rather than discord.

Deciding What You Need and Assigning People

For most projects, the staff assignment involves two steps: deciding what skills and experience you need for the work and then matching people to the tasks. You can create the description by writing out the individual competencies you need, and then see how the individuals you are considering would fill out the overall team competencies. (Competencies are defined as having the right qualities or abilities.)

If, after matching people to jobs, it still looks like you have the right talent available for the project, it's time to study the political ramifications of your choice of project team members. Also, you'll need to think about the location of the various people.

Risk Management

Sometimes an individual has such a unique technical skill that you must give him a supervisory or leadership role, regardless of how difficult he is to work with. You (and the rest of the team) will just have to learn to work with the difficult personality to get the job done. This is one of the standard challenges project managers must handle with aplomb.

Sometimes, all the people are in the same location, so it's easy. However, at times you may have people scattered all over the country or the world (see Chapter 19 on managing a virtual team)! Consider the political aspects of whom to choose, because you will need people from all the stakeholder groups to buy in. They are more likely to accept the project solutions if they have some of their people working on the project. Also, your boss may ask you to include someone on the project as a developmental opportunity as she might need experience to grow into her next job. You might think of this as an imposition. However, what you may really have is a bargaining chip to gain further concessions on other aspects of the project.

If you need to put a team together with resources from other departments, consider these questions before you go any further:

- Who will you have to deal with in other parts of the organization to get approval for a prospective team member's participation? Is this politically workable?
- How much will outside services cost? Would it be easier to use outside resources than to get approval to use the inside people?
- How much training does each team member require? Is it worth it?
- Will team members come willingly, or are you imposing your agenda on workers who would prefer to have no part in the project?
- Is another manager offering you a team member because he wants to get rid of the person? (This is called exporting the problem!)

A Survival Resource After the Project Starts

Skills inventories and contact lists also are useful after the project starts. Your goal should be to take an accurate inventory of the skills you need for the project, to prioritize the skills according to amount of experience required, and then to assess the proficiency of your project team members against that inventory. Why? What happens if a key staff member assigned to your project quits or gets sick? Pull out your skills inventory to identify potential replacements. If you don't have a network diagram and skills inventory ready, you will waste valuable time trying to find someone who can take over for the lost resource, and the project may suffer delays or other problems as a result. Always make this situation a part of your project risk plan.

The Best of the Best: Making Your Selections

After you've considered your options and the talent available to you, create a list of possible people and vendors for each task on your list. This list should include the alternatives available. For large, complex projects, rank the alternatives in priority order, and include the strengths and weaknesses of each choice. A worksheet like the one shown previously can be useful in identifying people and their strengths and weaknesses for a project team. (Guard your list closely and rarely share it with others!)

If you use a skills inventory, you will discover almost no perfect matches of people and project requirements on your list. Because no one can perfectly fit your needs, the selection process usually involves trade-offs. For planning purposes, identify people with the closest match of required skills, and ask yourself whether the skills deficiencies are workable. Can you use two people who complement each other's skills on the project? Can you make up for the lack of skills in other ways? The more critical the tasks, the more important the match of skill requirements to people becomes.

Sometimes You Have to Compromise

Obviously, you want the best people possible for your project, but even after making compromises and trade-offs, it's not always appropriate to use your first choice for every task, especially if another person's skills are adequate.

For example, if you were the project manager for All-Star Cable, you might have two people who could do the job of designing the new billing system. One of them has extensive experience in billing systems but is relatively new to the company, and you have not worked with him before. Another person does not have the experience of the first one, but you have worked with her before and know what to expect if she joins the team. So you will have to decide which trade-off you are willing to make—experience or familiarity. Which will it be? Every choice involves risks and trade-offs.

The other key reason for compromising might be budget constraints. With the example of the billing system design, the more experienced person might be your choice, but the person is too expensive. You don't have the budget to spend on the work that needs to be done, and the compromise might be to let the less skilled person do the work at a lower cost and just bring the more expensive person in on an as-needed basis.

The Problem of Imposed Team Members

You won't always have the advantage of being able to choose and organize every member of the team for your project. Other managers within your own organization may impose the team and its structure on you. Frequently people are selected because they are available and not because their skills or talent match what you really need. Imposed team members are common in every business for a variety of practical and not-so-practical reasons. Be sure to include the risks of imposed team members into your risk analysis, and determine the best strategy for mitigating that risk.

In dealing with imposed team members, there are a number of alternatives you can consider to make things work:

- Do the best you can with the people you have, but always document resulting problems as they occur (otherwise known as covering your rear end).
- If your team is not qualified in all required skills and training takes too long, consider hiring a consultant or an outside vendor to fill in the gaps. If you don't have the budget to do this, consider requesting more money and use your skills matrix as a selling tool.
- Compromise and negotiate for the team members you really need. If you have documented your own case with task requirements and skill inventories as suggested earlier in this chapter, a rational manager will usually listen. You may not get everyone you want, but if you identify the priorities, you may be able to negotiate for the people you really need.
- Approach the manager with specific alternatives in mind and a convincing argument as to why your proposed changes would result in a more efficient project team that's better able to deliver the project on time and within budget.

The Least You Need to Know

- Planning for the right kinds of people on your team is important to the success of the project.
- The core project team usually consists of the most important players involved in the project from start to finish.
- A comparison of project needs and people skills can help you match the right people to the right jobs on your project.
- Look for the right combination of skills and experience in team members, whether it's within or outside of your company.
- Part of your risk plan will need to include a strategy for replacing people you may lose over the course of the project.
- When you have team members imposed on you, analyze the risk that may entail and look for other ways to deal with the situation effectively.

Chapter 15

Getting What You Need: Supplies, Equipment, and Other Things

In This Chapter

- Establishing exactly what you need
- Getting bids from outside vendors, contractors, and suppliers
- Working effectively with the purchasing department
- The final steps for procurement

After you have defined the tasks, established a basic network diagram, and selected the team members, you must create a list of additional resources you'll need for your project. You have also determined your project schedule and budget, so you are ready to begin the process of procuring those additional items.

The Additional Resources You Need

As you figure out what you need to complete the project, you'll have to consider additional fundamental resources required to implement almost any project (we've already talked about people and money):

- Equipment
- Facilities
- Materials and supplies

You and the core project team need to identify these other resources for the entire project. Ask yourself what resources are already available. Professional project managers often use a resource inventory to list everything available for the project (including equipment, facilities, and supplies).

As you begin to plan for procurement, consider a variety of inputs to help you. You will need to review these items:

- Scope statement in your project charter
- Deliverables you are responsible for
- Procurement policies within your company
- Market conditions for the equipment, supplies, and so on, you need
- Constraints identified earlier in your planning process
- Assumptions you have made

After you (and the core planning team) use the worksheet to identify additional resources, you still need to know one more thing before you can complete your plan for project resources: the estimated quality and output of people and equipment resources. This is important because it allows you to make a trade off analysis between similar resources. If time is most important, choose the fastest resource. But if a slower resource really saves money in the long run and you have time to spare in the project schedule, then a slower but cheaper resource might be a better selection. If you don't make these estimates in advance, you won't be able to put the best budget and schedule together for your project.

Words from the Wise

If you need help building your estimates, check out one of the several estimating software programs available.

Planning for Outside Vendors, Contractors, and Suppliers

During the planning phase (where you are now), establish a list of probable vendors, suppliers, and contractors for your project and get estimates of cost and availability. Before you talk to vendors, you need to be crystal clear about the materials, equipment, and/or work you want from them. This will come into play during negotiations, and a well-defined statement of work (SOW) is essential. (If you need to revisit SOW, see Chapter 7.)

When you evaluate the need for vendors, consider doing a make-or-buy analysis. This technique determines whether you can effectively produce the items you need internally within the company or whether your best alternative is to purchase what you need. A good way to begin that analysis is to develop the specifications you need for your project, which include the following:

- *Design specifications* detail what is to be done in terms of the physical characteristics of the product. The risk is on the buyer.
- *Performance specifications* describe measurable capabilities the end product must achieve. The risk is on the vendor.
- *Functional specifications* express the way the item will be used as a way to stimulate competition and lower the cost since most products don't exactly match the functions to the usage. This is often linked to a performance specification. The risk is on the vendor.

Don't forget to include indirect costs when you begin this analysis. Often an internal source will look good until you factor the indirect costs into the equation. Also, keep in mind the overall perspective for the company and not just the project. For All-Star Cable, it might look like the resources for developing the cable box reside in-house. However, manufacturing several hundred thousand of them simply exceeds All-Star's capabilities. It would be better to hire a company that specializes in manufacturing to make them for you.

You might also need people with special training or experience to provide input into the procurement process. For example, when we did a project on pipeline maintenance for a major energy company, we looked for people who could give us expert advice on turbine engines. We decided we would talk with maintenance experts at a national airline on how they did the work on their turbine engines and see what we could learn and apply to our project.

Determine What Kind of Contract to Use

Different types of contracts will entail different levels of risk for you and the vendor. You will need to choose the right one for you and the risk tolerance within your company for these types of purchases. The three primary contract types used most often are:

- *Fixed-price or lump-sum contracts* let you know exactly how much you will pay for goods or services. They place much more risk on the seller's part, and therefore, most vendors will not enter into this type of agreement unless you provide them with a very clear and concise statement of work (SOW).

  Vendors who are hoping to work with you on a long-term basis on future jobs might bid the first job at a loss to blow away the competition and get the work. This is called *buying the job.*

- With *cost-plus-fixed-fee contracts,* you pay the vendors for their costs, both direct and indirect, plus a fee over-and-above those costs, which is the vendor's profit. This puts more risk on you as the buyer and less on the seller, but it allows you to offer incentives to the vendor if they meet or exceed certain targets for the project.

- *Time-and-materials (T&M) contracts* are a combination of the fixed-price and cost-reimbursable contracts and are often used for consultants or other personal services resources. T&M contracts resemble the cost-reimbursable contracts in that they are typically open-ended since the full value will not be realized until the project is finished. However, they resemble a fixed-price contract because you will negotiate fixed rates that you will pay for the services of different people (a senior programmer, for example).

Get an Estimate

No matter which type of contract you choose, you should ask for an estimated cost. You want to know the estimates are good ones and that the eventual commitments will be met. Follow these guidelines for getting the best estimates for your project:

- Whenever possible, get written estimates from suppliers with whom you have extensive and positive experience.

- Make sure all providers (people, materials, and equipment suppliers) bid competitively. Get a minimum of three bids or more if you can. When you have trimmed the list down, ask the final two providers to present you with any revised estimates. When two companies know they are down to the wire with only one other competitor, they will often sharpen their pencils and give you an even more attractive estimate to capture your business.

- Be aware that some companies are now beginning to hold what is called an E-auction for bidding that is similar to the auctions on eBay. This approach might be particularly appealing if you want to speed up the process due to a short timeframe.

Time Is Money

The amount of profit on a contract is frequently based on how the risks are to be shared between the vendor and you. The more risk the vendor takes, the more profit he will expect on your project.

Now you can get to the bottom line of working with outside suppliers. Never view an estimate as set in stone. Negotiation is a fine art. When you are ready to begin negotiations, you should plan for and include the following ideas in your thinking:

- Based on your WBS, determine what is the maximum and the minimum you expect to pay.
- Determine how you will evaluate the competing bids. Will you just decide on price or will quality or other factors be just as important as price?
- Decide whether you want a single source or multiple vendors for your project. Your answer will often depend on the risk assessment you have done.
- Review past performance on similar projects. You will want to make sure the vendor is capable of delivering on your project based on the experience of others.

Words from the Wise

Business people see me as a master negotiator because I usually wind up with what I am aiming to get. In other words, I negotiate to win and then I win.
—Donald Trump, chairman of Trump Enterprises

You need good estimates for your plans and good working relationships with your vendors to get these estimates. Work with suppliers, study the goods or services they sell, and check up on their reputations. Never let a powerfully persuasive salesperson push you into a commitment before you approve the plan. It may be harder to resist than you think.

If you follow these simple steps, you'll get more accurate estimates from suppliers of all sorts of goods and services:

1. Get written estimates for your service, supply, material, and equipment needs. On large projects, you may want to put together a formal request for proposal (RFP) to attract the maximum number of potential suppliers. Advertise the RFP if that's what it takes to get good estimates and quality vendors. Offer detailed specifications of your project and its needs by return mail, fax, or e-mail. Vendors will assume bidding is competitive, although the words "Competitive Bid" stamped on the RFP will help make it clear from the start.

2. Fully explain, demonstrate, and document your requirements for equipment, materials, and supplies for the estimate or in the RFP. Be as precise as the following sample bid request for professional services: "The Company expects the consultant to research and recommend billing technology that will satisfy the requirements listed in the statement of work and that will operate within the technical environment at All-Star Cable." In your RFP, here are some questions you might ask them to address:

    - What is your understanding of our need?
    - What will be the overall or life-cycle cost? The definition of life-cycle cost is the purchase price plus cost to operate over a period of time.
    - What are your technical capabilities to complete the work? Please give examples that illustrate these capabilities.
    - What is your management approach, and how will you use it to ensure the success of the project?
    - What is your financial capacity to fulfill the terms of the agreement during the life of the contract?

Time Is Money

Keep in mind that, as you develop the rest of the plan, your resource choices will affect the quality, schedule, and budget for your project. If you aren't able to get the resources you planned to use, you'll have to adapt the scope, schedule, and budget accordingly. It's a good idea to verify the availability of as many resources as possible before the project plan is approved.

3. Before you read a single proposal, sit down with your project team and develop the selection criteria. Determine if certain elements of your evaluation are worth more than others, and develop a weighting system that takes those priorities into account. Also, consider developing certain minimum standards that any

final vendor must meet to win the contract. You may be able to eliminate some vendors right away and not waste time on someone who wouldn't win against the competition anyway.

4. Make sure the vendors know acceptance and performance clauses will be inserted in the final order for goods or services. This means goods or services that don't meet specified standards will be returned and replaced at no cost to you or will be deducted from the invoice. Also, make sure the vendor will be responsible for picking up the shipping tab for return freight if materials or supplies are inappropriate or substandard upon delivery. Include delivery requirements in the description of your needs. (Ordinary but unavailable materials have sunk more than one project.) These specifications must indicate when the goods must be delivered and to what location; otherwise, the contract is void. If the company turns out to be a no-show, you're still in trouble project-wise, but at least you won't owe a bill for a shipment that arrives three weeks too late.

   Make sure you find out how changes will be dealt with. All projects will change over time, and you will need a clear process in place when you change the scope of work you have asked a vendor to supply. It will also help when one or more of the stakeholders requests a change because you will be able to explain to them how the price will change (increase) and what impact it will have on the schedule (delay).

5. When getting estimates from consultants or other service providers, ask for a formal proposal for their services. A formal proposal will tell you a great deal about a firm. Do they use "boilerplate" wording in response to your request? If so, it may mean they are not really familiar with your requirements but are hoping to impress you with their credentials. Be more interested in how they will work for you, not what they have done for others.

> **Time Is Money**
>
> If a process is highly technical, large, or complex in scale, ask for an answer back. In the answer-back process, the vendor takes your specs and builds a simple model that allows your experts to ensure that a clear understanding exists and that no significant parts or systems were neglected.

6. When hiring consultants or service providers, ask for a description of their current workload. Many will boast about current projects without realizing that what you're looking for is a person with the time to take on your tasks. The biggest concern most customers have is the classic "bait-and-switch," as we discussed in Chapter 14.

7. Check references, compare estimates, and use the estimate from the most likely choice of vendors for the rest of your planning purposes.
8. Hold a bidder conference to allow you to meet with several vendors at one time. A bidder conference is an invitation to all potential bidders to meet with you and some of your key team members. This will allow them to ask more detailed questions prior to submitting their proposals. Often, project managers will revise their RFP based on the questions they received during the bidder conference and then send it out to any vendors still interested in proposing on the contract.

Along the Critical Path

One way to get reliable bids and estimates is to have vendors develop their own WBS for their portions of the project, complete with the acceptance criteria and the list of resources they will use. Then they can assign individual costs to each task and resource in the WBS, just like you need to do for the rest of the project. This document can help you determine the quality of the estimate and the company's understanding of the work you want done.

Working with the Purchasing Department

Sometimes you won't be given the opportunity to get estimates or to order resources without going through the purchasing department. This can be a relief because it takes the work out of your hands. But the purchasing department can be the bane of projects (and project managers) if they are simply an organization that believes their job is to provide as much bureaucracy as possible.

Time Is Money

Look into using a database program to maintain the equipment inventory for your project. You can assign codes to equipment categories for easy sorting. Some of the more sophisticated project management programs allow you to include equipment inventories as part of the project data.

If you're lucky, you'll find a professionally run organization with experienced purchasing agents who take the time to understand your needs and to handle your bid requests with aplomb. Be aware, however, that you may be faced with the uphill task of (literally) fighting with your organization's purchasing personnel to place an order.

The only way to know what you'll be up against during a project is to test the waters. Begin by ordering something simple, such as a desk for a team member. The resulting cooperation of the purchasing department—or lack thereof—will let you know if you need to add tasks to your project that read: "Work with purchasing to explain need, secure bid, and gain approvals to order desks."

The best way to solve problems with a bureaucratic purchasing organization is to learn its procedures, follow its processes, and make friends in the department. If the department causes more problems than it solves, try to work around it when you can and learn to work within the process when you must. The test of the project manager's mettle is to make it all work, easy and hard.

The Final Steps in Procurement

For planning purposes, getting the bids for people, supplies, materials, and equipment may be enough to finish the budget for your project. But don't forget to build in some contingency funds for your equipment and supplies just in case circumstances change after the project starts.

After the plan is approved and you have the go-ahead to proceed with the project, however, you'll have to get an attorney or the corporate legal counsel to draft the actual work agreements with any suppliers or outsider vendors. Require vendor signatures on all agreements before work commences or money is exchanged. All these procedures are part of the procurement process, and procurement is a major portion of your job as the project manager.

The Least You Need to Know

- After you have identified all the tasks for a project, identify the specific resource requirements for each task or milestone, including people skills, material requirements, information needs, and other resources.
- Before you get your project plan approved, verify the cost estimates and availability for all the resources in your project. Otherwise, you can't put together a reasonable schedule or budget.
- Getting accurate estimates from suppliers of materials and equipment requires a clear description of your needs and a careful review of the vendors' capabilities.
- Establish a good relationship with the purchasing department and learn its procedures before you need to procure anything.
- Always check out the vendors before you sign a contract.

Chapter 16

Putting It All Together: Getting the Plan Approved

In This Chapter

- The importance of planning in project management
- Time for a last-minute reality check
- Putting the whole plan together
- Selling the plan to management and getting it approved
- What happens after approval

Okay, you've assembled a statement of work (SOW), a work breakdown structure (WBS), a network diagram, a schedule, a description of team requirements, and a budget. You understand the activities for the plan and the resources required. And you have determined how you will need to integrate the project deliverables into operations after it is completed. After all this effort, you may feel too tired to start working on the project, but you're not finished yet. You still need to integrate, evaluate, and get approval for all the work you have done to this point. That's right: you need to get your plan approved before you can start working.

This chapter reminds you of all the good reasons for planning in the first place and provides advice for getting your project plan approved so you can start working. Don't fret. You are almost ready for lift-off! With an approved plan in hand, you'll be ready to start working on the project. Finally!

Reasons to Plan in the First Place

Sometimes people complain that plans take too much time. They would rather start to work on the project than think about the plan. Some people think that plans are created only because other people want to see them. Your boss asks for a plan, so you write one. The customers want a plan, so you draft something to make them happy. Plans prepared slavishly rather than thoughtfully are a waste of time for the reader as well as the writer. Plans written only for the benefit of someone else rarely meet their goals of guiding the project to a successful conclusion. However, one of the biggest problems in business today, not just in projects but everywhere, is an attitude of ready, fire, aim. Don't get caught in that mentality.

> **Words from the Wise**
>
> One of life's most painful moments comes when we must admit that we didn't do our homework, that we were not prepared.
>
> —Merlin Olsen, member of Pro Football Hall of Fame

Finally, if you're not going to take planning seriously, don't bother. Just remember that without a good plan, you're like a surgeon who decides to remove an appendix with a can opener. You'll likely get the offending organ out, but you'll also make a mess of things in the process.

A good plan can help you avoid most problems, but not all. Even so, you should know that no amount of planning will make your project go exactly as you planned. Your plan will go off course because of things you didn't know in advance; and every project will encounter some things that cause you to deviate from the plan. Of course, you won't be able to think of everything. Remember that every project is unique, so you will be learning as you go. However, the better the plan, the more likely you'll get where you want to go. And the better you keep the plan up-to-date, the more likely you'll be able to make the best adjustments to keep the project on course.

The Reality Check Before Approval

Before submitting the plan for final approval, you need to perform one last *cross-check* of your planning efforts within the project team. This involves a line-by-line matching up of the WBS, schedule, budget, and network diagram, assuming you created these pieces. Computer-based planning software can help by finding impossible dates and durations on the critical path, missing network links (only if they're obvious), and missing activity data. Even when you use a computer, however, always check the logistics and flow of your project personally and carefully—don't assume things are accurate. Get your project planning team to help you with this effort.

def•i•ni•tion

One of the best tests of completion, whether for the doors on an airliner or the workability of a project plan, is **cross-checking.** To cross-check a plan, one person lists a procedure and another verifies it. With two people carefully verifying the plan, chances for errors greatly diminish.

Run all steps of the plan past your core team members before asking approval. The final fine-tuning of the project plan is no exception. After all, if you missed something, they might be able to fill in the gaps. If you've asked the impossible of a team member, you'll have an opportunity to hear about it before the work starts.

Follow these steps for cross-checking a project plan:

1. From the network diagram, match the activities, durations, and dates to the scheduling worksheet.
2. From the network diagram, match the resources to the scheduling worksheet.
3. From the network diagram, match the activity to those shown in the WBS.
4. Verify the numbers on the budgeting worksheet, and re-total them to make sure they match your existing estimate.
5. Study the activities on the critical path. Is the right path selected? Do any activities require more time? Have you separated the labor required from the duration on each activity?
6. Verify that the milestones (if you chose any) make sense as a means of summarizing the main activities in a project.
7. Check to see if the start and finish dates are still reasonable. Also verify that you have accounted for all holidays and vacations in the schedule.

If you didn't assemble either a network diagram or a WBS, it's almost impossible to cross-check a project. Reread earlier chapters on why these components are important.

If you're unwilling to prepare this level of detail in plans, whether formal or informal, be prepared for some surprises. A plan is an absolute requirement for success in project management.

What to Do If Discrepancies Appear

Inevitably, discrepancies will appear in the cross-checking process. As you might expect, larger projects tend to have more mistakes than smaller, simpler ones. After finding the errors, you must modify the plan to correct them. If more than 3 percent of the plan requires modifications due to your changes, perform the cross-check from scratch one more time after the changes are made. It's always possible to "fix" errors by introducing new ones. For that reason, review your notes from the previous procedure and do it again.

Time Is Money

An efficient way to present a plan is with a summary presentation backed up by hard copies of the plan's WBS, worksheets, and network diagram. Presenting a management overview will hopefully avoid a line-item review of each activity, its schedule, and its budget. If it comes to that, however, the backup data you've provided will do the trick.

One way to encourage review is to have a dedicated wall or cubicle where you can display the latest project data. Team members can check it and flag changes or problems. Team meetings take up a lot of time, so limit them. In today's networked world, you might consider additional "groupware" tools to share project information, but don't let tools replace your involvement as project manager.

A plan that changes more than 10 percent during the cross-check needs further work. Look at the errors to establish where they lie: schedule, budget, resources? If a definite pattern to the mistakes appears mostly in one part of the plan, consider redoing that part of the plan from the beginning.

Other Last-Minute Issues to Consider

Upon integrating the various components of the project plan, you might find issues that you have not addressed in your other planning efforts. Not all of these are worthy of an activity in the plan, but if you ignore them or don't address them somewhere in the schedule, the project will suffer. Typical things that get left out of the plan, but shouldn't, include:

- **Space and facilities.** Do you have basic office, manufacturing, and sleeping accommodations arranged that are suitable for your team? Do these costs appear in the budget?

- **Transportation.** Should your team need transportation above and beyond normal commuting, such as air travel and accommodations to other locations, and have you budgeted for this?
- **Permissions.** Do you require written or at least verbal permission to use specialized equipment, trespass on private property, to cross international borders, or something similar?
- **Licenses, permits, and clearances.** Do you need official permission to use hazardous chemicals, block access to a structure or roadway, enter restricted government facilities, move confidential equipment or materials, or something similar?
- **Insurance.** Are your team members and other resources underwritten for accidents and infringements that might occur? If insurance is required, what existing policies protect you, and how can you fill the gaps with additional coverage?
- **Weather.** How will the weather impact your plan? Can you hold the dates together if rain or snow delay construction, hinder delivery of materials and equipment, or impact team member performance?
- **Unavailable resources.** Is a strike possible within your organization or a major vendor? Is a key material in short supply? How will you address the problem and resolve it?

These are just some of the more common risk factors that might impact your project's timely completion. Before reviewing your plan with others, address all these items with contingency plans.

Putting It All Together

Use the following project checklist to see if you have all the plans ready for the review and approval process.

Project Planning Phase

❑ A. Develop project plan

❑ 1. Finalize scope definition

❑ a. Project objectives

❑ b. Project requirements and specifications

continues

continued

- ❑ 2. Develop work breakdown structure (WBS)
    - ❑ a. Identify work activities and performing organization
- ❑ 3. Develop organization breakdown structure
    - ❑ a. Match project work activities and performing organization
- ❑ 4. Work out project scheduling and cost estimating
    - ❑ a. Identify activity dependencies
    - ❑ b. Sequence activities
    - ❑ c. Develop project schedule
    - ❑ d. Estimate costs
    - ❑ e. Develop budget/funding profile
    - ❑ f. Determine scheduled start dates
    - ❑ g. Set project milestones
    - ❑ h. Establish measurement baselines for schedule and cost performance (project metrics)
- ❑ 5. Originate subsidiary management plans
    - ❑ a. Risk plan
    - ❑ b. Issues resolution plan
    - ❑ c. Organization and human resources plan
    - ❑ d. Procurement plan
    - ❑ e. Quality assurance plan
    - ❑ f. Project change control plan
- ❑ 6. Develop organization transition plan
    - ❑ a. Project communications plan
    - ❑ b. Change leadership plan
- ❑ 7. Deliver project plan memorandum to decision authority

The project planning documents are interrelated. If you make a change to one, you need to adapt the rest. For example, if you make a change to the scope of the project, it will affect the work that needs to be done (WBS), the schedule, the budget, and perhaps the project team members you will need to complete the new scope of work. If you don't keep the plan up-to-date, it doesn't matter how good the initial plan was. An out-of-date plan is a statement of what didn't happen—not a guide for the future. Typically, the plan will include additional narrative and organizing information to help readers (and team members) understand how the entire project fits together. The complete project plan for a large project might include a table of contents like the following example:

1. Executive Summary of the Project (or Project Overview)
2. Project Objectives
3. Project Assumptions and Risks
4. Project Milestones
5. Budget Details
6. Work Breakdown Structure (WBS)
7. Risk Analysis
8. Resource Details
   a. Human Resources
   b. Equipment
   c. Materials and Supplies
9. Project Organization
10. Operating Procedures
11. Quality Assurance Standards
12. Contact Points and Information Sources (if relevant)
13. Project Approvals

There is no magic formula for the right level of detail in the plan. If your project involves a large number of people and millions of dollars, you'll want to develop a detailed plan that allows you to coordinate the myriad resources properly.

The project planning stage dominates almost one third of this book, but the actual time required to complete the plan (including the work plan, resource assignments, schedule, and budget) is usually about 20 to 25 percent of the total time devoted to the project. But the quality and thought that goes into a plan, not the time, determines its value in the project management process. This is why it's so important to understand the issues in creating each component of the plan as we've covered them in previous chapters.

Write the Draft Project Plan for the Review Process

When you have completed the SOW, a WBS, a network diagram, a resource list, a schedule, and a budget, you have all the elements necessary to put together the plan.

Draft the final plan on your own if you have expertise in a project that makes you especially well-qualified to bring the major sections of the plan together. Also, if you are basing your project on a plan you used successfully for a previous project, this approach can work because you can compare what your project planning team has done to an existing plan that has worked before.

Of course, once you've completed a draft of the plan, have qualified individuals review it before you submit it to the steering committee. If you don't, you might encounter the following problems:

- It is more difficult to identify errors in the logic of a network diagram or WBS.
- You might not identify missing activities or incomplete activities.
- You might not have all the information you need to create an accurate schedule or budget.
- It is often difficult to see your plan objectively when you do it yourself. When other people review it, they should be able to understand what you are doing, when you are doing it, and what it will cost.
- People might feel left out, and you've missed a great opportunity at building support for the project with others, including stakeholders.

Conduct a Peer Review

Gather a group of qualified people who can review your project plan and give you feedback on various facets. For example, our project manager for All-Star Cable would probably want people from IT, accounting, sales and marketing, and customer service involved in the peer review. They will each have a different perspective on the plan and may point out risks or activities that you and your team may have overlooked. See Chapter 25 for more on conducting a peer review.

Review the Plan with the Key Stakeholders

Getting the key stakeholders involved in reviewing the project plan may require one or more structured meetings and probably advance preparation by each of the team members. As you prepare to present the information to the steering committee or whatever governance board will ultimately approve the project plan, put yourself in their place. What will they want to know? How can you best address their needs and concerns as you prepare to move into project execution? Who among your team members will they want to hear from and question about the project plan? Answer these questions before you prepare your materials for the meeting.

As you prepare the written project plan, also consider the following:

- How formal does the project plan need to be? In some groups, or for large, expensive projects, the project plan will need to be pretty formal—large notebooks with colored tabs and a Table of Contents. In other cases, you can do the project plan with PowerPoint slides and a few handouts.
- How does this group, or the key individuals in the group, like to see information? For example, many people respond very well to charts, graphs, and models. Others need pages of written text with only the occasional diagram thrown in. Again, tailor the information to the audience that will be reviewing the plan.
- This presentation can also be a test of how the steering committee will want to be briefed on the project as you progress, so pay attention to what they like about the way you present your project plan and what they don't like. Their reaction will give you clues on how to present the information in future status meetings.
- How much detail will you need to provide? Sometimes a steering committee will not want a lot of detail. If that's the case, leave the details out of the plan, but bring along any supporting information you have prepared. That way, if they ask you a question, you can respond quickly without having to say "I'll have to get back to you with that."
- At the conclusion of the review process with the steering committee or governance board, get the project plan signed by the project sponsor and any other

appropriate stakeholders, such as the president of the company, if they were part of the steering committee. You should view the project plan as a contract between you and the project steering committee and just like any contract, all the appropriate people need to sign it to make it binding.

Even after the plan is approved, as you bring new people into the project later in implementation, changes might be necessary if the new team members offer better or more appropriate alternatives for completing their assigned activities and reaching milestones. (When you start thinking about changing and modifying a network diagram with hundreds of activities during the life of a project and communicating these changes to multiple people, the rationale behind using computerized project management tools becomes apparent.)

Risk Management

While you work on a plan, your project might change in relevance, and you might be plugging away at something currently as important as yesterday's newspaper. Avoid this problem by continually feeding progress reports to your project sponsor and other key stakeholders during planning. And learn to take the company's pulse on a regular basis to see how the business climate might be changing.

Presenting the Project Plan

Before you present your project for final approval, study the presentation of the plan from an outsider's viewpoint. Do the activities explain themselves or do you need additional notation? Are the activities equal or almost equal in scope? Is the presentation clear and organized? Is the level of presentation appropriate for the scope of the project? Have the project sponsor review the project plan before you have any other decision-makers on the approval team look at it.

If you present your plan to a manager, customer, or review committee, be prepared to justify your choices, dates, and budgets. You'll need a compelling reason why each activity is required and the associated budget justified. (Even if the reviewers don't ask, you should be prepared.) Also be prepared to talk about risks and contingencies if things go wrong.

Use good judgment in what you present from the plan. Always start with an overview of the plan, and then move on to details. Remember, the people who approve the plan will have a copy of the complete document to review anyway; you don't need to go over every detail in the presentation. The goals of the presentation are to present the overall structure and objectives of the project, to answer questions, and to establish your credibility as the project planner (and project manager).

Too much detail in the presentation can be as damaging as too little. If you use too many activities in your presentation, you'll be bombarded with questions and arguments from management about the details. Managers might grandstand their opinions and try to save money on things they don't really understand. Avoid this by using milestone summaries of activities so that managers don't fail to see the big picture during your presentation. Keep the meeting short (one hour) and focused. Senior managers dislike meeting for longer than an hour. Keep it crisp, but make time for their searching questions and time to get their approval. Keep your antenna up for questions or suggestions that might cause a change in the scope of the project. If your scope gets changed in this meeting, it will impact your budget and schedule as well.

The result of your presentation will be either the approval (by signature) of the project (which is unlikely on the first presentation of a large project) or a request to make revisions. First make changes to the general plan (scope and strategy) and then to the details of the plan (the activities, network, resources, and so on). Remember, you must change both. You can't just adapt the schedule because the stakeholders don't like it. If you've done a good job of planning, you'll have to communicate this fact to the people who approve and sign off on the plans.

If real objections crop up, stop the presentation and reschedule the meeting after you have modified the plan. If more than three revision meetings are required, then either your plan has serious problems or the business or political agenda of the people approving it is likely to have changed and you are not in sync with it. Without full management commitment to your project, successful completion is unlikely at best.

If you get caught in a political situation, have one-on-one discussions with individual stakeholders to understand their concerns and then come up with a strategy for circumventing (or reducing) the politics from the process so you can go forward with the plan. Use your project sponsor to help you run the political maze that has your project ensnared.

Plan Approval

The final step before the ship sails, so to speak, is getting the project and its cross-checked plan approved by the people paying the bills. The people who approve the plan will vary by company, project, and assignment. As mentioned in Chapter 6 when we discussed the stakeholders on the project, make sure you know who will approve the work and the budget for the project. Sometimes multiple departments will be involved. Sometimes you'll get to sign the approval sheet on your own. In any case, the most important aspect of the approval is getting the money freed up (the budget) so you can start work on the project.

Along the Critical Path

In the real world, the plan for a large project (or even a small one) will go through multiple versions on its way to approval. Sometimes the steering committee will tell the project team to go back and make changes. Don't think of that as a failure! These plans may be debated, discussed, enhanced, expanded, and revised several times until the project plan is complete and approved.

Finally, you get great news: your plan is approved. They've signed on the dotted line. The accounting department has assigned a budget number and account codes for the project. You're ready to go!

The plan you created and got approved isn't the only plan you'll use during your project. You'll typically have three or more versions of the plan active at one time during a project. First, there is the original approved plan, which is usually called the baseline plan. Second is the actual plan, which reflects the actual work done to date. Third is the future schedule based on work done to date. Finally, you could have a number of contingency plans developed for a complex project over time.

Just remember to keep the plans numbered and up-to-date. A good computer program should be able to manage multiple versions of the project plan at a time so you can compare various stages of the project as you proceed.

From Plan to Action, Finally

After getting a plan approved, it might seem like you've done an awful lot of work and still not gotten anything done. The central role of the plan in the project management process often leads people to the mistaken conclusion that the creation of the plan is project management. But it's not. Most of the time spent in project management involves management. As you've already surmised, project management involves much more than just a plan.

Words from the Wise

The longer a project's duration, the less likely that changes in organizational priorities and happenstance will allow it to reach completion as originally planned.

—A project manager's standard axiom

Still, don't be surprised if people identify your project management skills with your ability to create an impressive-looking project plan. Worse things could happen, and as long as they pay you for it, well, you don't have to tell them that it wasn't really that hard.

You'll soon get to work and put your approved plan into action. Most project managers will tell you that planning a project is the easy part; executing the plan is the real work! Now the executing or implementation phase is about to begin. In the next part, we'll show you how to take the baseline and create both plans that reflect work done and schedules for remaining work. But that's to come. For now, just enjoy your completion of a demanding phase of project management.

The Least You Need to Know

- You need to cover all your bases in planning. A brilliantly scheduled research project in Switzerland will come in over budget if you don't remember to include the team's travel, food, and lodging expenses.
- Always analyze risky activities. If a less risky approach is possible, modify the plan to accommodate it.
- Scrutinize all planning documents from the WBS to the network diagram to ensure that they match and work together.
- You'll probably have to present your plan to management and customers before it gets approved, and it probably won't get approved the first time around.
- You must sell your plan to the stakeholders and get their commitment to the plan, its schedule, and its budget before starting work on the project.

Part 4

The Execution Phase

Well, you've done it! You've defined a project and gotten the plan approved. You're ready to begin, and the beginning is a very crucial time in any project. If you begin the execution phase (also commonly called the implementation phase) of the project the right way, it will enhance your likelihood for success.

To move toward the finish line of a project, you must establish your leadership, organize the team for top performance, institute operating guidelines, and yes, plan for good communications that will keep all your stakeholders informed and supportive as the project unfolds.

Chapter 17

Getting Started on the Right Track

In This Chapter

- Project kickoff activities
- Making sure the first project meeting goes smoothly
- Getting project members in synch and enthused
- Considerations when managing global projects

At this point, you have an approved project plan in hand. You have identified most of the key team members, sought permission to use them, and established a budget and a source of funds to pay them. You're ready to get started. Or are you? How will anyone know what to do? What's the first step?

For most projects, these questions are answered at the project kickoff event and the first project meetings with the group and individuals. These activities are the first steps in the executing phase of any project. The big kickoff event (or at least a small one) serves to get everyone in synch with each other and to build a feeling of camaraderie. The project kickoff is like the locker-room rally before a big game. It gets the juices flowing and reinforces the goals for the project. The first project meeting is like the initial huddle in the Super Bowl. You actually agree on your first play in the project and get the team lined up to win the prize.

In this chapter, we'll tell you how to hold a project kickoff that motivates the troops and gets everyone moving in the same direction—toward the project finish. You'll also see how to make the first project meetings part of the key strategy in your project game plan.

Always Get Your Own Act Together First!

Before you have the kickoff event, consider both your leadership style and your management tactics; the two are intertwined and are central to the implementation of projects. Your leadership skills and the appropriateness of the management tactics you adopt for each of the various people on your project team are of paramount importance in achieving project goals. The first time you get to try out these strategies and tactics will be at the kickoff event.

Time Is Money

Remember that you will never have everything completely in place and that changes will be coming no matter how carefully you have planned (we'll talk more about changes in Chapter 24).

In Chapter 18, you'll learn a lot more about becoming a leader on your project. We mention it now only because, to get a project kicked off, you must be both a manager and a leader. Use the project kickoff to gain the trust and respect of the project team so that people feel comfortable taking your direction. You can also use the kickoff to explain the reports and administrative procedures you'll use to help people get work done on time and within budget.

Do It Now and Do It Right

Once you've decided you're really ready, you need to decide how to kick off your project. Whether handled formally or informally, the kickoff events of the project or subproject need to accomplish the following objectives:

- Communicate the goals of the project to all team members to ensure that everyone is crystal clear on his own objectives and responsibilities for the project.
- Attain the commitment you need for the project and get people enthusiastic about making things happen.

- Establish the leadership style for the project and get the team ready to follow you.
- Identify critical deadlines and phases of the project.
- Review the overall schedule and work plan with the appropriate team members.
- Explain basic operating procedures including required reports, meetings, and other ongoing communications necessary between you and other team members.
- Explicitly give the people responsible for the initial tasks the go-ahead to begin work on the project.

If you add all these objectives together, you'll see that the overall goal of the executing phase is to establish a set of conditions so work can get done. These conditions start with clear communication about the plan and other procedures associated with your project. The project kickoff is the first step in opening up the channels.

The Formal Kickoff

Although some projects don't require more than a small meeting and a memo to get started, when a formal project kickoff event is appropriate, make it both celebratory and informative.

The type of event will depend on the size, importance, organization, and budget for the project. Use your judgment. Look at the kinds of events given in your company for similar projects, and ask about the events that worked and the ones that didn't. If a customer is paying the bill, keep the event simple and economical. One more reminder: if you hold the kickoff in a public place, make sure the competition is out of earshot.

It's a Go

Regardless of the sophistication or format of the kickoff event, the event should put team members on notice that the project is a "go." It should emphasize that each individual's contribution is vital to the success of the project. The kickoff event can also help individuals relate their goals and work responsibilities within the overall project to the efforts of other team members. This is a first step in establishing a "team" spirit.

In the more formal kickoff meetings like those described later in this chapter, always schedule the event so that your project sponsor and all other stakeholders, customers (if appropriate), managers, and key team members can participate.

Give the sponsor a spotlight (most of them love it) to endorse the project and "wave the flag." Remember the support of senior management is a critical success factor for projects. Seeing and hearing from one of the executives from the organization gives the whole project team a sense that the company really means business regarding this project.

The kickoff event should also establish the priorities, tone, and energy for the project. Avoid too many individual details; leave those for the first project meetings and one-on-one sessions with key project players. These meetings should take place during the first week after the project kickoff event.

Time Is Money

Start from the end result you want to achieve during the meeting and work backward. Express this as a written goal for the meeting and get everyone to agree to it before you start. Examples might be:

- Are you defining issues or making a decision?
- If the team is making a decision, are the decision-makers present and properly prepared to make a decision?
- If the team is defining issues to be worked on, are the proper people present to make work assignments?
- Do the meeting participants have the necessary content knowledge experts present (but not extra bodies)?

Between Kickoff and Team Meeting: Use the Time Wisely

The time between the project kickoff and the first formal project meeting (we recommend three days to a week between events) gives team members time to reflect on their roles. Feedback after the kickoff event is invaluable to plugging up holes in the project plan. During the period before D-Day (the day of the first project meeting), team members may approach you with questions or problems.

Based on any feedback, you can fine-tune your project plan and look into problems team members throw at you. You can also run issues and problems by senior management to level out small molehills before they turn into major mountains. Gathering feedback allows you to come to the project meeting prepared with answers to objections and explanations of issues that were inadequately addressed in the plan.

During that time, set up what is usually called a "war room." Often this is a conference room that is reserved for the exclusive use of the project team for the duration of the project. It should be outfitted with phones, Internet or intranet connections, and plenty of wall space to post information. Project members should be able to come here at any time and work, and other members of the company can stop by and see what's going on. While it is not top secret, you should also have cabinets with locks on them to store sensitive material.

The First Project Meeting

After the kickoff event, you're finally underway! Schedule the first team meeting to take place approximately one week after the kickoff. This first meeting will be the first true test of your leadership skills as the project manager.

Invite all working members of the project implementation team. (Do not invite customers and the executive management team.) Since this first team project review meeting is a meeting to get work started, it should accomplish the following:

1. Establish a model for future meetings:
    - Start on time.
    - Before the meeting, develop and distribute an agenda of objectives and ask people to review them before they come.
    - Conduct one agenda item at a time, and conclude it before moving on to the next item. (Avoid getting hung up on the order of topics.) Establish a "parking lot" for items that come up that are not on the topic. Write the list on a piece of chart paper and label it "Parking Lot."
    - Encourage open communication; meetings give individuals a chance to express suppressed ideas.
    - Take notes. Really the only notes that are probably relevant are action items assigned to people with due dates and any decisions made by the team.
    - Establish time and place for the next project team review meeting. We recommend you try to establish a regular meeting time, such as every Tuesday afternoon at 3:00. It's much easier for people to manage their schedules if they know that for the duration of the project, they need to devote their Tuesday afternoons to the project.
    - Agree on and reiterate any follow-up activities or required action items. Assign people to these tasks, and get their commitment to complete them.

- End the meeting on time. If you need to stretch the meeting a little longer, ask the group for permission and decide *how much longer* you will meet. Once that time is up, close the meeting down.
- Distribute (brief) minutes to all attendees within two days of the meeting.
- Make sure to indicate action items and responsibilities in the minutes so people don't conveniently forget what they agreed to do in the meeting.

2. Introduce the members of the team and their project roles.
3. Review the first priorities for the project and repeat/reiterate briefly the other objectives and overall schedule.
4. Review individual plans for getting work started.
5. Discuss methods and tools you will use to manage, control, and operate the project.
6. Deal with objections to the current project plan and work them out if possible.
7. If the group needs to make decisions, follow these steps:
   - Discuss the problems and seek opinions from all.
   - Don't allow one person to dominate the discussion.
   - Test for readiness to make a decision.
   - Make the decision.
   - Assign roles and responsibilities.

Here is an example of how minutes might look after a project team meeting for the All-Star Cable Movies-on-Demand project:

All-Star Cable Project Team Meeting Minutes

Meeting:	All-Star Cable Project Team
Date:	02/06/2006
Time:	2:30–3:30 P.M.
Chair:	Bob Braveheart

Attendees: Kim Winford
Jo College
Ben Adminovich
Joe Goniski
Mary Scarlotti
John Andreotti (by phone)

Decisions:
Agreed to the Case for Change and the Business Case for the project.

Items	Person Responsible	Date	Status
Action Items:			
Research vendors to build the cable boxes	Kim Winford	2/06/2006	Completed
Investigate the credit policy as reported by the project team	Ben Adminovich	2/06/2006	Completed
Review requirements for new billing system with Accounting	Joe Goniski	2/06/2006	In progress
Submit RFP for OTS software	John Andreotti	2/06/2006	In progress
Analyze reporting needs for management team	Bob Braveheart	1/30/2006	In progress
Parking Lot:			
Question of "adult" movies being part of the offerings to work with	Project manager Project sponsor	4/16/2006	Parked
GUI interface for customers	Parked until more items are completed	4/16/2006	Parked
Data storage and data mining	Parked until late February	3/30/2006	Parked

One-on-Ones: The Individual Starting Events

In addition to the kickoff and the first project meeting, you'll also need to meet with key individuals at the beginning of the project to make sure they have all the information they need to get started. These initial meetings with new players may continue throughout the project as different aspects of the project get underway.

def•i•ni•tion

One-on-ones are meetings (often scheduled and formal) between two people involved in a project. These meetings are used to discuss priorities, resolve issues, and communicate overall responsibilities to the project.

Use formal meetings with project team members, known as *one-on-ones*, to clarify priorities and to discuss schedules and plans. Many of these people will have worked with you on the project plan already, so you won't need to go over all the details with them. However, you will need to turn their focus away from planning and start delegating work to them so things start happening. This is a great place to review the network diagram and show each team member how her work fits into the broad project plan for the project.

Also schedule these one-on-ones with key players on a regular basis throughout the project. For a short project, the one-on-ones with key personnel might happen daily or weekly. For a longer project with more players, the formal one-on-ones might be monthly or even less frequently, depending on your other level of interactions.

In the first one-on-one meetings, clarify and review the following with each individual:

- Reasons he or she was selected
- Performance expectations
- Individual priorities, tasks, and milestones
- Administrative procedures and project management methods and tools in use, such as reporting of progress on work packages and time covering both the frequency and level of detail you want in those reports
- Challenges and issues
- Processes for solving problems
- A schedule for future one-on-one meetings
- Action items for future meetings

Always take notes in these meetings. Suggest the other participant does the same.

Setting the Right Expectations

Your ability to organize and control the first team meetings will be a major step in establishing your leadership of the project team. If you do this well, the meetings will serve as a model for subsequent project meetings and will set a tone of open communication and professionalism that will make managing your project a lot easier.

If you flub up the meetings, you'll not only waste the time used on the meetings, but you'll also lose credibility as the project manager. The number one criticism of most meetings is that they don't produce anything of value. Don't let that happen to your meetings. Preparation, organization, and focus are critical to making the first team meetings a success.

Information Everyone Needs to Get Started

The purpose of the kickoff and the initial team and one-on-one meetings is to inform people and get them in synch with the project plan. From the beginning, people who work on the project need access to relevant information in the plan so they can do their jobs. Tasks and schedules should never be a secret (although budget and other financial information may be held confidential when people aren't responsible for the costs). The project plan should generally be an open book to help guide people to the promised deliverable.

During the initial stages of the project, provide every member of the team with a summary of the plan. You can do this before the kickoff event, in a team meeting, or during a one-on-one at the very start of the project. For team members who will remain with the project from the beginning, we recommend presenting these documents prior to the kickoff event and then discussing them in the first project meeting and one-on-one sessions. As new team members join the project during later stages, make sure they get the information as well.

Every team member needs these pieces of information from the project plan in order to contribute appropriately to the project:

- **A summary of the overall project goals.** The project summary outlines and explains the purpose of the project, its goals, and the overall schedule.
- **The team member's role and task assignments.** Lay out in writing the specific tasks and milestones for each team member (or subteam). At the beginning, keep the milestones and task overview general and have specific tasks introduced by you or other supervisors and managers at a later date.
- **A list of who's who on the project.** The directory or list of key project team members should include a description of each team member, his or her role (and title) in the project, and contact information (telephone numbers, office location, and e-mail addresses).

In addition to information about the project plan, you need to inform every team member of the administrative procedures that will affect his or her life: reports, forms, legal documents, and so on. Don't drown team members in paper. If your reports to them are crisp and timely, their reports will hopefully be on time and accurate. For a large project, you may want to provide a "Project Administration Handbook" that assembles examples of all the forms, reports, and other documents required from project personnel, along with other relevant documentation of the project plan. For small projects, a simple list and an example report will probably do the job.

Along the Critical Path

Projects increasingly are becoming virtually staffed by transient, dispersed teams. Achieving to potential under these conditions requires distributed project leadership using "virtual walking around" techniques via computer networks, video conferencing, and the Internet. These techniques help people communicate, collaborate, and manage shared activities in an integrated way.

Also tell team members that you require regular status reports. Explain why the reports are essential to tracking the project and keeping it on time and within budget. Set the report intervals for weekly, biweekly, or monthly intervals, depending on the nature of the project. (Note that monthly would be for an extremely long project of more than two years. If you wait for a month to find out someone hasn't met his commitment, you are in a world of trouble with little time to catch up.) Present people with sample reports and completed forms that set the expectations for their reports. (We offer more recommendations on reporting frequencies and formats in Chapter 20.)

If confidentiality or other legal agreements are required for your project, now is the time to get them signed. If your organization contracts with the military or other government agencies, rules may be more strict. Look into the proper forms of agreement and reporting that are required, and make sure the appropriate team members understand the requirements at the beginning of the project.

Managing Global Projects

Having a project manager who must manage a global project is not as unique as it used to be. We are defining a global project as one that crosses boundaries between countries and is staffed by people from those countries. They often have different languages (although fortunately for many of us, the common language is English), and they certainly have different cultures.

Global projects, by their very nature, require a high level of sensitivity and awareness by the project manager. What may seem totally acceptable in one culture will not be acceptable elsewhere. You will need to consider these areas when you face the management of a global project.

Schedule

The schedule that you must develop for team meetings, for example, needs to take into consideration items such as national holidays in the various locations where your project team is located. They will vary greatly. Also, in some cases, the work week itself may be different. For example, the work week in many countries in the Middle East is Saturday through Thursday, and the work week in France is only 35 hours compared to the 40-hour week we generally take for granted in the United States.

Also, with time zones that can be several hours apart, planning how people who need to communicate and work together will do it can be a challenge. In one project we managed, people in Indonesia had exactly 12 hours difference from our location. It meant that someone would be up late at night (and early in the morning) any time they had a full team meeting.

Budget

With a global team, there will obviously be additional travel expenses. You will want to visit the project sites regularly, and you will want at least some of the team leaders to come to you to meet together occasionally. You will need to factor that into your budget and track it carefully. You can eliminate some of the travel costs using video conferencing, but again, find out what charges you will incur when you use those facilities.

Technology

Using technology to link the team members can be a tremendous help. However, plan carefully and arrange for shared drives so that team members can save their work and provide access to others who may need to see it or build on it. In providing a shared drive, consider security and access rights so the information you want to keep confidential (the pay rates of contractors, for example) stays confidential. Also, you may want to limit the access of some people to "read only" while others may have the right to edit materials. Finally, a common convention for naming and managing version control while the project is progressing will be critical to preventing problems later on.

Quality

Since you will not be on location to supervise much of the work being produced as part of the project, you will need to have a robust quality plan (covered in Chapter 25). Make sure your team members know how you will measure the quality of their performance. Also, a global project will require your team to have robust processes for the way work is produced and tracked including problems resolution. They will not be able to walk over a few desks and confer with their team mates when a problem arises like they would if they were collocated. All these issues need to be clearly communicated from the very beginning of the project.

Human Resources

In other countries, you may need to comply with other national or state laws as you manage your team members. Bringing members of your team to various locations may require visas for work-related activities. It's a good idea to find someone within your company's human resources department who can advise you on these kinds of issues, or hire a consultant with the background and experience to advise you on the correct course of action. You will need to know the rules from the first team meetings.

Risk Management

Do your homework to make sure you're familiar with certain customs. We know one project manager who had a kickoff meeting with his team at a local steakhouse that was known for great food. Unfortunately, part of the team consisted of people from India who would not even enter a steakhouse, let alone eat there, and therefore refused to attend the opening team dinner.

Procurement

Many countries will require you to purchase a certain amount of materials from the local or national economy, which you will need to factor into your budget. However, if those types of rules are also combined with a poor location infrastructure, you should consider that in your risk analysis. The best example is a project manager Mike met from Egypt who was managing a project in Sudan. His supplies were regularly disrupted due to the continuous eruption of civil war there. The project manager had to cope with local vendors who could not deliver at certain times. Again, getting expert advice from within your company or from a knowledgeable consultant is your best course of action in developing your procurement plan and negotiating the contracts.

The Least You Need to Know

- Getting a project started right involves communication.
- All projects need starting events that clarify project goals, responsibilities, and operating procedures. These events can be simple or elaborate but should always be commensurate with the size and importance of the project.
- Prior to the first project team meeting, have team members review the project and point out any holes in your plan that need patching.
- Managing a global project team will require extra thought and effort on your part.
- Focused, productive, and informative team and individual meetings are the best way to get things started on the right track.

Chapter 18

Leadership: Taking the Bull by the Horns

In This Chapter

- Establish your role as leader and manager
- Lead the way for change
- Develop a clear Case for Change
- Competing with other projects for attention
- Leading a technical project when you lack technical expertise
- The ever-changing roles of a project manager

Since it's up to your project team to complete the work specified in the plan, you as the project manager must employ appropriate methods to motivate, coordinate, facilitate, and administer your team. If you don't, the work may never get done. As a project manager, you must also identify and implement the appropriate leadership style to keep the team motivated.

The Importance of Establishing Your Leadership

Whether managing the remodeling of a major hotel in downtown New York City or the installation of a new Internet wiring within an office suite, you must take command to lead your project to success. You can use every technique in this book, but without assuming a leadership role for the project, you'll get nowhere. You must become the leader and the manager of the project if you want to succeed. And these are two distinctly different roles.

> **Risk Management**
>
> Project managers who are technically knowledgeable are sometimes prone to interfere with the work of their team members to the point that they actually become a hindrance to the team. Remember, as a project manager your job is to lead and manage the project, not approve all the details of the work.

As a leader, you must command respect and take responsibility for guiding the project. One key way to command that respect is to be a trusted and reliable source of information on the project. As a leader, your team will expect you to be honest, competent, and in charge.

As a manager, you will monitor and control the project to completion using specific techniques and procedures that establish the framework and structure of the project. You'll review the plan, complete reports, balance the budget, update the plan, fix the schedule, update the plan again, report on the updates to the plan, and yes, update it again. You'll also do a lot of other administrative stuff that will drive you crazy. You'll continue to "manage upward" by keeping the key project stakeholders informed and involved in project decisions.

Some people get so caught up in the management of a project that they forget about leadership. It's possible to complete the management part of the project and not attain the status and influence of a leader. That's why we've written this chapter—to make sure all those project management traits get transformed into leadership skills as well.

Wearing the Big Shoes

You must be a leader who provides strong guidance but at the same time offers a receptive ear to people with problems. Your team members may not always fill the big shoes you've offered them. The well-known Murphy's Law often ensures that anything that can go wrong on projects will, from the tiniest projects to the most colossal.

As a leader, you must also know the plan inside and out and be able to talk to the team about priorities without sounding frustrated or rushed. If a team member has a problem that requires discussion, as a leader you should always be seen as a resource to seek out rather than as an obstacle to avoid.

Managers go to meetings and complete paperwork. Leaders must gain the trust and respect of the project team. People must feel comfortable taking your direction; otherwise, they'll make up their own. Yes, as a manager, you must develop protocol and administrative procedures for ensuring that work is getting done on time and within budget. But establishing yourself as a leader is more important than any report or process.

Leadership style and your management tactics are intertwined and are central to the successful implementation of the project. Your skills and the appropriateness of the management tactics you adopt for each of the various people on your project team are of paramount importance in achieving project goals. Lots of hard-nosed books tell you how to become a leader, but we favor a simple, soft approach involving only eight tips:

- Listen to your people and ask lots of questions.
- Be a reliable source of information when your project team needs it.
- Observe what is going on and take notes.
- Know enough to know that you don't know everything.
- Be available when people need you. If you need to leave for any length of time, make sure your team knows how to reach you.
- Make decisions when called upon to make decisions, but also know when to defer decisions to other stakeholders with more authority.
- Delegate the work that needs to be delegated.
- Don't micromanage. You manage the project; your team members must manage their work.

A Style That Gets the Job Done

Business writers have described a wide range of effective leadership styles that can be adapted to meet the needs of different people, organizations, and projects. You'll need to choose from three basic styles to lead your project:

- Task-oriented leadership emphasizes getting the job done and concentrating on methods for assigning and organizing work, making decisions, and evaluating performance.
- Employee-oriented or people-oriented leadership concentrates on open communication, the development of rapport with team members, and an ongoing direct concern for the needs of subordinates.
- Reward-based leadership ties positive feedback and other rewards directly to the work accomplished. The reward-based style assumes that a high level of performance will be maintained if work results in meaningful rewards that correlate directly with the quality of the person's efforts. Rewards include pay and promotion but also encompass support, encouragement, security, and respect from the project manager.

The approach of matching management style to the specific needs of a situation is often called situational management or contingency theory. Project managers must effectively apply the best style for the job, whether task-oriented, employee-oriented, or reward-oriented leadership, to meet the needs of individual team members.

As you try to implement a style, don't assume that, because you like something done a certain way, your team members will have the same preferences. Individuals differ from one another in experience and personality. Each person has a different conception of how to do the job, who should get credit for the effort, and how each individual should be rewarded for his or her work. For these reasons, different leadership styles and management methods must be used to monitor and coordinate different projects.

How to Lead Change

It may seem odd to talk about leading changes as part of a project management book, but if you think about it, all projects are changing the way operations work. Whether the project is our All-Star Cable project case study, the construction of a new facility, or the introduction of a new technical system, it is always a change. As project manager, you must lead that change!

Projects always create changes in a variety of ways, not the least of which are …

- Work processes
- Procedures
- Performance expectations

As many experienced project managers will tell you, the operations group that ultimately receives your project will make some crazy assumptions that will only get you into trouble (because they will never admit that they might be the problem!). Here are some things to consider:

- Operations owns the project. Remember the premise from Chapter 1 that stated all projects are implemented to meet business needs. The operations people are the ones who actually have the business need that justified the project in the first place. If they don't own the project, you will always have difficulty defining and achieving success.
- Most operations people will underestimate the amount of effort that it takes to actually get operations ready for the project deliverables. You will often hear the operations managers say statements like "Just give it to me and my people; we're all pretty smart people and I'm sure we can figure it out." That is a sure recipe for disaster. If it fails, no operations manager will admit that it was his fault that his people weren't ready. It is always the fault of the project and the project manager.
- Most operations managers will not appreciate the time and money that it takes to evaluate and adjust the business processes to the new reality created by the project deliverables. It will be up to you as project manager to lead that effort and enlist the operations people in the effort.

Words from the Wise

A manager's personal style—how good he or she is at exchanging information—contributes more to … efficiency than the results of any structures or organizational brilliance.

—Mark H. McCormack, founder of the International Management Group, the world's largest sports talent and marketing agency

Building a Case for Change

In order to effectively engage the end users (or the business in general), the project manager will need to develop a clear Case for Change. The Case for Change is the way the project answers the fundamental question on everyone's mind as the project is launched: "Why are we doing this?"

In many cases, the people who are impacted, directly or indirectly, will be reluctant to change from what they know to some unknown (to them) solution. And they will quite naturally fear that the "cure" will be worse than the problem itself. Many project managers of information technology projects have faced that resistance. The Case for Change is designed to address those concerns at a high level.

Here are some general guidelines for developing a Case for Change. First of all, work with your project team and the business sponsor to answer the following questions:

1. Why are we doing this project from a business perspective?
2. What will change when the project is completed?
3. What will happen if we don't complete this project successfully?
4. What are the benefits of doing this project to us and the business?
5. What will we need to do differently?

Feel free to edit these questions as appropriate for your project and your situation. Remember to use words that will resonate with the people the project impacts. Nothing will turn them off faster than using language that is "project speak" or IT speak—well, you get the idea. That is where your business sponsor or business working committee members can help.

The project team should develop a first draft, and then the business or end users can edit it. When we need to draft this document, we usually start with the Business Case that was developed to justify the project. Of course, the audience for the Case for Change is not interested in all the gory details like cost/benefit analysis, return on investment, net present value, and the like. However, if you have a well-drafted Business Case, you can usually glean many of the answers to the questions we posed earlier; at least enough to provide the draft for the business people or working committee.

Our experience has been that it is far better to come in with a draft document that people can react to. We have been part of projects that tried to start with a blank sheet of paper, and that was a recipe for disaster. It leads to nit-picking and is rarely successful. Believe us when we tell you that you will have plenty of heated discussions just trying to edit the draft!

Let's take a look at how the Case for Change might look for a Customer Relationship Management (CRM) implementation.

Case for Change for Project Renewal

Question	Answer
1. Why are we doing Project Renewal?	◆ The current Customer Relationship Management (CRM) system (CTS) does not: ◆ Support a modern medical equipment and manufacturing operation ◆ Provide just-in-time manufacturing and delivery logistics tracking essential for effective manufacturing and high customer satisfaction ◆ If we do not do this project, we cannot: ◆ Respond to our customers' orders effectively ◆ Schedule the manufacturing of medical products in the quantity required by our customers ◆ Reduce the amount of inventory we need to keep on hand to handle rush orders ◆ Reduce rework by accounting and accounts receivable handling credits ◆ Diminish the number of "returns" caused by the shipping of the wrong items to customers
2. What are the benefits?	The new CRM application will allow us and the company to: ◆ Track our inventory in "real-time" ◆ Real-time inventory will change instantly with the "auto refresh" turned on. For transportation and rush orders, account representatives will know immediately what products we have on hand ◆ Present summary and drill-down views on customer information ◆ Allow us to do "what if" scenarios prior to entering an order to maximize discounts and promotions ◆ Easily enter orders with less paperwork and hassle ◆ Track our daily and monthly customer orders for more effective and successful projections of customer requirements

continues

Case for Change for Project Renewal (continued)

Question	Answer
	◆ Improve productivity ◆ Keep up with the dynamically changing industry and eliminate many spreadsheets and duplicate entry ◆ Make quicker decisions based on better knowledge management of our inventory and product mix in a volatile market ◆ Provide a tool to more accurately and efficiently pinpoint the value drivers within our product lines ◆ Provide more reliable tool that won't "crash" as often as CRT does

3. What if we don't change?	◆ Our current order entry system will be expensive and difficult to support in the future, and we will be left with outdated technology where:
	  ◆ The performance of the system cannot be improved
	  ◆ The system will gradually become less and less maintainable
	◆ We will spend too much time on administrative tasks
	◆ We won't be able to take full advantage of new product, business or market opportunities
	◆ We won't be able to efficiently capture the value and potential of our most profitable customers
	◆ We won't be able to efficiently model the future requirements of our business
	◆ We won't be able to efficiently pinpoint customer value drivers
	◆ We will continue to use our individual spreadsheets as our primary order entry tool, which puts us even further behind our competitors
	◆ We won't have a central repository for all of our customer data and buying habits

Question	Answer

4. What do we need to do differently?	We need to:
	◆ Use the CRM tool as primary tool for order entry and customer data and use our personal spreadsheets as secondary tools
	  ◆ Use the quick deal entry templates with a customized Sales Management Desktop
	  ◆ Use on-demand Sales and Marketing desktop analysis tools
	◆ Have sales representative input most orders including:
	  ◆ Standard orders
	  ◆ Customized orders
	  ◆ Odd-lot orders
	◆ Utilize the comprehensive audit trails
	◆ Develop and follow consistent processes, procedures, and policies

Hopefully you can see the power of providing your end users, in this case the sales and marketing people, with the answers to these questions. Immediately, instead of approaching the deliverables of the project reluctantly, you are building an expectation and excitement around the possibilities and potential of the project. If you deliver (and hopefully you will!), by the time you are ready to rollout the final product, the people who would normally be your biggest problem group will be actually begging you to deliver! They will start driving you to deliver it faster, and you might need to slow them down! Wouldn't that be a change!

Building a good Case for Change answers the basic question "why are we doing this?" and addresses the reasons for them to not only accept but also support the deliverables of the project.

The project team for All-Star Cable developed a Case for Change for their Movies-on-Demand project. Here is how it turned out.

Case for Change for All-Star Cable

Question	Answer
1. Why are we doing this project from a business perspective?	Movies-on-Demand will allow the company to move to the next level of service for its customers. All-Star Cable needs to complete this project to compete with other services, such as Netflix (movies by mail), movies provided over the Internet, and videos delivered to customer devices such as iPod.
2. What will change when the project is completed?	All-Star Cable will need to change our approach to: ◆ Customer service ◆ Billing ◆ Service delivery
3. What will happen if we don't complete this project successfully?	If we don't complete this project successfully, we will lose customers like we did once before when we didn't react fast enough. The company nearly went into bankruptcy and closed its doors forever.
4. What are the benefits of doing this project for us and the business?	If we complete this project successfully, we will benefit by: ◆ Providing our customers with the latest technology for their entertainment dollars ◆ Allowing the company to expand into a new area of service that can provide revenue growth ◆ Protecting our jobs and the viability of our company
5. What will we need to do differently?	◆ Think differently about how we do our jobs when MOD is operational ◆ Bring our customers a new level of service when they have difficulty with the service or their bills ◆ Operate at a new level of teamwork so our customers' experience is positive every time they turn on their television sets

Competing with Other Projects for Attention

Conflicts are part of any project, and project managers must be aware of other initiatives that may impact the success of their project. Let's look at some of the concerns that a project manager must attend to.

Communication Lines

A project manager must set up a method of communicating with the other project managers who have responsibility for these competing initiatives. The communication can be …

- Holding regular meetings to discuss projects
- Exchanging status reports
- Having lunch with another project manager regularly to catch up on the latest developments

There are other ways, too, but the important consideration is to have some formal process in place. If the communication is too casual or informal, it is likely to get knocked off the agenda rather quickly when time gets precious.

We will cover the importance of the communication plan in Chapter 21, but you might consider these other project managers as stakeholders for your project and ask them to consider you a stakeholder in theirs for communication purposes!

Where Do Projects Fit Together?

Rarely does any organization of any size have only one thing going on. Usually there are several, and all compete for time, attention, and resources (including money). Often, we concentrate so hard on making our project successful that we forget it is usually linked to others. For example, if an IT project requires training for the marketing personnel within the organization, the project manager must know of any other initiatives marketing has going because those initiatives may also have training requirements. Most organizations will not be receptive to taking their marketing personnel off the job for extended periods for training regardless of the importance and requirements.

As another example, if the company is doing an upgrade of the financial software package at the same time you are implementing your CRM project, you could easily overlook the fact that your data will need to flow over to the financial application for billing and accounting purposes. If you forget to check on their progress, you may find they have made some technical decisions that have an adverse impact on the way your project can send or retrieve data.

Also, you will need to analyze and handle any dependencies or overlaps in timelines so if one project comes off schedule, it will not throw others off, too!

Finally, within organizations, there are the people we go to regularly to help with important initiatives like projects. They are great, smart, and respected for their abilities. However, that is the problem—we go to the A-list people all the time! Often they will be advising other projects.

You will need to communicate with your project sponsor about such situations. Identify these people and be aware when they have a heavy workload. If you do not keep these considerations in mind, you may well push them too hard and not get the results you need. So communicating with the sponsor about creative ways to lighten their regular work to give them the proper time to focus on your project may be communication time well spent.

Critical Path Conflict

By its nature, the critical path (see Chapter 12) is very important to your project and to the other projects going on around you. You will need to develop a communication plan for keeping in touch with those project managers to make sure conflicts don't develop.

In the early stages of planning the projects, no conflict may be apparent, and everyone goes their way to implementation. But we all know that things rarely stay the same as projects begin to unfold. This is why communication is so important. A change in schedule on one project may suddenly put its critical path in conflict with another project when no conflict existed before!

Keep Your Project Front and Center

While program management is not an objective for this chapter or the book, some of you will probably see some of our suggestions as a form of program management. This will include working with your sponsor to fight for your project so you don't lose momentum or visibility, but you will need to keep your sponsor properly informed so he can handle these issues effectively and efficiently.

Words from the Wise

If a project is to succeed, it must have both a motivated project manager and a motivated project team. A project team takes its attitude from the project leader, so one of the greatest motivational tools the project manager possesses is enthusiasm, positive attitude, and confidence.

—From *Human Resource Skills for the Project Manager* by Vijay K. Verma (Project Management Institute, 1996)

Leading a Technical Project When You Don't Have Expertise

You don't have to have technical knowledge to provide leadership to a technical project or to supervise engineers working in a discipline you know little or nothing about. Instead, you need to be an efficient project manager capable of listening intelligently and understanding and handling the human and business issues at hand. Yes, it's possible that technical people may try to "snow" you with jargon, but you can work around these efforts to stall the project.

Words from the Wise

Sometimes a project manager who is the most skilled technical person on the team actually creates a problem. We were once asked to help a project team that was having considerable difficulty in maintaining its schedule. The problem was a very talented and technically superb project manager. He was so good that no one would make a decision without running it by him first. Needless to say, that created a bottleneck to progress. Once the project manager began to manage the project instead of trying to do all the work, the project began to move faster, and the project team gained confidence in its ability.

Always talk regularly to each member of the technical team, insist on periodic updates, and ask (with genuine enthusiasm) to see results, no matter how small. At the same time, never allow a single team member to be the only repository of key project data. Instead, insist that more than one member of the technical team understand, or at least be involved in, key technical areas. Keep copies of work descriptions on paper or on backup tapes/disks and archive them regularly (off-site!) as additional backup and protection from acts of God and disgruntled workers.

Being All Things to All People

As project manager, you change roles from day to day. One day, you may feel like a hands-on manager in charge of a group of productive, motivated employees. The next day, you may be relegated to a position that's really little more than that of petty bureaucrat, shuffling papers and sitting through dull appointments all day.

The role of project manager also changes as the project proceeds. At the beginning, during the initiation and planning phases, your role is to create a vision for the project and work with stakeholders (managers, customers, and other project beneficiaries) to reach consensus on the goals and objectives of the project. During this planning phase, the project team may occasionally complain that all they seem to do is crank out paper. However, gently remind them that all that "paper" will pay off when they move to the execution phase. Then, as the project proceeds into the execution phase, your role involves supporting, coaching, and otherwise guiding people to the promised land of project completion. You'll also have to spend time communicating the project status to the stakeholders so they remain happy with the results you are achieving as the project proceeds.

In all these roles, you will be expected to excel. Obviously, you can't be all things to all people. But as a project manager who is also a leader, you better be, at the very least, a lot of the right things to most of the project team.

The Least You Need to Know

- Project managers must lead change as well as lead the project team.
- Build a Case for Change to help you communicate with the project stakeholders in their language.
- No project is an island. Keep your project front-and-center to maintain support and momentum, and keep track of the situation surrounding your project.
- A true leader can fix almost any project problem by adjusting objectives and realigning the project team and stakeholders.

Chapter 19

What an Organization!

In This Chapter

- Creating an organization that works
- Casting people in your drama
- The four basic ways to organize people
- Choosing your organizational structure
- Tying outside vendors and the working committee to your project team

How can you know what the right organization is for your project team? How do you get people to move where you want them to go? Who should lead the work, and who should follow orders? In this chapter, we look at some of the pros, cons, and alternatives to help you organize your players for maximum impact.

No Easy Task, but Someone Has to Organize These People

The most important aspect of organizing your team will be to make sure everyone understands three things:

> **Words from the Wise**
>
> There are two ways of being creative. One can sing and dance. Or one can create an environment in which singers and dancers flourish.
>
> —Warren Bennis, professor and founder of the Leadership Institute and the University of Southern California

- The reason you chose each of them for the team; what he or she had to offer that you required
- The clear role and responsibility each person is filling on the project
- The standards you will hold them accountable for in completing the work with high quality

Structuring a project organization means more than just choosing team members and committing outside vendors to specific tasks. To function effectively, your project team members require clear reporting responsibilities and a road map to their location in the project. On top of this, your core team may require ancillary support such as administrative assistants, computer installers, technical help, and others who are trained, ready, available, and prepared for secondary but vital duties.

Turning all these people into a viable project team involves cementing relationships, making the right resources available in a timely manner to the right people, implementing reporting relationships, and establishing a schedule that works. Because people are involved, it sounds easier than it is.

The Human Drama: Personality, Politics, and Corporate Culture

To help you understand ways to organize the people in your project, compare your project team to the cast members in a play or a movie. This was a very effective metaphor used by Dutch Holland in his book *Change Is the Rule* (Dearborn Press, 2000). You have the producers and backers of the project (managers and other stakeholders), the director (the project manager), the main actors (the workers who play a key role throughout all or most of the project), the bit players (people who do one important task and then disappear from the scene), and the cameo players (the important people, such as consultants or advisors, who may add value to the project but don't necessarily stick around through the entire play). You also have the special-effects folks and the production crew, who have special skills but aren't as visible as other members of the cast. You may have prima donnas and stars on your project team, and these people need special care and attention.

Give Them a Script

One of the first considerations in developing your team is the same for actors in a play. They need a script to work from. What is your script, you may ask? Your script is your project plan. The members of your team need to see how the role they play helps the production (the project) be successful. Without that, they will make up lines, work on things that are not important, and possibly make some poor decisions. Just like actors, if you simply ask them to ad lib, unless they are very experienced, they won't do very well.

Avoid Casting Catastrophes

As you consider the organization of your cast, you'll need to develop some procedures to get things done. Lead players, bit players, and cameo players might possibly be directed (supervised) by assistant directors (other managers), and the production crew might work for lead crew or assistant producers.

Sometimes, after you have designed your ideal project organization, you'll find that the first choice for a team member in a particular role isn't even a possibility. For example, a person you would like to use in the project may not be available because of commitments to other, higher-priority projects. Or you may ask to use one person from an organization, but the manager from the group assigns a different person to your project. Thus, you may not get the experience you wanted in the cast and might have to adjust the schedule to accommodate for the less experienced actor to learn his lines.

If you say you need a person with a particular skill for your project and the line manager (middle manager) assigns a person to you, you usually must accept this person's judgment unless you can make a good case for someone you have more direct experience with. If you find out later that the assigned person lacks the required skills, you can negotiate or look at other alternatives.

Project managers often need to make these kinds of concessions to other managers to get people for a project. It's like signing up Sean Connery to star in your movie and then finding out that Eddie Murphy was assigned the role instead. Obviously, the script and direction will require some adaptations.

The Proud, the Few … the Project Team

When talented actors work on a play together, they all share and support the same goal (to produce a successful play). To this end, the actors, great and small, generally follow the lead of the director, and each player does his or her best to fulfill the specific role assigned in each play. Even the stars must follow the rules of the game. People on your project team need to play their roles in the same way.

For the people working on your project to become a real team, some specific things need to happen with your coaching and leadership as project manager. Project members need to …

- Realize they'll be working on activities that involve more than one person. Therefore, they'll need to communicate and cooperate with each other to get things done.
- Share common methods and tools for assessing and communicating the status of the project.
- Identify and solve problems together and then live with the results (together) and agree to support the common decision in public.
- Accept the fact that if one person makes a mistake, the entire team suffers. Therefore, they need to help each other avoid as many mistakes as possible.
- Realize that new people will be joining and other people will be leaving the project as time goes on, but the overall team structure and project goals will remain the same until the project reaches fruition.
- Recognize that changes will occur and they must be flexible enough to adjust and use the change control methods that we will describe in much more detail in Chapter 24.

When other organizations or departments are involved, positive interaction between the project manager and these organizations is also critical to creating a good team. The relationships among line, staff, vendor, customer, and project personnel must be tempered with mutual trust.

On Becoming a Team: The Basic Ways to Organize People

Even though infinite possible combinations of people are involved, you should structure the organization of a project in only a few basic ways. These include functional (or line) organizations, pure-project structures, matrix organizations, or mixed organizational structures. These structures may be distributed over multiple locations as well, making the organization more of a virtual team in cyberspace rather than a group of people in a defined location. And as you'd expect, each organization has its pros and cons.

The Functional Project Organization

On a project that uses people from the same organization, you can use the existing line organization to manage the project. This organizational structure is appropriate when the project is clearly the responsibility of one department. Many small projects use the *functional organization* as the project organization. A functional project is assigned to the functional department or division in a company that has the most interest and technical ability to complete the project. Almost all tasks in a project organized as part of a functional organization will be completed within the one functional area. Existing managers in the department often double as project managers.

def•i•ni•tion

A **functional organization** is one that is organized around common activities or expertise such as accounting or customer service.

The advantages of using a functional organization to complete a project include the following:

- **Familiarity of the team.** The team members are already familiar with each other, and the skill levels of the staff are clearly understood.
- **Established administrative systems.** The general administrative policies and procedures are already understood by the team and cost centers.
- **Staff availability.** The staff is readily available to the project because the line managers control the staff assignments. Thus, few, if any, interdepartmental conflicts arise over the use of resources.
- **Scheduling efficiency.** The scheduling of staff can be highly efficient. As a staff member is required, the person can immediately be assigned to a task and then return to routine work without serious logistical interruptions.
- **Clear authority.** The lines of authority and communication are understood. Thus, the conflicts between project authority and line authority are minimized.

The disadvantages of using a functional organization include:

- **Project isolation.** The project may be completed in isolation from other parts of the company and may fail to realize larger strategic goals as a result. However, if new collaboration, networking, and web-based tools are employed, this isolation can be minimized.

- **Limited resources.** The project is limited to the technical resources within the department, which may not be adequate to complete the tasks required. Of course, you can hire outside vendors and consultants, but expertise within other departments of the company is not readily available. This may lead to inefficiencies or redundancies in the project organization.
- **Bureaucratic procedures.** In a functional organization, the project manager usually has very weak decision-making authority. There may be more levels of approval than really necessary for the project because of the established bureaucracy in the line organization. This may impede progress and slow decision-making.
- **Lack of project focus.** The project may lack focus or priority in a functional organization because it is not the only work being done. Thus, routine departmental work may interfere with project work. In addition, motivation for project work may suffer because the project is considered "additional" or "optional" work as opposed to being a clear responsibility.
- **Department orientation.** The project may suffer from "department-think," which occurs when the priorities of the department become the project priorities, regardless of the actual goals for the project. Work outside the department's normal concerns is given little attention, and the "finished" project may not be complete or may suffer quality problems as a result.

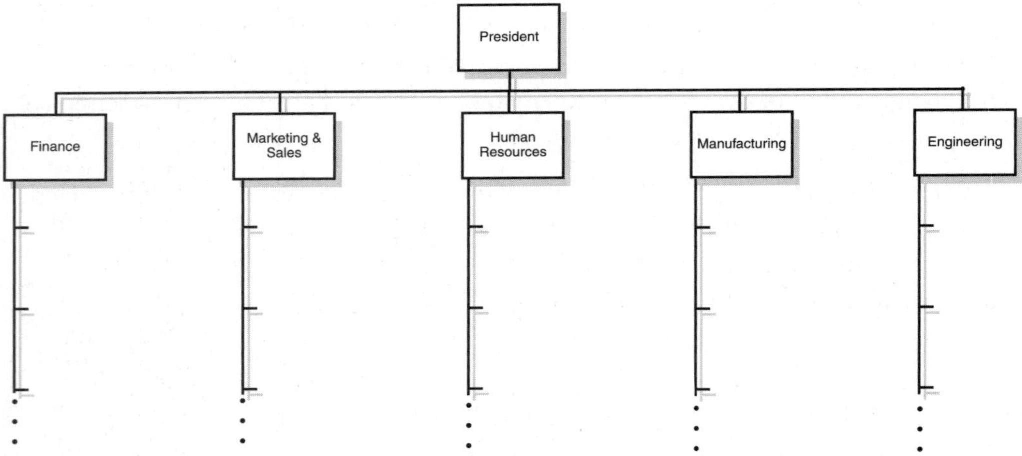

A functional organization.

The Pure-Project Organization

In a *pure-project organization*, a team or "task force" is put together to accomplish the project's goals. In such an organization, all the team members report to the project manager during the course of the project. The team members do not have responsibility to other managers or jobs during the course of their work on the project. When a team member's responsibility for the project is complete, that person returns to another job or is assigned to another project. Only one project and one job are assigned at a time.

def•i•ni•tion

A **pure-project organization** is one in which the project manager has full authority to assign priorities and direct the work of all the members of the project team.

In the direct version of the pure-project structure, every project team member reports directly to the project manager. This is appropriate for small projects with 15 or fewer people involved. In the indirect version of the pure-project structure (suitable for larger projects), the project manager may have assistant managers or supervisors to manage subprojects or functional areas within the project. As in an ordinary line organization, the supervisors and assistants report directly to the project manager, and the various functional teams within the project report to the second-level managers. Extremely large projects may have multiple management levels, just like a corporation.

Pure-project organizations are found in companies fulfilling large government projects or in some engineering-driven companies that produce predictable model updates for their products. Large construction projects often employ a pure-project organization as well. If work on a complex, priority project spans a year or more, a pure-project organization is often an advantage.

The advantages of the pure-project organization include the following:

- **Clear project authority.** The project manager has true line authority over the entire project. Thus, there is always a clear channel for resolving project conflicts and determining priorities. The unity of command in a pure-project organization results in each subordinate having one and only one direct boss, a clear advantage in most situations.
- **Simplified project communications.** Communication and decision-making within the project are simplified because everyone reports to the same project manager and focuses on the attainment of the same project goals.

- **Access to special expertise.** If the company will complete similar projects on a cyclic basis, specific expertise in the components of the project will be developed over time. It simply becomes a matter of transferring the experts to the right project at the right time.
- **Project focus and priority.** The pure-project organization supports a total view of the project and a strong, separate identity on the part of the participants. This helps keeps the project focused and integrated.

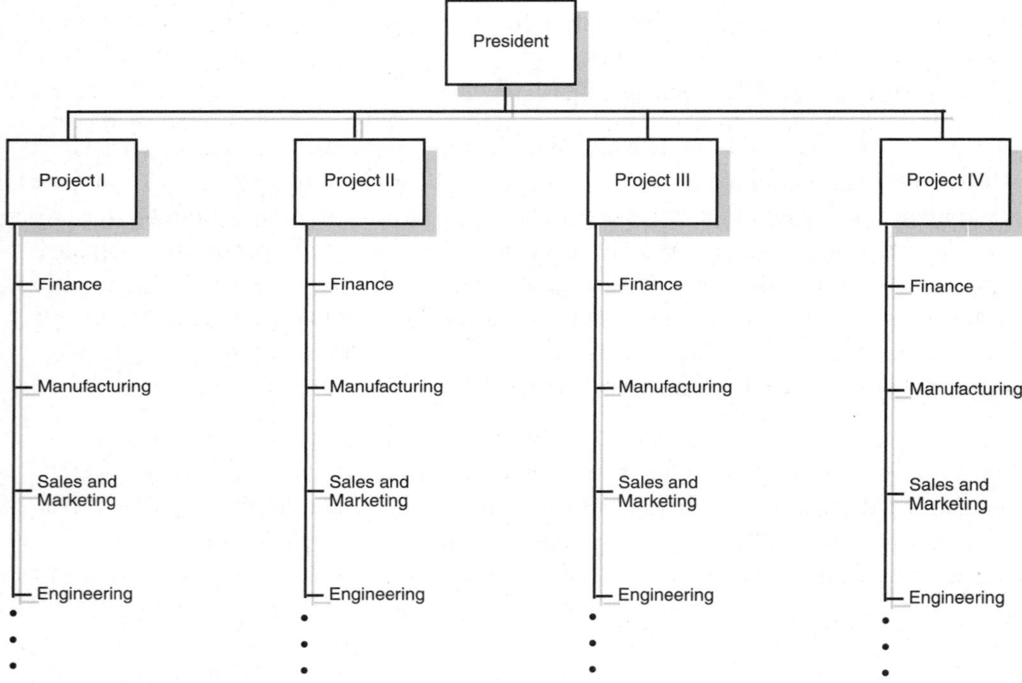

A pure-project organization.

However, there are distinct disadvantages to the pure-project approach, including the following:

- **Duplication of efforts.** If a company has multiple projects with important goals in progress at the same time, some efforts may be duplicated, making the overall cost of the projects higher than necessary.
- **Unclear loyalties and motivations.** Project members form strong attachments to the project and each other, which is good. When the project is terminated,

however, the team must be disbanded, which leads to uncertainty and conflict. Team members fear layoffs or anticipate assignments in undesirable projects in the future. Thus, keeping technically qualified people happy over the long haul becomes a major challenge. Your staffing management plan should clearly address this problem if you use this model.

- **Intracompany rivalry.** Rivalry and competition may become strong between various projects in a company that uses pure-project organization for its major projects. This may result in a company that competes with itself instead of with the competition—an ugly state of affairs.

The Matrix Organization

Implementing project management techniques sets into motion a significant change in the culture of an organization. One of the more common results of using project management in business is the introduction of "matrix management," a situation in which people report to multiple managers. Matrix management involves coordinating a web of relationships that comes about when people join the project team and are subject to the resulting multiple authority-responsibility-accountability relationships in the organization.

The *matrix organization* is an attempt to take advantage of the benefits of a pure-project organization while maintaining the advantages of the functional organization. It is rare to find pure-project or pure-functional organizations in business anymore. Matrix organizations are typical today, even when other project management tools aren't involved.

def•i•ni•tion

A **matrix organization** is one in which a project manager shares responsibility with the functional managers for assigning the priorities and directing the work of individuals assigned to the project.

In a matrix organization, a clear project team that crosses organizational boundaries is established. Thus, team members may come from various departments. A project manager for each project is clearly defined, and projects are managed as separate and focused activities. The project manager may report to a higher-level executive or to one of the functional managers with the most interest in the project. However, the specific team members still report to their functional departments and maintain responsibilities for routine departmental work in their functional areas. In addition, people may be assigned to multiple project teams with different responsibilities.

The problem of coordination that plagues other project structures is minimized because the most important personnel for a project work together as a defined team within the matrix project structure.

The management responsibilities in these projects are temporary; a supervisor on one project may be a worker on another project, depending on the skills required. If project managers in a matrix situation do not have good relationships with line managers in the organization, conflicts may arise over employees' work and priorities. Not everyone adapts well to the matrix structure for this and other related reasons.

The complexity that a matrix organization causes is clear: people have multiple managers, multiple priorities, and multiple role identities. Because of these complexities, before an organization enters into matrix organizational structures, the project or the enterprise should meet at least two of the following criteria:

- A need to share scarce or unique resources required in more than one project or functional area
- A requirement for management to provide high levels of information processing and communication to complete the project
- Pressure from the outside by customers or agencies to have one person or group centralize control of the project even though other groups in the organization may carry out the project

In cases in which projects meet these criteria, the matrix organization has the following distinct advantages:

- **Clear project focus.** The project has clear focus and priority because it has its own separate organization and management. A matrix organization realizes most of the planning and control advantages of a pure-project structure.
- **Flexible staffing.** Staffing is relatively flexible in matrix organizations because resources from various line organizations are available without job reassignment. Scarce technical resources are available to a wide range of projects in a company that regularly employs matrix-organized projects.
- **Adaptability to management needs and skills.** The authority of the project manager can be expansive or limited, depending on the priority of the project. If a project manager has strong authority, with command authority over most of the project, and is assigned to the project full-time, this would be called a "strong matrix" structure. If a project manager has weak authority, is assigned

only part-time, and the line managers have a strong influence on project activities, this type of organization would be dubbed a "weak matrix" structure. A structure called a "balanced matrix" structure falls in between. Thus, the matrix organization can be adapted to a wide range of projects, some that need strong support from line managers and some that require independent management.

- **Staff development opportunities.** People can be given new challenges and responsibilities that are not as likely to be offered in a purely functional organization. People can gain exposure to new technical areas, develop management skills, and have new experiences that maintain their interest and motivation at work. Ultimately, these new experiences can lead to more effective employees with high degrees of independence and flexibility. And because people tend to be more responsible for the quality of their own work in project-oriented groups, overall corporate productivity can improve.
- **Adaptability to business changes.** Matrix organizations can adapt more quickly to changing technological and market conditions than traditional, purely functional organizations, largely because of the high people-to-people contact in these organizations. In addition, matrix-organized projects encourage entrepreneurship and creative thinking that crosses functional responsibilities.

To take advantage of the benefits of matrix management, you must understand and deal with the disadvantages and potential conflicts within a matrix organization. The more frequently reported problems in matrix-managed organizations include:

- **Built-in conflicts.** Conflicts between line management priorities and project management priorities are inevitable. The question of who is in charge affects both the project and routine departmental work. The division of authority and responsibility relationships in matrix organizations is inherently complex. Matrix organizations are no place for intractable, autocratic managers with narrow views of organizational responsibilities.
- **Resistance to termination.** As in pure-project organizations, team members may prefer their project roles to their line responsibilities, creating interesting motivational challenges for managers. Because the team members have unique identities and relationships in their project roles, matrix projects often resist termination.
- **Complex command and authority relationships.** There is no unity of command in a matrix organization, a clear violation of traditional management principles. The team member is often caught between conflicting demands of

the line manager and the project manager. The discomfort and uncertainty of having more than one boss at the same time cannot be adequately described to someone who has never experienced the situation. Of course, if the two bosses are adequately trained and are open in their communications, many of these difficulties can be resolved or eliminated.

- **Complex employee recognition systems.** In a matrix organization, which manager should complete the employee's performance reviews or make recommendations for raises? If the reward responsibilities and authorities of the project manager and the line manager are not clearly identified, the employee may feel unrecognized. It is imperative that both line responsibilities and project responsibilities are accounted for in the employee's performance review process. Some form of reward system needs to be established for team members within the project; whether this is just public acknowledgment of a job well done or formal monetary rewards depends on the project and your budget.

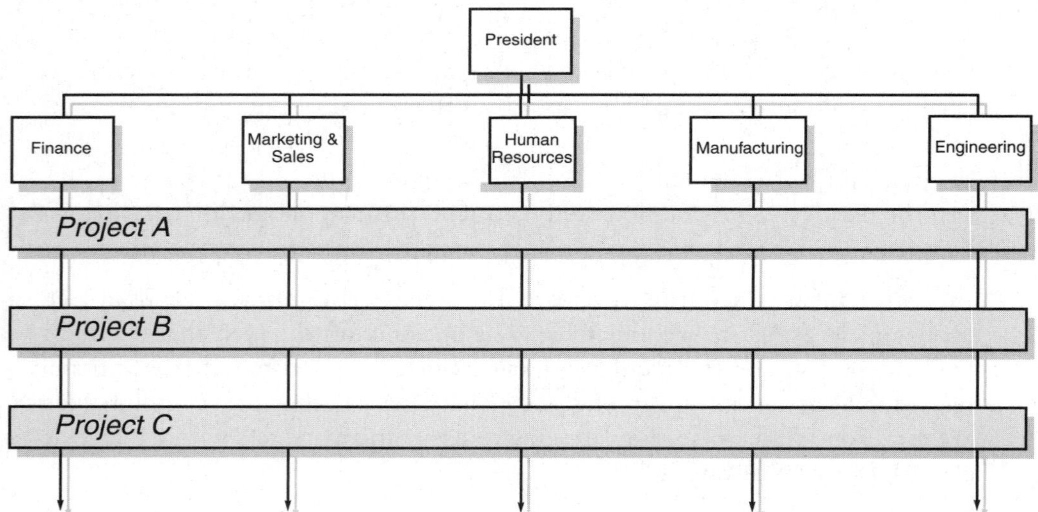

A matrix organization.

The Mixed Organization

Some companies employ a mixture of functional, matrix, and pure-project organizations to accomplish enterprise goals. In companies with a wide range of projects, a Project Management Office (PMO) may be set up to help administer projects as well.

The people in this office provide expertise and assistance in planning and tracking projects. In other companies, the PMO may become a division in its own right with full-time project managers and staff responsible for project-oriented activities.

When a project has more than one purpose, mixed organizational structures are usually the norm. The space shuttle missions are a perfect example. Getting the astronauts ready for a flight is one project. Building and installing a new robot arm is another. Although someone is responsible for coordinating all the projects and making sure they get done at the same time so the launch can happen as planned, the people are organized on a subproject basis. Each subproject requires a completely different set of team members and organizational structures.

Mixed organizations are not distinguishable from most matrix organizations because of the complexity of relationships, and most of the strengths and weaknesses of a matrix organization also apply to a mixed organizational structure. The unique problem in mixed organizations is one caused by the extreme flexibility in the way the organization adapts to project work. This leads to potential incompatibilities, confusion, conflicts, and duplications of effort if the managers are not adequately trained to deal with these complexities.

Which Structure Should You Use?

The organization you choose for most ordinary business projects will probably be an adaptation of a matrix or functional organization. No matter which organization you choose, always develop an organization chart that clearly shows who reports to whom so there are no mistakes or incorrect assumptions.

In the All-Star Cable case study, the project manager decided to use a strong matrix organization with a mixture of functional people from the company and consultants with skills and experience that were not available within the company.

Using a RACI Chart

A RACI chart is a special type of responsibility assignment matrix (see Chapter 14) that helps all the project team members understand who to work with on various decisions and issues as the project progresses. RACI is an acronym for …

- Responsible
- Accountable
- Consult
- Inform

Take a look at the following high-level RACI chart of the All-Star Cable project activities and people who are responsible for those activities.

Activity	Alan	Beth	Colleen	Duane	Ellie	Fred
Requirements	R		C		I	A
Design		I	C	R		A
Development	C	I	I	R	A	
Testing	C	R	I	I	I	A
Training	A	I	C	C	C	R

R = Responsible A = Accountable C = Consult I = Inform

Matching the Organization to Fit the Project

Project size, project length, experience of the team members, location of the project, and factors unique to the project all have influence on the selection of a project organizational form. For example, on a small, short-term project for creating a new process for bringing new customers into All-Star Cable, the organization of the project might be along functional lines that already exist with the involvement of a few outside resources and key vendors to complete specific tasks. On a larger project to design and build the next generation of cable TV, namely Movies-on-Demand, a matrix organization might be more appropriate because of the wide range of involvement and ongoing communication required across departments of manufacturing, marketing, engineering, and services.

Words from the Wise

If you are called to be a street sweeper, sweep streets even as Michelangelo painted or Beethoven composed music or Shakespeare wrote poetry. Sweep the streets so well that all the hosts of heaven and earth will pause to say, here lived a great street sweeper who did his job well.

—Martin Luther King Jr., civil rights leader

Managing the Working Committee

Remember the working committee we covered in Chapter 6? Now we really need to get them working. They come from different parts of the organization, and their role is to provide feedback on the impact of project decisions and deliverables on their departments.

Develop clear ties between working committee members and members of your project team. For example, in All-Star Cable, the project manager will develop a working relationship between the business analysts working on the accounting portion of the project and the accountant sitting on the working committee. As the project team works the options around decisions, the business analysts should be talking regularly with the accounting representative about those options.

Schedule regular meetings of the working committee to give them status reports, but you will rarely excite people about going to a meeting where they only hear about the status of the project. Focus most of the WC meeting on working through issues that have an impact across the organization. For example, our project manager for All-Star Cable has options around how to handle financial data that will impact sales (re commissions), accounting, invoicing, and accounts payable. He will have the WC consider the options and develop a recommendation for the project team. That will ensure the buy-in of the commercial side of the business once the project has been completed.

The Least You Need to Know

- As project manager, you're like the director of the play for the team. Make the roles clear and assign people to specific parts, or the cast won't know how to work together to stage a successful play.
- In addition to the right team members, the correct organizational structure (functional, project, matrix, or mixed) is key to managing a successful project.
- Get the vendors involved at all stages of the project and connect them to the project to manage them effectively.
- Remember to organize the working committee as well as the project team.

Chapter 20

Operating Guidelines: Setting Up to Get Things Done

In This Chapter

- The process groups within every phase of the project
- The Plan-Do-Check-Act cycle
- Getting the work done
- Setting up a WAS
- Establishing administrative procedures
- The importance of keeping a project diary

When you initiated the project with the stakeholders, you already established some basic rules for the project in the statement of work (refer to Chapter 7), including authorities and reporting requirements. Now it's time to extend those rules and expand the operating procedures for the entire project team.

Before we talk about procedures, though, let's talk about processes.

The Project Processes in Each Phase

In each phase of the project, basic management processes will aid you in organizing the project. We can further divide these project processes into the following categories:

- **Initiating process.** This process begins a phase of the project and authorizes the work in that phase.
- **Planning process.** This process defines and refines the goals for a project phase and includes selecting the best course of action from all the alternatives.
- **Controlling process.** This process ensures that the goals of the phase are met by monitoring and measuring progress regularly to check for any deviation from the project plan so corrective action can be taken when necessary.
- **Executing process.** This process consists of coordinating people and other resources needed to carry out the activities in a phase.
- **Closing process.** This process brings an acceptable and orderly end to a phase.

In each phase of a project, you need to use each of these processes. Arrows represent the flow of information and the links among the process groups within a phase.

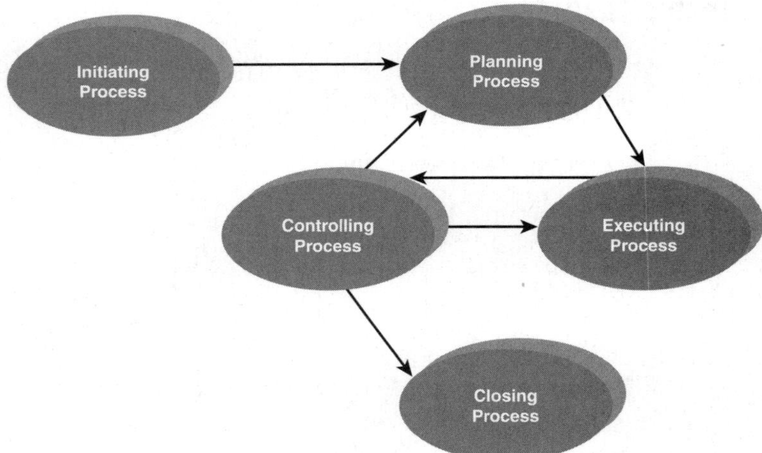

The general project processes may vary in intensity depending on the project phase. For example, the initiating processes are much more in evidence during the beginning of any of the four project life cycle phases. Focusing on the initiating processes during the beginning of each phase helps to ensure that the project stays focused on the business need it is supposed to deal with. Controlling processes are important during the execution phase of the project, but they should be recognized and used from the beginning to control costs and schedule. Finally, the processes overlap, so that the closing of one phase provides input for the next. For example, in the All-Star Cable project, the closing of the project definition phase requires the acceptance of the project charter document by the steering committee. In addition to closing out the definition phase, the project charter defines the activities that will be undertaken during the project planning phase as the project team plans for Movies-on-Demand.

Project Processes vs. Project Procedures

Unlike the project processes, the operating procedures for your project should help you guide people to work on the right tasks at the right time. Operating procedures also help you stay abreast of the status of every activity and cost associated with your project. You need to delegate the work and gather information without demotivating the team with too much administration, paperwork, and redundant communications. In other words, your operating procedures should help you manage the project but not keep you from getting the project done.

Operating procedures should also allow you to gather the information necessary to make changes in a timely fashion, thereby maintaining control of the schedule, resources, and costs and ultimately guiding your project to completion on time and within budget.

Project Processes and the Plan-Do-Check-Act Cycle

An underlying principle within the project processes comes from the work done by W. Edward Deming, a professor and author, and others in the Total Quality movement of the 1980s. The planning processes correspond to the Plan, the executing processes to the Do, and the controlling processes to the Check and Act components. And since a project, by definition, has a definite beginning and end, the initiating and closing processes are designed to address that finite nature of projects.

The Plan-Do-Check-Act cycle was the basis for upgrading manufacturing. This model was adopted by the Total Quality movement and contributed to improved design, service, product quality, testing, and sales.

The Plan-Do-Check-Act Cycle

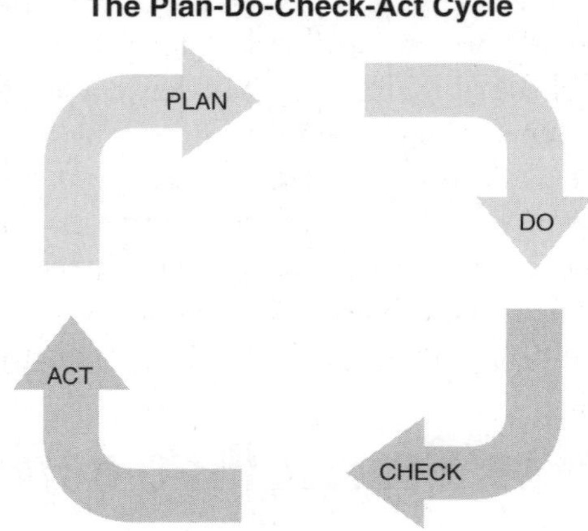

The Things That Need to Get Done

Getting work done on the project should always be the first priority. To get the actual work started, you'll need to delegate all work that isn't your own responsibility. Do this in meetings, in written communications, and through reviewing the project plan with team members and the working committee. As you start the project, however, you'll also need to develop a process or work schedule for the many activities that won't necessarily be found on the work plan or task list for the project.

Handling Business Process Changes

Once your project has developed the case for change (see Chapter 18), the next important series of tasks to get both the project team and the business users working on is the business process changes that will occur.

> **Risk Management**
>
> Not paying attention to the business process changes that your project creates will get you in deep trouble quickly, particularly on a large project that touches a large number of people.

The business process changes occur naturally as part of any project deliverables, but it is critically important that both sides work together to analyze the various changes that will occur and then let the business decide how to address these changes. Let's take a look at a decision-making process and then an example of how that might play out in our case study.

The model shown in the following illustration may be useful in making decisions around process changes.

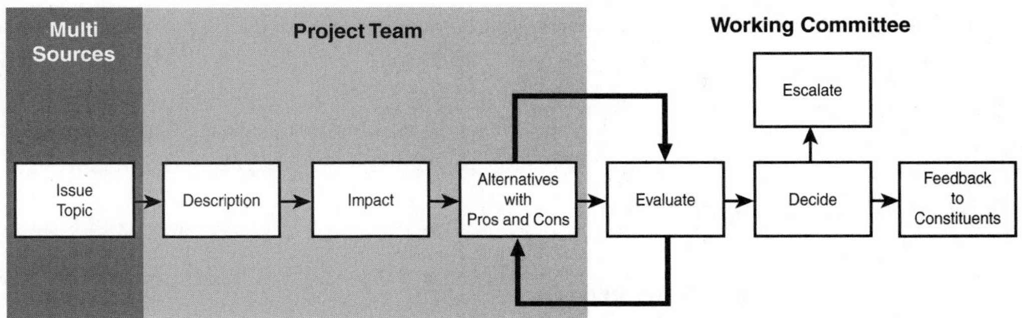

Issues or decisions may come from a variety of sources and then move from left-to-right through the project team, to the working committee, and finally to either the senior management or the constituents (the organization affected by the issue or decision).

Start with the Project Team

Issues that create the need for process changes may come from a variety of sources such as the business analysts on the project team, the new technology vendor, or the business itself. For example, the business may decide that the project is an ideal time to make a change in a business policy or procedure that is not created by the project but provides the natural opportunity to address it.

Regardless of where the issue of a process change originates, the project team's business analysts need to do the following:

- Develop a complete description of the proposed process change
- Evaluate the impact on the business as they see it
- Develop a list of alternative actions that may address that process change with the accompanying pros and cons
- Conduct a cost-benefit analysis on each of the potential options

Starting with the project team is an important step and one you should not shortcut. Very few people are capable of making these kinds of decisions when working from a "blank sheet of paper." The decision-making process is always much faster and effective if those who must make the decision have something to react to and work from.

Now It's Time for the Working Committee

At this point, the working committee takes over and conducts a detailed evaluation of the alternatives provided by the project team or even develops other alternatives if they identify possibilities the project team did not anticipate. Use the following list as a template to evaluate the business process changes in a measured and methodical way.

Process area

Process change

Background information

Issue
(What decision do we need to make?)

Constraints

Alternatives

Plan
(How should we move forward?)

Test
(How should the project team test to make sure this works?)

Communications
(What do people need to know? When? Who should provide the information?)

Training
(What must people be able *to do* after training is completed?)

Leadership
(What support does the management team need to provide for success?)

Benefits

Transition
(How do we handle this issue until the project is fully implemented?)

Once the working committee has completed its evaluation, it will need to make a decision as to which alternative to use. This is important for several reasons, but the most obvious is that the business will make the decision based on the best way for the business versus the best "technical" way according to the project team.

Making the Decision

Part of the decision-making process should include having the various working committee members network the alternatives, including pros and cons, with other members of the constituencies they represent. This is important for two reasons. First, it gets input from others who will later be asked to support and adhere to the decision. If they have had input along the way, they are much more likely to support those decisions. Second, this wider audience helps to ensure that the working committee members have not missed something. This can happen! Often, these people may be managers who are not familiar with all the intricate details of a process and so may overlook, or be completely unaware of, an important detail they should consider before a decision is made. We are *not* advocating some sort of democratic vote around these decisions, only suggesting that more people need to be consulted. The ultimate decision should rest with the working committee since it will be held accountable for all the decisions it makes.

Escalating the Decision

You will need to have an *escalation procedure* in place prior to the first "deadlock." If you have no escalation procedure in place, the situation could develop into a power play for some individuals and seriously delay the project team. A general rule of thumb suggests that the working committee has three attempts to make a decision, and if it is unsuccessful after those three attempts, then the decision is passed on to the sponsor or the steering committee for resolution. Of course, as project manager, you must alert the sponsor or steering committee at the first sign of trouble. Don't let them be surprised by a problem coming to them! If they know the situation in advance, they may even be able to work behind the scenes to get a resolution. Also, an escalation procedure has the added benefit that most people will work to resolve an issue and make a decision if they know a time limit is imposed. If there seems to be an open-ended process, then people can get into playing games or striking poses for other purposes completely unrelated to the project.

def•i•ni•tion

An **escalation procedure** is a defined process or procedure used to elevate a decision to the steering committee of a project.

Finally, once the decision has been made, the working committee needs to communicate the decision to the organization.

Set Up a Work Authorization System

When your project team begins to work, the question always arises: when should I start the work I've been assigned? The answer to that question is that you must put a *work authorization system* (*WAS*) in place from the beginning.

> **def•i•ni•tion**
>
> The Project Management Institute defines a **work authorization system (WAS)** as a written method that sanctions the right work is done in the right order. It also provides direction that allows a team member to begin work on a specific activity or work package.

A telling story involved a project manager who did not have a WAS in place. During the course of the project, customers would approach project team members and ask them for minor modifications in the work they were doing. In their attempts to be accommodating to the customers and keep them happy, the project team members would say "okay" and begin to work on the modification. The project manager had no idea this was happening until a few days later when he asked for the work package. Because it was not ready, he discovered the reason. If the WAS had been in place, the team members would not have been able to accept the modifications. They would have had no authorization to do that work. It would have also provided the team members with a convenient way to say "no." They could have referred the customer to the project manager by saying, "I would do that for you, but I need the authorization from my project manager. Please see him/her, and I'll get started as soon as the work is approved."

In large projects, make the authorization to begin work formal and in writing so that it can be tracked in a project audit if it is required. In smaller projects, it can be more informal, such as an e-mail "okay". However, under no circumstances should it be just verbal as you pass in the halls. If a conversation does occur and you approve work passing in the halls, always follow it up with written authorization!

Administrative Procedures That Won't Hurt

Eventually, in spite of your good attitude and informal chats with people, you'll have to ask them to do administrative tasks, such as writing reports and reconciling expenses. Most people won't like it, but if you have a positive work environment, they'll usually comply with your guidelines (as long as you make the requirements clear in advance).

As you develop administrative procedures, try to collect only the information you'll use. At the beginning, you may collect more information in the form of reports and updates than you really need. When you realize you're gathering too much data, give the troops a break and tell them to simplify or shorten their reports. For the data you really need, store the information for ready access and make it easy to retrieve when you need to analyze it.

Words from the Wise

When people fill out time reports weekly, without writing down what they did daily, they are making up fiction. Such made-up data are almost worse than no data at all.

—From *Fundamentals of Project Management* by James P. Lewis (Amacom, 2002)

If your project is one of many similar projects in your organization, established operating and administrative procedures are probably already in place to help you complete your ongoing responsibilities to the project. These include report formats, time frames for project review, and other tracking procedures.

If review procedures and administrative reports are not already well-established in your organization, you need to develop basic administrative procedures before you begin work on your project.

The Reports You May Need

Your stakeholders, managers, and customers deserve informed communication about the project in a timely fashion. A regular status report, targeted toward project stakeholders, contains information on current progress, schedule changes, and budgets. Other reports may also be required to both inform and motivate team members. On large projects, a daily or weekly update report targeted toward the project team, including vendors who are part of the team, may be a good idea. An update report emphasizes important priorities, issues, or deadlines. The purpose of the update report is to convey information that might otherwise fall through the cracks. (If a major snag crops up, the update provides information to keep troops focused on their own work while you deal with the problem.) Cost-variance reports, load-leveling reports, supply inventories, and other formal documentation should also track specific aspects of the project.

Simple Forms to Create Useful Reports

Reports allow your team to follow the project "roadmap" and stay on track, but the reports need to be easy to produce. We suggest using a good project management program (see Chapter 30) or simple forms for gathering regular report information. These forms, which we often use on our projects, may be useful for yours:

- **Status reporting forms.** Consider investing in a groupware reporting system on a computer network that reminds people about status reports and other administrative requirements (a paper system can accomplish the same goal but it is not very effective). Have the status report provide the following information:
  - Tasks completed since the last status report with completion dates
  - Tasks in progress with forecasted completion dates
  - Tasks planned with expected completion dates
  - Budget expenditures
  - Issues that need attention
  - Recommendations for project improvements or changes
  - Questions or items that require other people's approval or input

When everyone uses the same format, it's easier to summarize, synthesize, and analyze the status information for the formal status report you'll write as the project manager.

Every Report Needs a Purpose

For each report (or form) you choose to use on your project, document the following:

- How often is the report produced? Some reports are produced weekly; others are submitted monthly or quarterly.
- What is contained in the report?
- Who is responsible for producing the report?
- What is the objective of the report?
- Who will follow up on action items identified in the report?
- Who is the intended audience for the report? For example, there are three potential audiences for status reports: team members on the project, company

management, and customers or key stakeholders (if involved). The report to management and customers is typically more formal but less detailed than the report made to the team members. The reports team members send to you (as project manager) probably have the most information; some of this information is for your eyes only, however, so always filter what you summarize for other staff and managers.

Writing status reports for various audiences allows you to synthesize the formal and informal monitoring you've been doing. It allows you to relate your progress to the original project plan and to understand any risks to meeting your planned goals.

Ask Two Final Questions Before You Start

Before any report or procedure becomes part of the bureaucratic process associated with your project, ask yourself the following questions:

- Is this report or procedure the best way to communicate this information?
- Would some other form of communication or action be more expedient and just as useful?

Chapter 21, which discusses how to make the most of your communications, will help you answer these questions.

Why You Should Keep a Project Diary

In addition to taking notes at meetings, gathering information from project participants, and making general reports, a prudent project manager makes a personal project diary part of standard operating procedure. The daily diary should include notes on progress, problems, and any issues that impact the project in a positive or negative light. Unlike a young girl's "Dear Diary" entries, this notebook resembles a captain's log from a ship. Entries are to the point, dated (by page), and contain as much or as little information as required to document project progress and issues. The diary also tracks discussion points, decisions that were made, and any action items that you committed to at any given time. It should contain information about the outcome of key meetings, accomplishments, conflicts, and extraordinary events affecting the project's health and well-being.

The purpose of the project diary is threefold:

- It tracks your progress and can be reviewed later. The diary may pinpoint project sinkholes that are hard to identify by reading a pile of status reports. Long-term problems, such as a failing team member, become easily visible as you flip through the book. Unloading the team member is easier when you can document his or her nonperformance through the written record.
- If management complains about a problem, such as budget overages or tardy delivery, your meticulously kept diary serves as the perfect memory of what really happened so you can explain the situation.
- Your diary is an excellent tool for doing a better job next time. Review it occasionally to see what worked and what failed last time. Employ the positive and reject the negative. A good project is fuel for laughs years down the road.

The Bottom Line

In implementing all the operating aspects and creating the administrative guidelines for your project, remember the management and leadership of the project make the difference in your success, not the forms or the computer programs. You must act as a manager and a leader, not just as an administrator. With this in mind, we're ready to attack some of the best ways to keep all the "adminis-trivia" under control and make communications more effective.

The Least You Need to Know

- Every project needs the project processes to track progress, report its status, and move successfully from one phase to another. But no project needs long-winded reports with irrelevant details or meetings without objectives.
- Use the project team and the working committee to handle business process changes.
- Establish a work authorization system (WAS) to manage the work of your project team.
- Make sure your reports have a meaningful purpose and are not a bureaucratic exercise.
- Be sure to establish the administrative procedures you want at the beginning of the project.
- Use a project diary to capture your notes and ideas as you move forward.

Chapter 21

Making Your Communications Count

In This Chapter

- Know your audience
- Build and execute a communications plan
- Communication and strong leadership go hand in hand
- Effective ways to get your message across
- Be a good listener

According to the Project Management Institute, about 80 percent of a project manager's job is communications. If you consider all the meetings, presentations, status reports, and telephone calls that a project manager handles in just one day, you can begin to see that the PMI estimate may not be far off. However, many project managers learned the technical parts required for a project, but not some of the softer sides, such as communications. That's the purpose of this chapter—to help you develop your project communications.

The Basics of Communications: It's All About Perceptions

Much of our understanding comes from our perceptions. Every time you communicate with people, your project team, stakeholders, or anyone else, you must keep their perspective in mind. The following figure illustrates how perspectives influence people's understanding. Before you communicate anything to anyone, analyze your audience. Ask yourself the following questions:

- What information do people need?
- Does the message I'm sending communicate a particular feeling or attitude? (You may need to alter the tone depending on how you answer the question.)
- What is the best media for delivering the information?
- Who is the best person to deliver the information?
- How should I deliver the message?
- When should people receive the information?
- How will I receive feedback on how people react to the information?

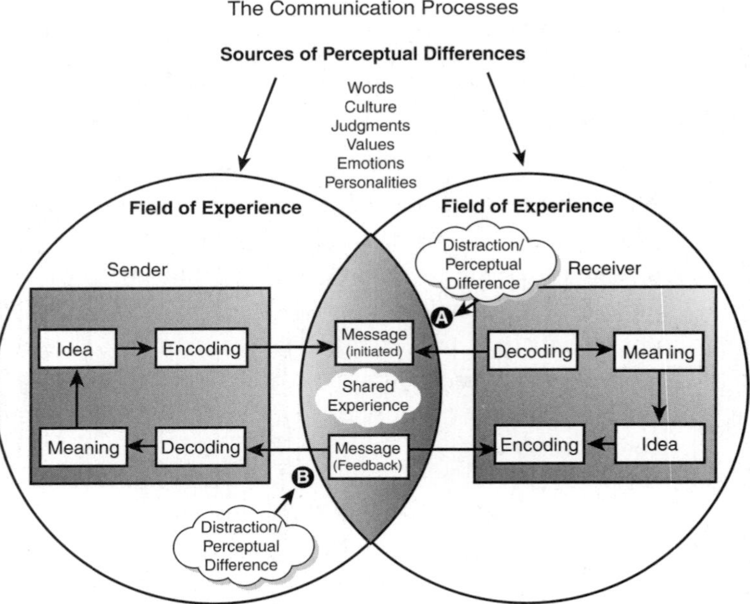

A basic communications model demonstrates that perception comes from our experiences, culture, word choice, values, and judgments. We use all these elements to encode and decode messages, and communication only occurs when the circles overlap. Otherwise, misunderstandings are inevitable.

From Human Resource Skills for the Project Manager *by Vijay Verma*

Recently, Mike had a customer who was in a tough situation that all project managers find themselves in at one time or another. The project was coming into the final months; things had gone very well up to that point, but the final few months threatened to undo all the goodwill that had been built up over the previous 18 months. While many of the issues that surrounded the project were more complex than is necessary to detail here, there was a basic flaw in the strategy. The project manager had fallen into the habit of communicating with the business users through e-mail only. As most of us know, between the tremendous amount of e-mail (much of it unnecessary) coupled with spam, many people will ignore e-mail after a while. And that is what happened to this project. The project manager had to go back and build a new and more robust communications plan to help the project finish with the amount of goodwill they deserved based on the terrific job they had done.

What Does a Communication Plan Look Like?

Building a communication plan is critical to the success of any project. It is the most common way of letting the end users of the project know what will happen to them and when. We'll look at several components of the communication plan in greater detail:

- Stakeholder analysis
- Sensitivity analysis
- Information needs
- Media requirements
- Delivery personnel and power bases
- Timing requirements
- Common definitions
- Feedback loops
- Macro and micro barriers
- Jargon and acronyms

Stakeholder Analysis

Some stakeholders will have more interest in a project than others. In the case of a project to develop a new customer information database for the company, the front office of sales and marketing personnel are probably much more interested in this project than others in the manufacturing facility, but all of them have an interest! The purpose of doing a stakeholder analysis is to see if we can determine how they will be concerned. These examples illustrate the point:

- **Sales** is concerned about how the information will help them sell more products and services to their existing customers and if it can help them land the business of some prospects that are not currently customers.
- **Marketing** is concerned with getting information that will help them identify buying trends that may be the result of marketing literature. They also hope to see trends that will indicate the types of new products customers are likely to buy in the future.
- **Research and Development** takes the information that Marketing provides and works to develop products that will meet the new demands and can be manufactured at a price that will produce a profit.
- **Manufacturing** is interested in the order entry so they can plan their production schedules in a way that will ensure enough products are on hand for sale, but not too much that will require storage in a warehouse.
- **Purchasing** wants the system to feed information into their financial systems so they can track customer purchases to make sure they are not exceeding their credit limits and provide information to track their payment records.
- **Management** wants visibility into the buying patterns of their customers so they can make rational decisions about where to invest limited capital and human resources that will allow the company to continue growing.
- **Stockholders** want the profits to grow relative to the money invested.
- **Governments** want the tax revenues that are generated by a successful enterprise and its employees.

Sensitivity Analysis

All these groups will have some sensitivities the project team will need to consider when developing their communications plan. For example, sales professionals will be sensitive to any system that seems to add a layer of bureaucracy to the tough business of selling goods and services. They will rightly complain and follow with a statement like "What would you rather I do, sit around all day entering information into a computer or be out on the street selling products?" The answer to that question is obvious, but the project team that does not take that into account will run

> **Words from the Wise**
>
> The most important thing in communication is to hear what isn't being said.
>
> —Peter Drucker, management guru

into some serious resistance later on as they try to implement the new customer database.

The management team and all others will have different concerns, but the way the team addresses them will be just as important during the course of the project.

Information Needs

Different groups need different types of information. Sales people will be much more concerned about how information is entered into the system since they will be the ones most likely asked to do that. Accounting and marketing people will be much more interested in the reporting capabilities and the accuracy of the information for invoicing and payments. They will want to know how much and what type of information they can extract from the system. They will be bored by the level of detail the sales people will need on order entry. Likewise, each group will have its own unique information needs. You will need to build each type of information requirements into your communications plan.

Media Requirements

Think about how, exactly, you are going to deliver information to each of the stakeholder groups. When we talk about media, we mean the vehicle you will use to deliver that information. You will want to deliver the information in such a way that it has the best chance of success—that people will actually pay attention to the information! Let us reiterate a basic point that has hurt hundreds of projects over the years: sending out e-mail messages is not communicating! While e-mail can be one component of the overall plan, you really need to make it a minor media at best. Consider, instead, a variety of other delivery mechanisms, such as:

- Town hall meetings
- Presentations
- Staff meetings
- Written memos
- Wall charts
- Web portals

The following table illustrates the various types of communications commonly used; the check marks indicate the situations where it is generally most effective.

Types of Communication and Their Characteristics

Type of Communication	Group	Individual	Written	Spoken	Formal	Informal
Memo/e-mail		✓	✓			✓
Letters		✓	✓		✓	
Reports		✓	✓		✓	
Meetings	✓			✓		✓
Presentations	✓		✓	✓		
Teleconference	✓			✓	✓	
Telephone		✓		✓		✓

Delivery Personnel and Power Bases

Consider who would be the right person to deliver the message. That will depend on thinking through the power base that is required to complete that message successfully. As you can see in the following table, different sources of power will give you different results. For example, you'll notice that the most persuasive power base is expertise. As a project manager, that tells me that if I have a message where the desired outcome is to persuade people, I need to have that message delivered by someone who is considered an expert (whether internal or external) to the people being targeted for the message (hence the "+++"). If I ask an executive to order people to comply, I am likely to get a poor outcome (the "–"), which means I might actually be worse off than if I hadn't communicated at all!

The rule of thumb, then, is to pick the source that matches the result you want.

Power Base	Action	Results
Expertise	Persuasion	+++
Admiration	Ask	++
Reward	Promise	+
Position of authority	Order	–
Coercion	Threat	––

As you can see from the chart, what you need to accomplish determines the power base you come from. If you will need to persuade the stakeholder group, then a power base of expertise is the best direction. How would our project team apply that to the customer database implementation?

Let's say we need to make a shift in the way sales reps keep track of their information on existing customers. We might think that having a leader such as the Vice President of Sales make a declaration on the way it must be done would be a reasonable idea. However, we can tell from the chart that it may not achieve the results we had hoped for. However, if the project team were to provide one of the real "stars" of the sales department (someone recognized by the entire sales staff as successful) a demonstration or prototype of the new tool and get their suggestions on how it could enhance their ability to generate sales, and then ask the sales rep to speak to his or her colleagues on the benefits they see, what difference do you think that would make? The difference would be dramatic! The sales people will really listen to one of their peers because they are respected as an expert, not by position (like the Vice President of Sales) but by performance, the test that really counts for sales people.

Timing Requirements

The right timing for the message is important. If you provide information too early, people may ask questions you can't fully answer just yet! They may want more details than you can give them—particularly early in the project. If you wait too long to relay information, then the project is moving forward at a pace that will not allow people that are impacted to keep up, and they may feel like you are making decisions without them. While you don't really need their consent, timing your information correctly will make them feel like you are seeking, and receiving, their approval. It will really provide excellent buy-in from the ultimate customers!

Common Definitions

Often certain industries or even companies within an industry will have a unique, set language. It will be important that the project manager know the unique definitions within this language. This is particularly important if you are coming in from the outside. Again, your internal subject matter experts (such as the working committee) can be helpful here.

On one of his projects, Mike was installing a new software application that allowed energy traders to input their trades easier and faster. However, as his team did the

> **Risk Management**
>
> Make sure all the key people on your team are familiar with the common definitions associated with your project.

analysis of changes, they discovered that many of the definitions for fields, for example, were going to change with the new application. By the time they finished, they had 18 pages of definition changes that mapped the old definitions to the new ones. Mind you, not every person used every definition, but that was a long list!

Feedback Loops

In any communication plan, you will need to build in a feedback loop to assess how the information has been received. Occasionally there can be unanticipated interpretations or consequences based on the communications. If you consider for a moment, it makes sense. Making sure everyone involved understands common definitions is one way to prevent those misunderstandings from occurring. However, different interpretations of the information can lead people to different conclusions than you had anticipated. Therefore, the only way you will know that has happened is if you have a feedback loop.

One way to build a feedback loop is to develop a relationship (or have your team members do it) with a key person in various stakeholder groups and contact them after a key communication has gone out. Ask them what the reaction was—what people said around the water cooler. That will help you realize if your communication was successful or if you'll need to refine or modify the message next time.

Another benefit of a feedback loop is that it lets you know what rumors are circulating about your project. Address those rumors as quickly and fully as possible. Nothing will build the credibility of your project more than having a message delivered about a rumor that only started a few hours or days ago. The stakeholders will believe you are listening to them, and this will reduce their anxiety about your project considerably.

Macro and Micro Barriers

As you build your communications plan, think about macro and micro barriers. Some of these barriers are obvious; others are not so obvious, but all are important to consider and plan for to be effective.

Macro barriers are those large barriers that prevent effective communication. One such barrier would be simple geography. If the potential customers are scattered over multiple locations, obviously the ability to communicate is more difficult. You will need to consider how to handle the situation and overcome the barrier. Another macro barrier would be different languages; different languages, including culture, will be a major consideration as you plan your communications. Getting a project team member from that language or cultural group to assist in the communications will be critical to success.

Micro barriers are much more subtle. One obvious example would be attitudes that people, as a group, have about the deliverables of a project. Maybe a similar project was attempted a couple of years ago and was a complete flop! Now everyone thinks the business concept is flawed and will never succeed. Other similar micro barriers may surround the project and will need to be considered as you figure out how you will communicate to people.

Jargon and Acronyms

When you communicate, use only jargon and acronyms that are used by the stakeholders of your communication plan. For various functional groups, it is easy to slip into using jargon and acronyms that are common or popular with that function, but are not familiar to others. A simple example of an acronym might be the use of AMA. If you were talking to a group of business people, they would probably assume you were referring to the American Management Association. However, if you were speaking to doctors, they would assume you were referring to the American Medical Association.

Execute the Communications Plan

A plan is only as good as your ability to execute it. After spending the time to develop a communications plan, don't leave it on the shelf. Put the tasks into your project plan and execute them like you would any other task (or give some of them to your team members) during the project. Don't forget to assign some of those tasks to members of the working committee, too! You may need to coach or assist them by drafting the communication, but don't do it for them. Remember that all projects are really undertaken for business results, and you shouldn't let them off the hook for messages that really need to come from the business leadership. Also, just like any other part of the project plan, review and update tasks as circumstances change.

Communications and Leadership

Good communication and strong leadership go hand in hand. The project managers who consistently succeed in bringing their projects in on time and within budget are those who effectively manage the interactions and communications between people and organizations. The people working on your project and other members of the project team need to be comfortable with bringing issues to your attention. This goes for people who report directly to you, their managers, and your managers as well.

Three types of communications must occur for a project to be managed effectively:

1. **Vertical communications.** These are the up-and-down organizational communications based on the hierarchical relationships established on an organizational chart.

2. **Horizontal communications.** Horizontal or lateral communications involve communicating and coordinating activities with peers.

3. **Diagonal communications.** The diagonal relationships are rarely shown on organizational charts, but they are almost always important to the success of a project. Diagonal communications involve upward relationships with managers and officers from other departments. They also include downward diagonal communications with third parties, such as contractors, suppliers, or consultants.

If you have established the required communications in all three dimensions before conflicts occur, when the inevitable conflicts do arise between organizations, styles, procedures, or priorities, the channels you have established will be available for resolving issues.

Always think through the purpose of your communication. Do you want the recipient to do something? Do you want the recipient to think or feel a certain way? To determine what kind of response you want, complete this sentence: *The purpose of my message is ….* If you can't complete the sentence, how will those with whom you are communicating understand your purpose?

Developing Effective Messages

Communicating on a project is an art. The better you get at it, the smoother your project will flow from beginning to end. You must provide enough information to keep team members informed without boring them. Every word counts. What you send, to whom you send it, and when you send it are always issues. If in doubt about a message, always wait. When you decide you need to say something, however, these guidelines should help you decide exactly what you want to say (regardless of the medium you choose):

- Always draft the message and then carefully edit it before you send it. This will help you be more concise in the message and ensure that you have covered all the points required.
- Think about the audience's expectations, any actions required as a result of the message, and your expectations after the message is delivered.
- Justify your choice of delivery medium for the message and the timing of it.
- Start the message with an introduction that identifies the issue, context, or opportunity of interest.
- Make any required actions clear and specific in the message.
- Be as concise as possible without seeming insensitive or rude.
- Never surprise someone with information. For example, if you will be discussing something important in a meeting, make sure the right people know what you will say before you get there.

Listening Is Part of Communicating

The ability to listen is one of the most important communication skills a project manager can possess. Only through listening can you determine whether your messages are understood. Focused listening helps keep you abreast of project progress better than any status report. Observant listening can also help you foresee political issues before they start bogging down the project.

Here are some tips for becoming a better listener:

- Stop talking and let others tell you what they want to say.
- Let people finish what they are saying. Try not to interrupt because you'll never hear the person's complete intent if you do. If there is a brief pause in the discussion, don't jump in pre-maturely. Allow the other person to finish before you take your turn.
- Eliminate distractions, such as telephone calls or people coming in and out of the office. Give the person your full attention.

- Listen with purpose and intent. Try to hear between the words for the underlying meaning of the message. Notice body language and facial expressions as people talk. These are often the clues to dissatisfaction or issues that are not being addressed. If you see something wrong in the person's face, ask some probing questions to get at the real concerns.
- Restate what you hear people say to make sure you have the message right. You must receive and understand the message for good communication to occur.

The Least You Need to Know

- Plan the communications as thoroughly as you do the work for the project.
- Remember all the elements that you must examine as part of the communications plan.
- Be sure to get the leadership involved in the communications.
- When developing important communications, create them carefully and ask others for their feedback before you send it.
- Be sure to keep your project communications plan evergreen and execute it!
- Being a good listener is an important part of being a good communicator.

Part 5

The Controlling Processes

Like any good project manager, to maintain your lead in the project, you need to exercise control. Control of a project starts with a detailed plan, good communication, and clear operating procedures that you've developed for the project.

To actually maintain that control over time, however, you need to deal with changes, problems, and unexpected circumstances. You need to compare the time, cost, and quality of your project at every stage, and then make adjustments to the activities, resources, and plan to keep things moving toward the ultimate goal. Sometimes you may need to slow things down to avoid an accident. Other times, you'll need to step on the accelerator to keep pace with the changes.

Finally, you will need to learn how to prepare the operations group for the final deliverables from your project.

Chapter 22

Monitoring and Controlling Schedules and Expenses

In This Chapter

- Why control is a good thing
- What project monitoring should accomplish
- Understanding earned value analysis (EVA) and Gantt charts
- The project review meeting
- Controlling with a project audit and peer review
- Monitoring the budget

Once a project is underway and you establish the operating procedures and start working on perfecting your leadership style, your key responsibility is to keep things going on time and within budget. After meticulously planning your project, you might assume that team members will simply stick to your plan and get things done as you have specified. Unfortunately, this almost never happens. On occasion, you'll need to intervene.

In this chapter, we'll give you some basic control techniques that can help you deal with any problems.

Taking Charge and Getting Control

Once a project is underway, it takes on a life of its own. If you were the project manager for the All-Star Cable Movies-on-Demand project (our case study), you'd know the company's future depends on getting the project done on time and within budget. Your job and your reputation are on the line. But how will you know if people are doing what they have promised to do? How can you meet your objectives and still get everything else done? It can all seem too overwhelming.

The purpose of controlling a project is to ensure that the project is staying on schedule, that the work is being completed within the budget constraints, and that the project is meeting the quality criteria. If any of these go awry, the business case for the project may be lost, and it no longer makes economic sense to continue. Controls within a project ensure that all the key stakeholders, from the project team to the steering committee, can monitor the progress toward completion, compare achievement against milestones, and help correct problems if they appear.

Getting a handle on your project isn't really that hard. You have a plan, and now is the time to use it. Your plan is your main tool for maintaining control of the project through its lifetime. To move forward and keep everything in gear and well-lubricated requires careful management of both the plan and its resources, especially the people. Although change is an inevitable consequence of moving through time (see Chapter 24 for more on change), you must measure and manage its effects. Otherwise, you won't meet the goals established at the project's outset. The schedule, budget, and procedures you've put together to this point provide you with the structure you need to evaluate where you are at any time.

Control can imply bureaucracy, headstrong authority, or excessive power. Because of these negative connotations, people new to project management may be reluctant to implement project control. The controlling phase is not about domination, however; it's about gathering information so you can measure, monitor, and make course corrections as you progress toward your project goals. That's a good thing because, otherwise, you'll never know if your project is on the right course.

Success Criteria for Project Control

How you use your status reports and operating procedures (discussed in Chapter 20) to control your project will directly affect the end results your project will achieve. These guidelines for using reports and operating procedures will help you achieve positive control of your project:

- Use the project plan as the primary guide for coordinating your project. We have devoted a major portion of this book to preparation of the plan because of its centrality in the project management discipline. If you diligently follow the steps laid out in previous chapters, your plan is most likely a good one and something worth following.
- Consistently monitor and update the plan and the other control documents including the statement of work, the requirement specification, the blueprints, and the functional specifications (if you are using these documents for your project). A plan or supporting specification that stays in the top drawer of your desk will not help you control your project to a successful conclusion. Instead, for your plan to be useful, you must update it regularly. It must always reflect the current status of the project and any changes that become necessary because of new information, budget constraints, or schedule or product modifications.
- Remember that quality communication is key to control. Never provide too much information or offer too little. Every person on your project org chart requires ongoing communication at various levels of detail. Higher-level management requires summary reports on the project. Operational members of the team require more detailed information. Some communication will be formal, and some will be informal. The objective of communication is to keep people informed, on track, and involved in the project.
- As we've emphasized throughout this book, monitor the progress of the project against the plan on a regular basis. Managers must compare the time, cost, and performance of the project to the budget, schedule, and tasks defined in the approved project plan. This should be done in an integrated manner at regular intervals, not in a haphazard, arbitrary way. You must report any significant departures from the budget and the schedule immediately because these anomalies affect the business case and success of the entire project.
- Get involved. You won't have time to sit in your office waiting for results and accolades from the big boss. Instead, roll up your sleeves and get down in the trenches with the team. That way, you not only have a finger on the project's pulse, but you also actually contribute to a workload that may otherwise weigh heavily on team members' shoulders.
- Adapt the project schedule, budget, and work plan as necessary to keep the project on track. As the project progresses, changes in the original plan may be required for several reasons. We'll cover the more common causes for changes in Chapter 24. The project manager's responsibility is to make sure these changes are appropriate, valid, and approved.

- Document project progress and changes, and communicate them to team members. Keep the quality and level of detail of your reports and communications consistent, reliable, and appropriate for each level of the project team.

What Should You Monitor?

To keep things running smoothly, monitor the following elements for every project, regardless of size or complexity:

- The completion of work packages as compared to the plan to check if you are on schedule
- The scope of work being performed to make sure you don't have scope creep
- The quality of work being performed (see Chapter 25) against the requirements for the project
- The costs and expenditures as compared to the plan to check your budget
- The attitudes of people working on the project or involved with the project, including key stakeholders and management
- The cohesiveness and cooperation of team members

Time Is Money

Remember in managing a project, you need to control time, cost, quality, and scope.

Note you need to monitor more than just the tasks, the schedule, and the budget. The level of communication and cooperation between team members and the quality of the work being performed are also obviously important aspects of the project. In addition, you must monitor the use and availability of equipment. For example, you may be responsible for the usage of computer equipment on a large project like All-Star Cable. You also want to make sure the equipment doesn't suddenly disappear because no one was paying attention.

On a large, complex project like All-Star Cable, the effort required for monitoring and control may take more time than you actually spend working on the project. This is okay. It is your job as project manager to be the Chief Integrator to bring the project to a successful conclusion. If you find yourself doing a lot of the work, that should be a red flag for you. Of course, on smaller projects, the degree of monitoring and control should be much less time-consuming.

Using a simple scorecard with the colors of a stoplight, such as the one shown in the following table, can be a useful yet simple way to show the status of the project. However, be aware that some people are colorblind and may not be able to see the status if you only use colors without additional words or symbols.

Project Scorecard

Cost	Yellow	Danger of a cost overrun in the development of the customer GUI
Schedule	Green	No significant problems in the schedule for the project
	Yellow	The vendor who is building the remote control is running a little behind but believes they can catch up
Quality	Green	Peer review set for May to test the technical interfaces
Best practices	Green	Reviewed "Critical Success Factors for Projects" to remind ourselves of what to do
Functional issues	Green	To discuss for billing structure with Accounting
	Green	New customer input decision for credit to be concluded next week
	Green	Ron to chair database working group
	Green	Lisa to chair group reviewing video streaming requirements document
	Green	Andrea working rollout issues with Marketing
Communication	Green	Project team to review and respond to Marketing queries
	Green	Project team to send out documentation that will be refined within the steering committee before the GUI is approved
	Green	Project group to provide complete list of known issues for the steering committee to resolve
	Green	Charles to obtain more information from vendors on their quality assurance plans
Risk	Green	None

Red = High Risk **Yellow = Marginal Risk** **Green = Minimal Risk**

The use of the appropriate level of reporting can help minimize the time spent monitoring activities on both small and large projects. As we cautioned in Chapter 20, keep your reports simple and concise. In addition, the use of appropriate project management software that is adapted to your project needs can help reduce the time required to understand the impact of current activities and changes in the project plan. (See Chapter 30 for more information on choosing an appropriate software program to help you track progress.)

What Monitoring Should Accomplish

The tasks, milestones, and budget you documented in your project plan are the starting point for project coordination and control. These tasks and milestones form the checkpoints you should use to monitor progress. Whether formal or informal, project monitoring should serve one or more of the following basic functions:

- Communicating project status and changes to other project team members
- Managing the expectations of stakeholders (clients or customers) about the status of the project
- Providing the justification for making project adjustments
- Documenting current project plans compared to the original project plan

Consistency is very important in the monitoring and control process. You must monitor the project from start to finish because problems can occur anywhere along the way.

Inexperienced project managers may start out full of energy and monitor everything during the first few weeks. Then, when things seem to be going okay, the monitoring begins to disappear. These managers often end up with a big mess at the end of the project because they failed to keep track of progress and problems. Don't let this happen to you! Maintain your zeal throughout the project.

Using Earned Value Analysis to Determine Project Status

Earned value analysis (EVA) is an industry standard for doing the following:

- Measuring a project's progress
- Forecasting its completion date and final cost
- Providing schedule and budget variances along the way

The basic concept is that as project activities are completed they will "earn value." EVA integrates three measures to provide a consistent, numerical indicator so you can evaluate where you are versus where you should be:

1. **Budgeted Cost of Work Scheduled (BCWS):** Planned cost of the total amount of work scheduled to be performed by the milestone date
2. **Actual Cost of Work Performed (ACWP):** Cost incurred to accomplish the work that has been done to date
3. **Budgeted Cost of Work Performed (BCWP):** The planned (not actual) cost to complete the work that has been done

Before you can calculate EVA, you need to have the right elements in your project plan to make EVA work. That includes having done your work breakdown structure (WBS), as described in Chapter 9, by using deliverables and work packages to define the activities to be completed by the project team. And each of those work packages and deliverables has a cost associated with them.

These simple calculations can help you to manage your budget and schedule:

- **Schedule variance** or **SV** (BCWP minus BCWS) compares the amount of work performed (BCWP) during a given period of time to that scheduled to be performed (BCWS). A negative number (variance) means your project is behind schedule. For example, if BCWP = $49,000 and BCWS = $55,000, the schedule variance (SV) = –$6,000, and the project is behind schedule. If the number is positive, the project is ahead of schedule.
- **Cost variance** or **CV** (BCWP minus ACWP) compares the budgeted cost of work performed (BCWP) with actual cost of that work (ACWP). A negative number (variance) means the project is over budget. For example, if BCWP = $56,000 and ACWP = $49,000, the cost variance (CV) = +$7,000, and the project is under budget. If the number is negative, the project is over budget.

While the input and manipulation of data can create a considerable amount of work and quantifying the work can be difficult at times, there is definite value in using EVA to control your project. It can help eliminate the guesswork in measuring performance and forecasting and can also help eliminate some of the "fuzzy" measures used in controlling a project.

Using Gantt Charts to Control Your Project

Gantt charts (we defined them in Chapter 10) display information in two ways: the left side displays it as a table and the right side as a chart. The table portion displays information about the project's tasks, such as when they start and end, how long they are, and what resources are assigned to them. The chart portion displays each task graphically, most often as a task bar. The bar's position on the timeline and its length indicates when that task begins and ends. In addition, the position of one task bar in relation to another indicates whether the tasks follow one after the other or are overlapping.

The best use of a Gantt chart is to see how activities are progressing over time. You can track progress by comparing planned and actual start and finish dates and by checking the completion percentage of each task. Although you can't see them in this chart, the bars are represented in different colors to indicate various aspects of the project status. Black represents the original plan, blue indicates the float available for the activity, and red indicates where the activity has slipped and taken more time than anticipated.

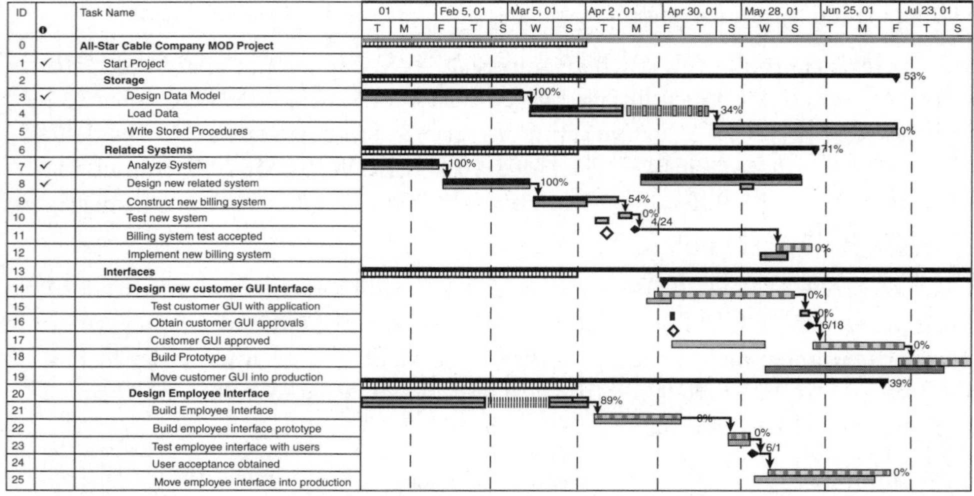

Using program software such as Microsoft Project can help you track your project. This tracking Gantt chart compares the project plan for the All-Star Cable MOD project with the current status of the project.

The Project Review Meeting as a Control Process

Analyzing reports from your office chair will never be enough to help you guide your project to completion. Resolving conflicts, problems, and staffing issues is almost impossible using just reports, so meetings with people are always a necessary component of project control.

Time Is Money

When working with outside vendors, suppliers, and agencies, strike up friendships with their support personnel. That way, if things start running off the rails for any reason, your friends can alert you before your project misses a milestone.

The project review meeting is an opportunity for key team members, not just managers and supervisors, to get together to resolve issues. It's also a time to discuss the current project status and to project performance toward meeting future milestones. Project review meetings are often held at the completion of a major milestone or before or after a key phase of the project. Some project review meetings are held on a periodic basis in place of formal reports. For example, a short subproject, such as the training design for new cable subscribers, is best handled with brief reports and regular meetings because the project is of a short duration. A project like All-Star Cable's Movies-on-Demand may have less frequent meetings at certain stages and then more frequent meetings when more coordination is required.

If a project meeting is necessary to resolve issues, have one now, not later. It's best to take action as soon as you are aware of a problem instead of waiting for a regularly scheduled meeting. Make the meeting short and focused on the single issue that you just became aware of and then adjourn. Long, drawn-out meetings that wander into other issues can dampen enthusiasm and obfuscate the problem. At the end of three hours, no one cares anymore.

The Project Audit

The most formal type of project monitoring (and the process project managers most fear) is the audit. Sometimes audits are required as a part of the contract; sometimes they are necessary because the project is really off track and the source of the problem remains a mystery. The goal of a project audit is to get an accurate picture of the quality of work, current expenditures, and schedule of the project. (These are the goals of all monitoring activities, so the audit is really no different from putting together a big status report.)

Audits are commonly performed on large government projects, projects involving multiple companies and big budgets, and projects involving customers who need outside assurance that work is proceeding as planned. Audits may be initiated both during and at the end of a project. Project managers and team members can also perform internal audits at key milestones in a large project.

In most cases, (allegedly) objective outsiders perform an audit by reviewing progress, costs, and current plans. After discussions with team members, reviews of reports, and direct observations, the objective auditors (who usually work for the customer or the government) report their conclusions on the current status of the project to the project manager or to executive management. They often make strong recommendations giving better ways things should be done to keep a large project under control.

If your project ever gets audited, you'll be okay if you've followed all the tips for monitoring and tracking progress we've given you in this chapter. If you've done a good job of communicating and monitoring, the audit shouldn't reveal any surprises, but if it does, take them to heart and take action. Just because you didn't discover the problem is no reason to ignore the suggested solution.

The Project Peer Review

Another monitoring strategy is to gather some of the sharper minds both inside and outside the company for a peer review. Such reviews usually last from one day to a maximum of one week. The objective of the peer review is to ask knowledgeable people to review your project from a technical and business standpoint and to alert you to any risks or problems you and the project team may have overlooked. You know it's funny, but if you work on something day after day for quite a while, the whole team can begin to make the same assumptions that turn into oversights.

In a project like All-Star Cable, where you are trying to beat the competition, you might consider asking people from vendor companies (with whom you already have nondisclosure agreements) to participate in the peer review. Consulting firms might also offer valuable insights; just make sure you have nondisclosure agreements with them. If you are using an outside consulting firm, make it clear that the review is not an opportunity for them to sell work for their firm.

Words from the Wise

Always remember the distinction between contribution and commitment. Take the matter of bacon and eggs. The chicken makes a contribution. The pig makes a commitment.

—John Mack Carter, Editor of *Good Housekeeping* magazine

Monitoring and Controlling the Budget

Reports and meetings are great for tracking schedules and performance, but budgets and cash outlays require special monitoring techniques. The way the budget tracking is set up depends on the accounting systems already in place in your company. As you make expenditures or sign contracts with vendors, establish a formal tracking method to measure your actual commitments.

In most companies, if you rely on expenditure reports from the accounting department to provide the financial status of your project, you'll likely go over budget or think you have more money than you actually do. Money is often "spent" in the form of contracts or agreements long before it is accounted for in the billing and invoice cycles of the corporation. Accounting reports typically deal with invoices that have been "paid to date." Unfortunately, they don't usually report on invoices that have not been paid or have yet to be billed. Think of it the same way you would your checking account. You need to account for outstanding checks before you can get a true picture of the balance you really have in the bank.

For this reason, you must track actual expenditures to date in addition to reviewing the accounting reports. Ultimately, your expenditures and the accounting department documentation should match, but it might take as long as 90 days for the two systems to be reconciled. Most of the available project management software packages will allow you to track expenditures as well as tasks and people.

You and each person on your project team who will be making financial commitments to vendors or suppliers must account for all monetary commitments as they occur. At a minimum, all expenditures should appear on the formal status reports. For larger projects like All-Star Cable, you may want to have someone with accounting skills on the project staff who can assist you in tracking and auditing the project expenditures.

When you get reports from accounting that don't match your budget file, you will have the documentation necessary to reconcile the differences. If you don't have such a file, you'll be at the mercy of your accountant or finance officer (not a desirable condition).

Time Is Money

When you collect data from your team, collect information on all aspects of the project at one time (tasks, budget, quality, and issues). If you keep going back to people for additional information, you'll irritate them and diminish productivity.

Putting It All Together

The project team is your best source of ideas for keeping the project on track. Once you have complete input from your team, you can analyze project status and decide on new actions to take (if any) to keep the project moving toward a successful conclusion. This includes two steps. The first step involves—you guessed it—updating the project plan to reflect the current status. The second step is a review with the stakeholders and team to gain consensus on the revisions to the plan. We'll discuss this second step in detail in Chapter 24. For now, let's tackle updating the project plan and the related documents.

Your plan documents, including the SOW, product specifications, blueprints, budget, and schedule, are the most important control tools you can use. They allow you to present the work that's been agreed to and to communicate necessary changes.

If you're comfortable with your cross-checking of project tasks, schedules, and budgets after gathering data on the current status of the project, compare the reality with the approved plan and other project documents as appropriate (such as comparing the SOW and product specifications to better predict what's going to happen from here on out). For large projects, this is most easily done with computerized tools (see Chapter 30). Plugging in the status data may predict required changes to the schedule, budget, and critical path. (Computerized project management tools allow you to see comparisons of the old versus the new by highlighting changed paths, dates, tasks, and budget variances.)

Once you have used the new data to forecast a new schedule and budget, look for the problems causing the variances. If your critical path suddenly goes late, follow the lines back to see what tasks are late and who or what is responsible. If the critical path changes, it may or may not be a major flag. Again, study the flow to see what went wrong.

Tracking the budget is a matter of having good accounting practices in place that can give you timely figures on the committed costs and expenditures of the project. The process of comparing current to planned expenditures is similar to matching work completed to the planned task network. Graphs and spreadsheets are useful for demonstrating cost variances and projections. Good project management programs will offer a number of graphing techniques to allow you to visualize the budget through time.

Risk Management

If your managers feel that your project is doomed or is seriously in jeopardy, they may take resources, including staff, from your project to work on other projects. The best way to avoid this problem is to keep everyone informed of positive results and to keep the project on track through careful monitoring and control.

The Least You Need to Know

- Control requires knowledge of the project status. Since the status is constantly changing, you'll need to regularly monitor the project and compare it to the plan in some way.

- If you keep the plan and other key project documentation up-to-date to reflect changes and adjustments, you can more accurately determine your status.
- Use important project methods like EVA to help you understand the status of your project.
- Use project audits and peer reviews to help you maintain control.
- Monitoring the budget takes time and effort, but it's part of good project management.

Chapter 23

Preparing Operations for the Project Deliverables

In This Chapter

- ◆ The five requirements for operations integration
- ◆ Develop a training plan
- ◆ Warning signs that operations are not ready
- ◆ Dealing with resistance to change

Very often in projects, managers forget that the final product or products from their projects will ultimately be transferred into the everyday operations within the company. In other words, the product moves from being a project to being the operating procedure or tool or equipment people will use every day to help them do their job. While many tasks must be completed before handing the project deliverables over to the operations group, one of the most important is getting the operations group ready to receive those deliverables.

In this chapter, we discuss why it is important to focus on these preparations and when the project manager should begin to concentrate on this aspect of preparation.

Five Requirements for Operations Integration

In developing the plan for *operations integration*, you must meet these five requirements if you are to succeed:

def•i•ni•tion

Operations integration means that people are using the product or service (delivered by the project) exactly the way it was intended in the business case.

1. Create and communicate the conclusion
2. Have skills in place for using the product
3. Give users incentives to use the deliverable
4. Help users make the change the deliverable will require
5. Let stakeholders know the schedule for when events will happen

Let's look at each requirement to see why it is important and then discuss ways to implement that requirement for success.

Create and Communicate the Conclusion

You must create a vision for what the workplace will look like after the deliverables are in place. Some people have dubbed this conclusion "a day in the life," and that might work, but what you are really trying to do is paint them a vivid picture of how they will use the deliverables from the project in completing their everyday work. The communication must not just say "you'll be able to work faster," but it must explain why and how they will be able to work faster. And it must borrow from the Case for Change you built (described in Chapter 18) to answer the question "why are we doing this?"

Have the Skills to Use the Deliverable

You'll need to explain to people how they will develop the knowledge and skills necessary to use the project deliverable effectively. Much of the resistance to change that project managers face when handing over their project is that the operations group is worried that they will not be properly prepared and therefore look foolish or incompetent. Very few people, regardless of their mindset, are going to let someone make them look foolish without putting up a fight. You will need to explain, in detail, the training (discussed later in this chapter) they will get and assure them repeatedly that they will be ready when the project is ready. One of Mike's colleagues, Cindy Sepety, coined a great phrase that sums up the situation quite well: the project gets the deliverables ready for operations, and operations ready for the deliverables.

Give Users Incentives

When we prepare to transition the project into operations, we'll likely need to provide some incentives for the users/operators to try it. Companies have done this for years when they develop a new product or service; they give a substantial discount or sometimes even give a free sample, just to get people to try it. For example, the project manager for All-Star Cable might offer subscribers free Movies-on-Demand for a month to get them to try the new service. Not every project will be able to use that tactic, but it is worth considering.

We know that some people can be called "early adopters." These are people who like the latest products and will readily try out a new item. As you plan for the transition, try to identify these people, and begin to pull them into the process of handing the project deliverable over to operations. Usually they will not need incentives because of their eagerness to try a new product. In the IT world this is called User Acceptance Testing. This tactic may have application beyond the introduction of new software.

> **Words from the Wise**
>
> If people don't want to come out to the ballpark, no one is going to stop them.
>
> —Yogi Berra, Hall of Fame baseball player

One effective tactic Mike has used is to have a lunchtime demonstration of the new product. To entice people to attend the session, he provides free soft drinks and cookies. It's amazing how many people will attend if they get free food! At other times, when the budget would allow, he has provided a full lunch (free, of course) for the influential users/operators whom he wants to support the implementation. Again, it's the idea of an incentive for coming and seeing!

Brainstorm with your team and the business people in your working committee to determine the right incentives to stimulate participation and ultimately buy-in.

Help Users/Operators Make the Transition

It is very important for people to have the right help in making the transition. One obvious form of help is the training you will provide. If you follow the suggestions for developing a training plan outlined later in this chapter, you'll be training people to use the project deliverable in their actual job. That will help tremendously in building confidence among the target audience.

Also provide extra help, such as a hot line, for people to use in the first weeks to get information they need if they forget how to do something in the interval between their training and when you actually roll-out the deliverable. And depending on the geographic locations, you might even have experts wandering around the floor or worksite on the first few days so people can easily call someone over to their workstation if they need some immediate help.

Let Stakeholders Know the Schedule

Most people are very aware of the fact that something will be happening to them. Knowing when these events will unfold is some comfort. They want to know when …

- They will get their training.
- They will start using the project deliverable.
- The old way of doing things goes away and the changes go into effect.

Giving stakeholders enough detail to help them know when various events will happen will give them the security that there will be no surprises.

> **Along the Critical Path**
>
> Innovative companies deliver training in a variety of ways. Because many companies are located all over the world these days, project managers are forced to be creative in helping people to develop the knowledge and skills they need. In addition to standard classroom-style training, they deliver training over videoconferencing, through compact discs (CDs), over the Internet through webcasts, and even through what is called Podcasting, via iPods and MP3 players!

Developing the Training Plan

Often project managers take a superficial look at training and only ask the question "What will people need to *know* to make the project deliverable work?" If they ask the training professionals within their organization, they will typically get the same sort of answer because many of those trainers come from an educational background.

However, training should instead focus on the question "What will people need to *be able to do* to make the use of the project deliverables successful?" Focusing on "doing" rather than "knowing" is a critical difference because it changes the paradigm from a learning solution to a job-focused solution. If people only need to "know" something, then it probably belongs in the communication plan, not the training plan.

Basically, people *do* work, hence the focus on doing rather than knowing. There will be process changes, and there may be new equipment, tools, or systems. Developing the training plan should incorporate information from the process changes as well as any technical training in the use of a project deliverable, such as a software application.

The key stakeholder group in the working committee should approve the training plan by looking at two types of training, T1 (product training) and T2 (job-focused training):

- **T1 training** focuses on the technical function and features of the final project deliverables
- **T2 training** focuses on "how" individuals will use the deliverables within the workflow and demonstrates how to use the product to do their work

In our All-Star Cable example, let's look at how it might apply to the customer service people after Movies-on-Demand goes to people's TV sets. If we consider T1 training, it would focus on giving the employees the ability to …

- Navigate the screens to find the customer's name and address.
- Input data correctly when they are taking an order.
- Create searches for billing information if the customer has questions about their bills.
- Display and print reports.

Now these are very useful and helpful abilities, but they may not really help the employees become the kind of customer-focused people that All-Star Cable wants for the future, nor will they help the company in achieving the business case.

Therefore, we must focus on T2 training. Now we will be helping our employees …

- Navigate the screens to help a customer solve a problem by being able to access that customer's needed information.
- Input data accurately to place the customer's order in the right priority category so the correct discounts and incentives are applied during billing.

- Create searches for information so that marketing and sales representatives and product development people can begin to assess and predict buying trends.
- Display and print reports that allow customer service representatives to recommend other services that a particular customer might be interested in purchasing.

If the training plan is developed correctly, people will feel confident that they know what they are doing and the resistance to change will drop dramatically.

Words from the Wise

Executives are like joggers. If you stop a jogger, he goes on running on the spot. If you drag an executive away from his business, he goes on running on the spot, pawing the ground, talking business. He never stops hurtling onwards, making decisions and executing them.

—Jean Baudrillard, philosopher and developer of the theory of hyper-reality

Symptoms That Operations Is Not Ready

Some warning signs may suggest that operations may not be ready for the project deliverables. In other words, you and the project team are nearly ready to turn things over to operations, but they are not ready to receive them. If this is the case, you will begin to see telltale signals. If you notice any of these, take corrective actions to try to alleviate the problem. For example:

- Key people or groups are not aware of the project or do not seem to support it in actions or words
- Training is not well attended by some groups, which means their management is probably not providing the support you need
- Incentives that you have provided are not producing the results you had hoped for and may need to be adjusted
- Key people or groups are not aware of the timeline for the implementation

If any of these signs occur, you'll need to confer with the working committee and develop some remedial plans to address them. The worst thing you can do is ignore the problem. Try to determine why people are not on board and plan for corrective action as quickly as possible. Your working committee is the best source for uncovering that information. Why? Remember who is on that committee—people who represent the needs and concerns of the group. People within the company are much more likely to talk with them about their concerns or reservations than the project manager or project team.

Overcoming Resistance to Change

Many people naturally resist change in their lives, whether it's moving to a new house or city, finding another job, or any other situation where they must give up the tried-and-true for the unknown. People may be resistant to the changes your project deliverables will bring for a variety of reasons, including …

- Fear
- Feelings of powerlessness
- Simple discomfort
- Absence of self-interest

Any of these emotions can cause people to refuse to accept the changes that the project will bring. You will need to build actions and communications to help them address the root cause and gradually bring them into a mindset that accepts the project.

Fear

For some people, when they hear about changes that a project will cause, they immediately assume a worst-case scenario. This is particularly true if they have previously been subjected to poorly implemented projects. They believe that their reaction is normal until proven otherwise.

Others may fear a reduction in the workforce based on the implementation of the project: "They aren't going to need all of us after the change, and I'm the one who will go!" Indeed, a reduction may happen as the result of a project, and if that is the case, you must communicate it clearly. Work with the management team to send the right messages regarding any reduction in force that may occur. If a reduction is not part of the plan after implementation, that you must also communicate frequently since people may not believe it initially. They may think management is hiding the "true" intent, so don't be surprised. And don't give up!

Some people may fear they won't be personally competitive in the new operating environment. You must give them a clear idea of how you will prepare each and every person to handle his job confidently and competently as you transition into operations. Obviously, training will be a centerpiece of that effort, but so will the use of job aids, a help desk they can call when they have questions, and any other elements you have planned to prepare people correctly. Make sure everybody understands the new environment.

Another common fear is that mistakes will be punished because the company has spent a lot of money on this change. Some might fear the first one to make a mistake will be fired. Hopefully, that is not the case; however, this has indeed happened in some organizations, but not when you have the type of extensive planning and preparation we are talking about. You will need to communicate how mistakes will be handled and the real level of tolerance that management will have as the transition to operations proceeds. And then you must hold both management and employees to the approach you have communicated.

Feelings of Powerlessness

Often, resistance occurs because there is a general feeling that people's ideas are not valued. They will state, "I told them the problem the first time the idea came up. I told them how to make it work, and they didn't listen." Again, the working committee will be very helpful for these people. They should solicit ideas and feedback from them before decisions are made and then follow up with them after decisions have been made. In this situation, you may need to help the working committee with the messages they deliver, to make sure all of them are consistent.

Other people tend to view themselves as outsiders and feel management only cares about a certain privileged few. The best way to handle this is to communicate the plans so that they see how things will happen and when. Usually they will realize that everyone is being impacted and the plan appears organized and comprehensive. That will reduce the anxiety and give them confidence that management is not "playing favorites" as the project moves to operations.

Risk Management

Constantly monitor the working committee members to make sure they are communicating with everyone, not just to a small, select group. That will be a recipe for disaster if you are not careful. You are playing right into the hands of this group because they aren't being consulted.

Discomfort

Let's face it, some people are just happy with the status quo. They take the attitude of "If it's not broken, don't fix it!" That is not unusual. Many of us like things the way they are and consider the future a foreign place we would just as soon not visit! The good news is that if you have painted a strong picture for them and clearly explained how the job will work in the future, when it finally happens, it will likely be a non-event, and they might even look forward to the change!

Absence of Self-Interest

Usually, people who are driven by self-interest (and aren't we all to some extent?), don't understand the perceived benefits when the project moves to operations. They are basically asking "What's in it for me?" or thinking "I'm putting more into this than I will get out of it!" Strong communications must constantly reinforce the benefits that they will reap from the successful implementation and operations after the project is completed. Now remember, because people are looking at their self-interest, they may not be persuaded by the benefits the company will accrue. They may also believe that the benefits of the project are long term or will go to others before they will receive any benefit. "I'm suffering now for 'maybe' benefits in the future" is another common complaint of this group.

You will need to communicate how this project will help them in both the short term and the long term. Much of the information will probably come from the business case, but put the case into everyday language that will help people understand the benefits to them personally. The only way to do that effectively will be to do a careful audience analysis prior to developing your communication plan for these people and get the working committee actively involved in selling the benefits.

Finally, you may hear the cry "It's not fair!" from people who believe that the project is just "one more change" inflicted on the workers who are carrying the company. To address this type of concern, you should work with key members of the working committee and use the Case for Change and communication plan as your basis for addressing this problem. In our experience, this is usually more a perception problem than anything else.

As you work to handle the resistance to the changes your project will deliver, you will need effective leadership from operations. As you analyze the sources of the resistance, remember the power base for messages we discussed in Chapter 21. At times you may need an authority figure like a vice president and other times a respected person who is known for his or her technical knowledge of the business to explain what is going on, and why, to those who are resistant. Be sure to pick the right person to deliver the message that the change is coming and they need to be ready. But remember it is your project that is going to operations. You will usually need to develop the content of the message for the person who will deliver it. Don't expect the vice president or working committee chairman to do it!

The Least You Need to Know

- Resistance to change will occur if you don't fulfill the five requirements for operations integrations.
- You will need to prepare a training plan for your project deliverables.
- Deal with resistance to change as soon as you begin to see it.
- Watch for warning signs that operations is not ready to receive your deliverables.

Chapter 24

Changes, Changes, and More Changes

In This Chapter

- Developing a process to deal with changes
- Estimating the impact of change
- Balancing a project
- Understanding the trade offs and the options for change
- Handling conflict during a change request
- Creating an issues log

One of the most difficult challenges for any project manager comes when the scope of the project changes. Although many factors cause change, two reasons are most common. One cause of change would be to overcome a technical problem not foreseen in the original project plan; a second cause for a change in scope would be a shift in the business drivers for the project.

Remember from Chapter 1 that the reason for the project in the first place is to solve a business problem and/or to enable the organization to perform at a higher level. So it's reasonable to expect that over the course of a large project that will take 18 to 24 months to complete, the business requirements for producing that higher performance will change. And with that your project scope will probably change, too!

Some changes are under your control. For example, you might be able to shorten a schedule because you learn faster ways to do things as you proceed through the steps of the work plan. On the other hand, if the vendor who was manufacturing your cable boxes closes because of a strike, you'll have to change the schedule, like it or not. In both cases, you'll have to anticipate the impact of the change and adjust your project plan accordingly. Because change is inevitable, managing the impact of change is a key aspect in controlling your project.

A very common change is a change in requirements when you are already in the execution phase of a project. Recognizing that changes impact schedule, cost, and quality, you must balance those factors as you manage the change.

Develop a Process for Change Control

During the planning phase, you and your team will need to develop a *change control system* that you will follow, and expect the stakeholders to follow, when a request for a scope change occurs. To handle these requests by using a process is particularly important because the process will be an important part of managing the expectations of various stakeholder groups.

> **def•i•ni•tion**
>
> The Project Management Institute defines a **change control system** as "formal documented procedures that define how project deliverables and documentation are controlled, changed, and approved."

Let's turn to our All-Star Cable Movies-on-Demand case study to illustrate this point. During the project planning phase, the project manager was told that so-called "adult films" would not be part of the MOD package. However, during the execution phase, the marketing department convinced the management team and steering committee that adult films would be needed if they were going to get the revenues predicted in the future. So the company president summoned the project manager to his office and told him to include adult movies in the film library. The project manager then had to do an assessment of the impact of adding this new category of movies and informed the steering committee what impact the change in requirements would have on the schedule and the costs to the project.

What Might a Change Process Look Like?

The answer to this question is not as simple as it may seem. The first consideration is to do a quick assessment of how difficult the change may be. The simple changing of the color of the background on a screen may not be too difficult as opposed to a dramatic shift in the scope of the project. In either case, begin with a formal request.

Follow that request with a review of the impact on the project—its schedule, cost, and quality. Depending on how big the impact is on first assessment, you will need to make your first decision about who to put on the evaluation of the change request. Pick people who are able to devote some time to the evaluation without impacting your overall project schedule. However, these people also need to have enough experience and knowledge to provide a reasonably accurate assessment.

The next step is to develop a high-level cost/benefit analysis. Construct this analysis against the original scope requirements and specifications. Remember, the reason organizations invest in a project is the increased performance results they expect to achieve.

Finally, a decision needs to be made as to whether this request requires an authorization beyond the decision-making authority of the project team. If your team decides that the impact will make a serious change to the cost, schedule, or quality of the project, then the decision is something that you should definitely take to the steering committee. However, don't surprise them. This is where managing stakeholder expectations comes into play. If you believe that a decision may be elevated to the steering committee, then immediately brief your project sponsor on the situation. Let him or her know that you may be coming to them for a decision. Give the sponsor a rough idea of the nature of the request and reasons you think it will require their approval. Then encourage the sponsor to begin networking with the steering committee members to let them know what's going on. The key is to make sure they know that the project team will make a request and provide them with alternatives to consider.

Along the Critical Path

It is not the project manager's job to prevent change. It is the project manager's job to assess the impact of the change and to make a decision (or ask the steering committee to make one) based on his or her analysis.

Managing change and reviewing the project go hand in hand. As you monitor your project over time, you'll get feedback on the general issues, problems, and other factors that may be affecting your progress (positively or negatively) in completing the project. Lots of things enter the picture as the project proceeds; some are desirable, others are unpredictable, and once in a while, one can be disastrous. (We were working on a project at a major airport and were almost finished when 9/11 occurred. No one could have predicted that event, and needless to say, it had a dramatic effect on our project.) The good ideas and the unpredictable problems will all result in the same thing: the need to change the project plan in some way.

Through project review, new ideas and new ways of doing things become apparent. The realities of what can and cannot be accomplished shift tasks and goals, as do changes handed down from senior management or the customers.

The Rules of Change Control

Now that you've accepted the inevitability of change, these four rules will help you anticipate changes on your projects:

1. During the planning phase, you established a decision-making process regarding changes that are requested. Be sure to follow that policy now.
2. Establish a change control board that is a subset of your working committee or governance board. Use them to evaluate changes that have an impact on the stakeholders and the project. They should handle the politics of changes within the organization.
3. Establish emergency decision-making authority in case things need to be done too quickly for even the change control board to meet and discuss a change. In our All-Star Cable case study, a major decision needed to be made quickly on the movie library that All-Star Cable would use to pull movies. A vendor was in financial trouble and needed to make a deal to improve its second-quarter financial reports. Unfortunately, this occurred at the end of June, when most of the members of the steering committee and the change control board were on vacation. Fortunately, the project plan included an emergency authorization for the project sponsor to act on behalf of the steering committee, and All-Star Cable was able to secure a very favorable contract.
4. Maintain a change control log (see the following example) that tracks all change requests and documents the vital information needed to complete the lessons learned during the close-out phase (discussed in Chapter 27).

Use a change control log such as the following to track the information, including the tracking number that corresponds to the numbers on the work breakdown structure (WBS). You would normally keep a record like this in a spreadsheet or database application, not a written form.

<table>
<tr><td colspan="4">PROJECT CHANGE REQUEST
☐ APPROVED ASSIGNED CHANGE REQUEST NUMBER:__________[1] ☐ REJECTED
DATE:_________ DATE:________</td></tr>
<tr><td colspan="4">Change Authorization Decision Required (Date/Time):</td></tr>
<tr><td colspan="2">Project Name:</td><td colspan="2">Category of Change:</td></tr>
<tr><td colspan="2">Customer:</td><td colspan="2">Decision Maker:</td></tr>
<tr><td colspan="2">Project Sponsor:</td><td colspan="2">Project Manager:</td></tr>
<tr><td colspan="4">Description of Change Requested: (Attach any additional documentation required to access necessity for change)</td></tr>
<tr><td colspan="4">Justification for Change: (Include the reasons for the change as well as the consequences if the change is rejected)</td></tr>
<tr><td colspan="2">Cost Impact:</td><td colspan="2">Schedule Impact:</td></tr>
<tr><td colspan="4">Other Impacted, Re-planning Activity Required (Attach Supporting Documentation);</td></tr>
<tr><td>Submitted By:</td><td>Printed Name</td><td colspan="2">Signature and Date</td></tr>
<tr><td>Project Sponsor:</td><td>Approval Signature & Date (if req'd)</td><td>Project Manager:</td><td>Approval Signature and Date</td></tr>
</table>

[1] See Change Log for next available sequence number.

The project change request form has several key items to consider. First is the impact of the change so that later on you can track how the impact was assessed to see how correct you were. Second, it tracks who authorized the change. That may be important if someone questions a change later.

Risk Management

There's always someone associated with your project who "knows" how to do things better than you're doing them. Sometimes you need to be assertive and keep this person from getting in your way. Establish a clear process for suggesting and reviewing changes so that people offer constructive advice. And if you fail at a project because of outside interference, guess who will get the blame? We bet it won't be the person with all those "good" ideas.

Understanding and Estimating the Impact of Changes

If you want to stay in control and help your project evolve in the right direction, a well-documented project plan is your first line of defense in managing change. If you want the results you expect as opposed to the consequences that just happen, you need to keep your plan up-to-date. Period. With a plan in hand, you can quickly assess the impact a change will have on the project's budget, schedule, and resources. You can also use the plan and your current status analysis to show why a new or different user requirement may have a negative impact on the final results of your project.

As you review your plan, you'll see that really only six major components in any project can be changed. They are the same components you used to create your project plan in the first place:

- The business reason the project was undertaken in the first place, as articulated in the business case which you translated into project goals and objectives.
- The people who work on the project.
- The money (budget) you have to spend on the project.
- The material and technical resources you have available to support your project.
- The time you have available to complete the project.
- The quality requirements that were acceptable for the finished deliverables.

Any change in your project plan will affect one or more of these project components. Most changes will affect all six in some way.

The Balancing Act

Balancing a project, or managing changes in the project plan, can take place at three levels of authority, depending on the severity or immediacy of the change needed:

- **Project-level balancing** involves making adjustments to keep the project within its approved cost, schedule, and quality outcomes. The project manager and core team members should have enough authority to make these decisions.
- **Business-case balancing** is necessary when a project cannot achieve its approved cost, schedule, and quality goals. When this becomes obvious through project monitoring, the business case for the project must be reevaluated. Maybe the project will be useless if it doesn't come in on time. Maybe there isn't enough money (or profit) left in the project to make it worthwhile. Business case changes are beyond the scope of the project manager's authority alone and must involve the review and approval team of stakeholders.
- **Enterprise-level balancing** is required when a firm has to choose from various projects to spread limited resources out. This could result in a project being cancelled (terminated) or postponed. This is primarily a business management decision that is well beyond the scope of the project team, although the key team members will likely be involved in the process.

Once the changes are decided upon, document these changes on the original plan, date them, and communicate them as you would a new project plan. On large projects, the documentation of the changes is often called configuration management, and it can require a full-time staff in the "project office" responsible for controlling the different versions of the project plan.

Risk Management

It's important to always get formal approval for revisions from the powers-that-be. Even if the disruption is minimal, managers and stakeholders should be fully cognizant of changes. For changes that impact delivery dates or the budget, written correspondence should accompany your request. Remember, if they're not in writing, agreements are easily forgotten.

After the new plan is approved, inform all team members of the changes to their tasks and delivery dates. Make sure all team members are aware of exactly what you will expect of them and how the changes will impact the project. You'll also need to let team members know how the effect of the changes will be measured so that things don't end up going on just like before. Do this measuring through ongoing monitoring, reports, and communication. (And yes, you might need to change some of your project reports or procedures to make sure you get the new information you need.)

In balancing a project where changes impact its time, cost, or quality objectives, here are the basic things you can do:

- **Reduce the scope of the tasks.** Sometimes the best way to get a project done is to scratch some of the work from the list. This can turn an impossible list of tasks into a doable (and scoped-down) project. Before promising to do less as a way of dealing with change, however, make sure the downsized project is really worth doing. Also make sure the stakeholders agree to the downsizing. If they don't, you'll need to negotiate what you really need, more time or resources or a bigger budget, to get the project done right.
- **Increase productivity by using in-house experts.** Some people are simply more productive than others. By reassigning people, you may still be able to meet your original cost and schedule performance. Be sure there isn't a better way to make the staff more productive, such as training people or prudently using new technologies.
- **Use outside resources.** Assign part of the project to an external firm that can manage and complete it within your original guidelines (outsourcing). This moves the work to outside experts who will hopefully be more productive. However, this may create more risks in terms of lost in-house control and the gamble that the outside experts will actually do what they say they can.

Words from the Wise

People can get frustrated with endless rounds of picky changes. To avoid this frustration, limit the self-induced changes to those that are truly necessary and important.

- **Use overtime.** Use it prudently, however. It can backfire in lost productivity and morale problems if this option becomes the default action. If you're using hourly employees as opposed to salaried ones, it can end up pushing the budget out of control.
- **Crash the schedule.** This involves compressing the tasks on the critical path to reduce the time required to meet the desired finish date. You'll need to produce a cost/schedule/trade off analysis, which can help analyze the cost of reducing the schedule. Sometimes the increases in cost to get things done faster will outweigh the need for speed.
- **Adjust the profit requirements for the project.** A reduced profit margin can free up cash for needed resources. If the project won't bring in enough money to meet the business case, however, this is a bad idea. A decision to reduce profit is clearly the territory of the company executives, not the project manager.

- **Adjust the project goals.** This is like playing on thin ice. Although it may be appropriate to reduce some of the functionality or scope of the project end results, to reduce the performance characteristics (quality) of the project is not usually a good idea. Remove some of the functionality only when it doesn't affect the performance of the overall product.

Comparing Changes with Trade Off Analysis

Trade off analysis is one method of dealing with change that lets you evaluate the impact of various alternatives. "We can do this if we skip that. Which is more important?" Analyzing trade offs is also a way to understand the pressure change is placing on the project. Understanding trade offs clarifies the changes that will affect later tasks and milestones. Here are some considerations for understanding the impact of various options (or trade offs) when implementing a change to a project:

- Determine the underlying rationale for the change. Are the changes motivated by rational thinking or a political agenda? Does the change really make sense?
- Are the project goals still appropriate? Will the change also affect the eventual outcome of the project?
- Do the options affect the likelihood of completing the project successfully? You should have already reviewed how the various options impact schedules, budgets, and team member availability. When changes increase the risk of failure, this problem needs to be carefully analyzed and then clearly communicated to all involved.
- Analyze the options at all levels. Try to hold the budget and objectives constant, and then evaluate how you can accommodate the changes. Look for alternatives, tasks that can be deleted or shortened, or dollars that can be moved around in the project. This is usually an exercise with your team leads. Be patient when trying to come up with alternatives. Don't always jump on the first ideas. Only after looking at all options should you ask for more money or more time.

Communicating a Scope Change

You may remember from our discussion of scope in Chapter 7 that a change in scope means that something we were originally not going to include in the project is now included (the adult videos example from All-Star Cable). A variety of people may need the information about a scope change—whether or not they approved that change.

1. **Inform your project team.** Sometimes changes will occur, and you need to make sure all team members understand the nature of the change and will support the change. Make certain they are on board before you do anything else. Nothing can destroy the reputation of the project more than having project team members openly, or covertly, grumbling about a change.
2. **Go to your communication plan and see which stakeholders are impacted by the scope change.** Then follow the same format for communicating the scope change. Start with examining what information they will need and when. Then decide who is the right person to deliver the message and what medium to use. You should probably start with the project sponsor and the working committee. They should have already sanctioned the change, but it is a smart tactic to remind them of that formally in the communication. You can handle small changes through e-mail or the regular project updates you already have in place. However, large changes should be handled in a richer forum such as a town hall meeting.
3. **Log the change into your change log.** Notice in the project change request form shown earlier in this chapter that the authorization is noted in the log. Later, when you conduct your lessons learned for the project, having that information will be helpful in writing your final report.

All these things require that you update your plan (including the SOW) for the project. As we've emphasized, updating the plan means making changes to the goals, tasks, workflow, schedule, budget, or people and getting them approved by the appropriate stakeholders. Be prepared for change. It's not a question of what to do *if* there is an issue; it's what to do *when* there is an issue.

When Conflicts Occur

When a change has been requested, even before it has been accepted or rejected, conflicts may occur. People will have legitimate differences of opinion on the wisdom of the change. In that light, a project manager must understand how to handle those types of situations.

Many people have studied conflicts and how managers resolve them. In general, these studies have identified five general ways to resolve conflicts, all appropriate at one time or another:

- **Withdrawing** means that the manager retreats (withdraws) from the disagreement. This is often an option if the conflict is petty, of inconsequential impact to the project, and not worth spending time to figure out.

- **Smoothing** is used to emphasize areas of agreement to help minimize or avoid areas of disagreement. This is the preferred method when people can identify areas of agreement and the conflict is relatively unimportant. However, this is a weak approach; chances are the conflict will flare up again even though sparring parties shake hands and make up. Use it to get the project moving until you can find a better solution.
- **Compromising** involves creating a negotiated solution that brings some source of satisfaction to each party in the conflict. Compromises are best made after each side has had time to cool down if the conflict has escalated to the anger and hostility stage. The best compromise makes each party feel as though he or she "won." A well-constructed compromise will hold the project together. A poor or weak one will come apart in the future, so be ready for it. The solution to a collapsed compromise is usually another compromise. This works best when people have a give-and-take attitude and a shared focus on the priorities of the project. (The delicate art of negotiation is described in Chapter 25.)
- **Forcing** is used when someone exerts his or her position of power to resolve a conflict. This is usually done at the expense of someone else, and we do not recommend it unless all other methods have failed to resolve the conflict.
- **Confronting** is not quite as strong as forcing, but it is the most used form of conflict resolution. The goal of a confrontation, if handled professionally, is to get people to face their conflicts directly, thereby resolving the problem by working through the issues in the spirit of problem solving.

Create an Issues Log

Whenever conflicts or issues arise, an issues log is a great tool for the project manager. An issue may be a difference of opinion on how to solve a technical problem that the project must deal with. Smart, honorable people may have legitimate differences of opinion on the way to solve the problem. In that light, an issues log makes a great deal of sense because it forces everyone to be as objective as possible. This log contains detailed information about the conflict or issue and includes the following elements:

- A description of the issue or conflict
- The person assigned to work it through
- The impact the issue has on the project
- Individual who authorized the accepted solution
- The date on which the issue was successfully resolved

Always keep track of any issues that arise during the course of the project. And then use the issues log to make sure you have addressed all the conflicts (note that doesn't mean they are solved to everyone's satisfaction). You can also use the log at project close-out as part of the lessons learned. Here's a sample issues log:

Issues Log

Issue	Impact	Assigned	Due Date	Resolution
Coding language	High	Bob Braveheart	4/15	ABOP chosen
Union request	Medium	Julia Robins	5/02	In progress
Software acceptance	High	Ben Samuels	5/10	Accepted as tested

The Least You Need to Know

- Changes are a natural and expected aspect of any project, but changes made through a defined process will be easier to control.
- When you must consider a change, for whatever reason, always do an impact analysis and understand the trade offs and options available.
- Be sure to balance the project when changes create situations that impact workload and schedule problems.
- Requests or the need for change will almost always cause some friction. Be prepared for it and use the techniques for managing that conflict so it won't adversely impact your project.
- Create an issues log to record all the issues and how you solved them. It will be a great resource for you later on.

Chapter 25

Quality Management: Making It the Best It Can Be

In This Chapter

- The meaning of quality in a project
- Planning for quality
- Useful tools and techniques to ensure the quality of a project
- Quality assurance
- Controlling quality during the project

The issue of quality will always surface as you attempt to balance the four main elements of your project: time, cost, quality, and scope. We've spent a lot of time on monitoring and controlling your schedule and costs (see Chapter 22), so now let's work on assessing and ensuring the quality of the project's deliverable. In reading this chapter, keep in mind that even though we refer to the "product" of the project as a deliverable, in reality, it can mean a service as well as a physical good.

What Exactly Does Quality Mean in a Project?

In its simplest form, the definition of quality is conformance to requirements. Remember when we talked about developing the requirements in Chapter 1? That's the starting place for developing your quality plan. During your quest for quality, you need to identify which quality standards are relevant to your project and determine how to satisfy them.

Often, a project team may confuse *quality* with *grade* and end up hurting the project overall. For example, a software product may have high quality because it does what it is supposed to do with few problems. However, it may have a low grade because it has very few appealing features. On the other hand, we have all had software that had not only a ton of features but also so many "bugs" that we wanted to throw it away. That product would be defined as having high grade (a lot of features), but low quality (too many problems).

def•i•ni•tion

The Project Management Institute defines **quality** as conformance to requirements. **Grade** is the ranking we give products that have the same functional use, but different characteristics.

Determining the right balance between the quality and the grade is the work of the project manager along with the project team. In our case study of All-Star Cable, the project manager and the project team will need to see how many features they can successfully add to the Movies-on-Demand product while still meeting the requirements for cost and schedule they have developed.

Planning for Quality Is the Starting Point

When you begin to plan for the quality of the product your project will produce, first go to the statement of work and review the scope of the project. Review with the team what is clearly in-scope and out-of-scope on this project. For example, the project team at All-Star Cable decided they would initially target their existing customers as the primary audience for this service (in-scope) and not target new customers with MOD (out-of-scope). Also, they decided to use a film library from an outside source (in-scope) since they didn't want to maintain a library of movie titles (out-of-scope) and outsourcing the library would allow them to change titles more frequently. Continue reviewing the requirements and specifications given to you when you were handed the project and the process you used to refine them during the definition phase.

When you begin to plan for quality, a key consideration will be the criteria that the key stakeholders will use to accept the final deliverables. These familiar examples illustrate the point:

- **Major functions:** Are all the required functions built into the Movies-on-Demand system?
- **Appearance:** Is the appearance consistent with the other services we offer our customers?
- **Accuracy of information:** Are the customer's bills accurate in both customer information and billing information?
- **Reliability:** Is the MOD system up and running every time our customers want to order a movie?
- **Security:** Have we built security into the system so children can't run up huge bills using MOD without their parents' permission? Have we built security into the system so children can't order adult or inappropriate movies through MOD?

There are many more than these. The key will be to understand what the operations team will use as criteria for judging the quality of your project team's work.

You will also need to review other aspects of the project to gauge the impact on quality. For example, you may need to review the procurement process for selecting vendors who will supply you with products or services to be sure that the quality requirements for the vendors you choose will meet your project requirements. This will also help you control the quality of the vendors' work during the course of the project. The project manager and the project team for All-Star Cable developed a very specific set of requirements on the size, features, and video signal capabilities for vendors before they sent out the request for proposal (RFP) for the cable boxes and remote controls for Movies-on-Demand.

Quality Planning Tools and Techniques

You can use several tools and techniques to plan the quality of your project's deliverables. Here we'll cover the more common ones.

Cost/Benefit Analyses

One of the most useful techniques is to do a *cost/benefit analysis* as part of the planning for a project. As you work to balance time, cost, scope, and quality, you will need to weigh different factors and come up with alternatives to satisfy your stakeholders. For instance, to determine which features to include in the Movies-on-Demand screen menu, the project manager for All-Star Cable will do a cost/benefit analysis of the features. Some of them may be almost a given, such as a parental control feature that prevents children from ordering movies without their parents' knowledge or consent.

def•i•ni•tion

A **cost/benefit analysis** is an estimate of the costs and benefits of various alternatives and then using financial measures, such as Return on Investment (ROI) or payback period, to determine which of the alternatives is the most desirable.

Other features may be far more optional, such as the length of time the customer will have access to the movie after ordering it. In this example, allowing the customer to have access to the movie for 24 hours versus 72 hours will have a very different economic impact on the company. The project manager will need to show the steering committee how these two alternatives might affect the profit margin for MOD by discussing the options with them, providing them with the cost/benefit analysis, and letting them make the decision.

Benchmarking

Benchmarking can also be a very useful tool in quality planning. This involves comparing your project plan or practices to those of other projects to generate ideas for improvement or to provide a sound standard you can use to measure your project's performance. You may want to benchmark against other projects within your organization if they are available, or you may want to use standards developed by the Project Management Institute. Either way, it should help you plan and execute your quality process within your project.

Cause-and-Effect Diagrams

Cause-and-effect diagrams, also called Ishikawa diagrams or fishbone diagrams, can help identify how a problem may be solved by showing the linkage between various factors. The basic idea is to find the cause of a problem and separate that from the effect it is having (similar to a doctor noting a high fever—the symptom or effect—and the cause—an infection or a virus). As you measure the progress of your project, any potential quality problems should begin to show up, and you will need to take corrective action. The cause-and-effect diagrams can give you and your team a visual linkage between factors to see if the problem lies with manufacturing, people, a technical specification, and so on. Also, you will need to collect data that helps:

- Define the problem using what has been observed or reported
- Identify where the problem is occurring
- See any patterns for when the problem is occurring
- Determine how often the problem occurs

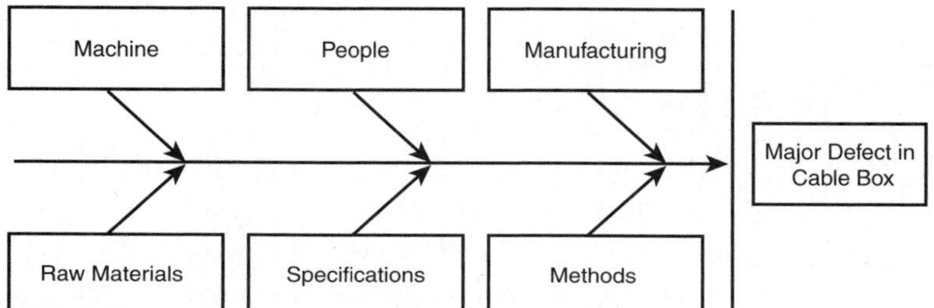

Cause-and-effect diagrams can help the project team to uncover problems by showing how various parts link together.

Finally, system or process flow charts can illustrate how information flows during a process or throughout an organization. The project team can also use them to help show where quality problems might occur so they can plan to prevent them. The pictorial representation can help people see what is happening and when. As a result, detecting the source of a problem, or potential problem, may be easier to identify.

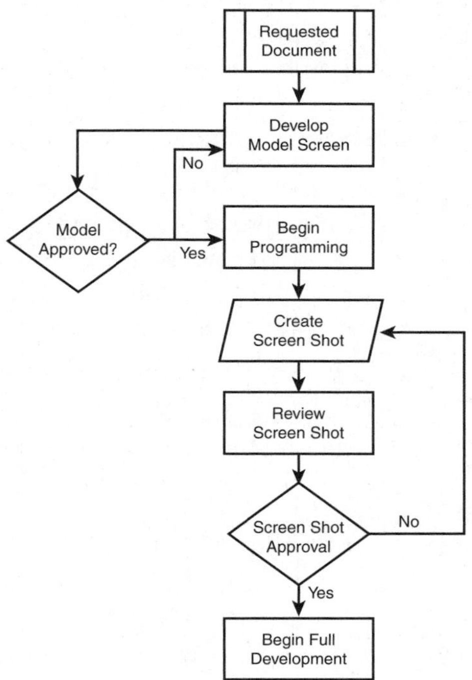

Flow charts can help the project team spot potential areas for quality problems.

As you use these tools, you and your project team should develop a quality management plan that explains:

- How you will implement your plan
- What operating guidelines you will use to measure quality
- Which checklists you will be using to verify that you have implemented your plan

Quality Assurance: The Real Proof

There are a variety of ways to ensure that the project will meet the quality requirements set out in the quality management plan. The tools mentioned earlier are a great start. Doing benchmarking to see how a successful project operated is an easy way to ensure your project team will know how to succeed. All the quality tools are also helpful in keeping the quality of your project deliverables on track.

You may also consider conducting a peer review, which we discussed at length in Chapter 22. This formal review of the project, usually during the design phase, can provide an unbiased assessment of your project plans. To set up your peer review, gather a small group of people (probably no more than 10) who have the knowledge and experience to effectively evaluate your project plan. They should probably not come from your stakeholder group since you want an unbiased review. However, you should give the stakeholders a briefing on the results of your peer review when it is completed. For All-Star Cable, the project manager would probably invite people who know a lot about cable systems from the perspective of various disciplines, such as IT, accounting and billing, content management, marketing and sales, and operations and management.

These people evaluate the plan and provide insights on potential risks that may be present but that the project team had not considered. Don't ask the reviewers to approve or disapprove the project. They are just there to evaluate and help the project team with a "sanity check" on the approach to the project.

> **Words from the Wise**
>
> Good project management in an organization is, in itself, a quality management process.
> —Lynn Crawford, DBA, University of Technology, Sydney, Australia

We have been involved in dozens of peer reviews, and they are one of the best quality tools around to handle quality assurance.

Quality Control: It's All About Results

In quality control, as project manager, you and your project team are monitoring very specific project results to make sure they meet the requirements of the project. Some organizations have a quality control department; if yours does, get them involved early on in the project so they can help with quality planning. Or maybe you have a quality expert on your team; if so, also involve him or her in the planning process. If you don't have that expertise, don't fret, there are still some things you can do.

One of the most common methods of quality control is simple inspection. For example, as project manager for All-Star Cable you might want to assign a team member to visually inspect and test the cable boxes that the manufacturer is producing for the company. The purpose is to make sure that the boxes conform to the requirements established in the quality management plan. It's far better to learn of some mistakes *before* the customer gets those faulty boxes!

If there are too many boxes to inspect individually or you are short on time, you can conduct a statistical sampling. This means that instead of inspecting all the cable boxes, the team member will look at a certain percentage of them, say, every tenth cable box being made. Or maybe she will look at 3 boxes in each large container of 25. A number of books on the market give detailed approaches to sampling and the evidence that it works. This sampling can also reduce the cost of conducting quality inspections, usually a primary consideration in cost-conscious projects!

Once you've inspected the product, you can use a Pareto diagram to put the information you have collected into a usable format for control quality. A Pareto diagram is basically a histogram that shows how many results were generated by an identifiable cause. It will show you where the problems are and help you and your team establish priorities for tackling any defects.

A Pareto diagram is a special type of histogram that helps us identify and prioritize problem areas. It involves collecting data and types of problems from the various sources. In the diagram, the sources of problems are the video signal, audio signal, remote control, power cable, and cable connection. This is the source of the famous 80/20 rule that says that 80 percent of your problems will come from 20 percent of the sources. You are trying to evaluate where the greatest source of problems is occurring and take corrective action. In this case, the video component seems to be the greatest source of problems, so it becomes the highest priority for corrective action.

Using checklists and the whole suite of available quality tools will aid you tremendously in getting the results you and stakeholders want.

Pareto diagrams can help the project team set priorities.

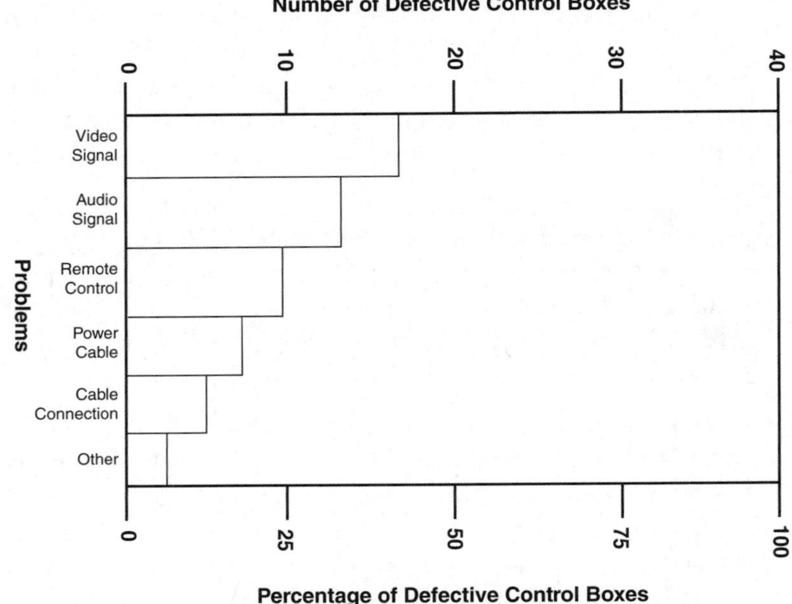

The Least You Need to Know

- Focus on quality, not on grade.
- Plan for quality right from the beginning.
- Use quality tools to help you.
- Use peer reviews as a way to ensure quality assurance.
- Remember that quality control is all about results.

Chapter 26

Common Project Problems: Get Them Before They Get You

In This Chapter

- Ways to recognize the urgency of the problem before you take action
- A dozen or so common problems to expect on any project of any size
- Identify problems in the making before they undermine project objectives, schedules, or budgets
- Strategies to help you solve or avoid the most common project problems

Okay, you've read every chapter so far, but as hard as you try, some of your projects aren't getting done any better. They're taking too long. They're not reaping results. Your team doesn't seem interested in meeting the deadlines. Your boss keeps asking for changes. The customers want more results. Even Dogbert's advice and Dilbert's humor don't seem to help when deadlines are slipping and expenses are skyrocketing.

If you think that project management techniques will eliminate all your problems in getting things done on time and within budget, think again. All projects have problems. In some ways, project management success depends on problem-solving techniques more than any other processes.

Recognizing All Problems, Large and Small

The successful project manager is able to maintain a perspective that allows honest, objective evaluation of each issue as it comes up. Like personal conflicts, not all problems require immediate action, and some don't require any action at all. You just need to monitor them to make sure they don't get out of hand. At this point, you might want to review Chapter 3 and the seven key reasons why projects fail.

> **Words from the Wise**
>
> You know, by the time you reach my age, you've made plenty of mistakes, and if you've lived your life properly, you learn from them. You put things in perspective. You pull your energies together. You change. You go forward.
>
> —Ronald Reagan, former U.S. president

Large problems typically have multiple owners and involve many people and/or significant amounts of money with jeopardy to budget, schedule, and quality. These frequently require immediate attention and take a great deal of time to resolve. On the other hand, small problems may be solved quickly and with the help of only one or two people. Nonurgent problems are those that can be deferred until later without impact to the project, the customer, or the organization. In fact, a great many of these disappear as time passes.

The good news is that most project problems, whether large or small, are predictable. To help you anticipate problems in your projects and thus minimize their impact, we'll describe some of the common project problems. Like a Boy Scout, expect to encounter them and be prepared to minimize their impact.

The Floating Start Date

Some projects just never seem to get off the ground because other priorities keep getting in the way. Unfortunately, even though a project may start late, everyone expects it to finish on the original schedule. If you find that your project never gets started, consider these strategies for solving the problem:

- Re-analyze the business case for the project. Maybe the project really isn't that important after all.
- If the project really needs to be completed as scheduled, work with your project sponsor to communicate the problem to management and adjust your own work habits to make time for it.
- If the project starts late, communicate (in writing as well as verbally) the new finish date to management and the project team. If you need to keep the original date, complete a trade-off analysis of time, cost, and quality that the changes will require, as described in Chapter 24.
- Analyze your daily activities and determine whether you are wasting time on less important tasks. If you need time-management training, get some. Many good books offer guidelines for identifying the time traps in day-to-day work; get one and implement its advice.

Risk Management

Never assume that people will be available when dates slip. If you don't ask about the new schedule and people's availability, you may be the last to find out that you don't have the people you counted on to get things done.

There's Not Enough Time, or They Need It Faster

Sometimes, despite our best efforts, we fail to estimate the time it takes to complete the tasks in our work breakdown structure. Things seem to take longer than we anticipated, and there are more things than we have time to do. Shortening the schedule is a frequent request because of predictable business demands, especially competitive pressures to get products out faster or to generate the revenue anticipated from the completion of a project.

In a search for solutions to the ever-present problem of finding more time for the project or compressing the schedule, look into the following alternatives:

- If the team is falling behind, don't try to catch up all on your own. Delegate more of the activities, and involve other people in the prioritization and assignment of work.

- Eliminate work that isn't really necessary. Always question the necessity of each task on a project. Skip tasks that don't count.
- Review your project plan to see if you can *fast track* or *crash* any of the project work.
- Change the priorities for the work. Some things may get done later than originally planned, but this is better than nothing getting done. Of course, you must communicate this change to the other people working on the project.
- Work longer hours when this is an option, but don't overdo it for too long, or you and your team will become burned-out and be less productive and less motivated. All work and no play are ingredients for disgruntled project teams and poorly executed projects.

> **def•i•ni•tion**
>
> **Fast tracking** is a project schedule compression technique that rearranges work into parallel tasks originally scheduled to be completed in sequence. **Crashing** is a technique for either reducing the amount of work or adding more people to complete the work.

The 90-Percent-Done Syndrome

Many people are optimistic about their ability to make up for lost time. Others simply attempt to look good on paper. For these reasons, the phrase "90 percent done" on a project status report usually indicates a big problem. What is hiding behind that unfinished 10 percent that no one wants to admit? Why does it seem that 90 percent of the effort only takes 30 percent of the time, and the last 10 percent takes 200 percent of the original schedule?

If you see that 90 percent or some other large percentage of a complex task is completed very quickly but then the work only inches up to 91 and 92 percent over the next couple of status reports, you need to figure out what is really going on by talking to the staff in an environment of support and understanding.

Use these guidelines to get to the root of the 90-percent-done syndrome:

- Investigate the scope of the remaining work through meetings or one-on-one sessions with key project members. Are there technical difficulties that the team doesn't want anyone to know about? Should the task be broken down into smaller, more measurable work packages?
- Consider whether the remaining 10 percent of the work is really predictable. Creative tasks, such as inventions or coming up with ideas, are often difficult to

schedule. In the development of a new technology and in other high-creativity situations, the breakthrough required to complete a project may not happen as scheduled. Creative tasks need to be more realistically assessed. You can't schedule spontaneity, so don't try. Just be honest about the creative blocks, and document the schedule changes accordingly.

- Help the team be honest in its assessment of project status by encouraging open communication and by pointing out the problems with being too optimistic about risky endeavors. Team members may be giving you the estimates they think you want to see, not the real ones. Reward yourself and the team for honesty and effort rather than false statements of accomplishment or unrealistic commitments to impossible dreams.

Moving Target Objectives

Changes in project plans are valid for many reasons, as we discussed in Chapter 24. However, sometimes the changes in project goals and objectives seem to occur more frequently than they should. Because there isn't time to plan and adjust for these daily or hourly changes, you might not bother to update the current plan. This is a bad idea. Not adjusting the plan is just about the easiest way we know of to end up with a project disaster. When changes are requested frequently and arbitrarily on a project, it is an indication of a lack of consensus regarding the original plan or some other political problem between your customer or client, the project, and the stakeholders. Here are some ways to save yourself in this situation:

- Make sure you clearly document the authority for making project changes in the project plan.
- Don't start a project until the plan is approved by all appropriate levels of management and other appropriate stakeholders (customer or client).
- Don't promise to implement changes in a project until you have time to analyze and document the impact of the changes. Follow all the other rules for making project changes discussed in Chapter 24.

The Key Person Always Quits

Projects shouldn't depend on the special skills of a single person, but sometimes they do. If this person leaves, the project could be damaged. However, here are a few basic ways to keep the departure of a key person from becoming a catastrophe:

- Keep the key person happy in the first place. Listen. Be aware of problems in advance. Most people don't just walk out; it takes time for them to become disgruntled or lured away by more money. If there is a reason, try to find it and fix it.
- Remember the Responsibility Assignment Matrix from Chapter 14? Cross-train people as work proceeds on the project. Combined with some additional training, this can minimize the impact of losing a key person on the team because others will be familiar with the work packages they were scheduled to work on for the project.
- Make sure the key person is documenting his or her work. If the key person works in isolation, the impact of this person's absence could be disastrous. On the other hand, if he documents the work, you can usually hire someone else to take over where he left off.

Costs Spiral out of Control

Budget and cost-control problems occur for many reasons, including lack of skill or discipline in estimating costs in the original plan, inadequate detail in the plan that results in vague or inaccurate budget allotments, schedule delays that cause more resources to be used than planned, unforeseen technical problems, changes in material or service costs that weren't anticipated, and changes in the scope of a project that are not reflected in the updates to the budgets along with a myriad of other "justifiable" events.

In spite of excuses to the contrary, you can control costs in only one way: keep on top of expenses through regular monitoring and appropriate accounting controls. There simply is no other solution.

Cost overruns don't just happen. Costs increase because of poor communications, lack of control, inaccurate reporting, or inadequate documentation of project changes. Through diligent monitoring of expenditures during the project, you can deal with money problems when budget concerns first appear, before the costs get out of control.

The Staff Has More Enthusiasm Than Talent

Unfortunately, the most likable people are not always the most competent. If you choose people for their personalities alone and not their skills, you can end up in a situation where a congenial team just doesn't get the work done. What should you do when you have a great group of people working on the project, but they just don't seem to deliver what you need? Try these guidelines to help you decide:

- Develop an objective skills appraisal system to select team members at the beginning of the project. This can help keep friendly but unskilled people off the team.
- Watch the team to see if they are spending too much time in social activities. Sometimes the problem isn't a lack of competence at all; instead, the schedule suffers because of too much socializing during work hours. Usually, a simple meeting to reemphasize the priorities of the project can solve this problem.
- If a congenial but unskilled person (or group) is willing to be trained and has potential, additional education is sometimes a solution. However, getting people up to speed is only an option if the schedule can absorb the time required for training.
- If competence is the root of the problem, a consultant or outside vendor can sometimes make up the difference in skills, allowing the friendly person in question to remain on your team in a lesser capacity.

Words from the Wise

Desire alone is not enough. But to lack desire means to lack a key ingredient to success. Many a talented individual failed because they lacked desire.

—A project manager with 30+ years' experience

Ultimately, you may need to tell your "friends" that they aren't making the grade. Give people every opportunity to do the job, but if everything else fails, you will have to find someone else for the team. When this is necessary, cut the ties earlier rather than later. Getting rid of dead wood on the team is one task that most managers dread and put off. In business, if the goals for the project are important, the project must take priority, no matter how much you like the person (or the group). See Chapter 14 for more on building a strong project team.

The Impossible Remains Impossible

In an attempt to look good, novice project managers often commit to more work than is possible. Even worse, they commit to projects that are impossible from the start. The budget and schedule may be so unrealistic that there is no possibility for completing the work as specified. Sometimes there are valid reasons to accept a project that can't be completed on-time or on-budget, such as a project to extend the relationship with a customer. Here are some tips for what to do in that event:

- Make sure you and your sponsor are very clear about the statement of work (SOW) and everything necessary to complete the project.
- Do an extensive risk analysis of the danger involved and discuss how to mitigate those risks with your sponsor and/or steering committee.
- Develop a project plan with two or three options to complete it within the impossible schedule or budget. Highlight the trade-offs in each option, and recommend the option you think has the best chance of success. Remember to try crashing or fast tracking the schedule to see if that will work.
- Try negotiating a change in the measures of success for the project. Determine how much over budget or how late in the schedule you can be and still have the project considered a success with your leadership team.

Words from the Wise

Failure is good. It's fertilizer. Everything I've learned about coaching, I've learned from making mistakes.

—Rick Pitino, coach at the University of Kentucky and NCAA Champion in 1996

It is difficult for project managers to admit defeat, but often the best solution is to realize that some things just won't happen as planned. If you find yourself caught in an impossible situation in spite of your realistic communications, the best way to get out is as quickly as possible. Prolonging the agony makes the problem worse and has brought many a company (and project manager) down in the process.

Politics, Politics, and More Politics

Politics in human endeavors is unavoidable because people always have different opinions and motivations. If the political attitudes are annoying but don't affect the end results of your project, ignore them. It's only when political agendas start undermining project goals that they pose a problem. When this happens, treat the politics as any other conflict, and resolve the situation by following the conflict resolution options covered in Chapter 24.

Management by Best-Seller

Senior management may push one of many ineffective, concocted-over-cocktails ideas on your team. Gently agree to consider the idea no matter how stupid or insufferably dopey the book or seminar from which the idea came. Then, if forced into management-by-fad, put the process into practice but complement it with the basics of good project management, inspired leadership, and common sense to make sure you actually get things done.

Taking Care of Yourself to Remain Sane

Does your family treat you like a boarder because they never see you? Does aspirin seem like candy in relief of your headaches? If this sounds familiar, it's time to get a life. Sometimes the best way to handle problems is to take care of yourself first. Stop everything! Get a handle on the problems that are causing you to live at work, and then use your leadership to fix the problems. Or choose to scale back or step down from the project. Your life is worth more than any project, even if your boss may express other sentiments.

A Parable of Last Resort

As project manager, you'll be faced with pressure from both above and below in the organization. Things often seem impossible when you have too many roles and too much to do. When you feel that way, consider the following story, which according to a computer industry joker, probably originated at IBM.

A new project manager proudly walks into her new office. She arrives just as her predecessor is walking out the door in disgrace. The departing manager tells her he has left three envelopes numbered 1 through 3 in the top desk drawer. The departing manager instructs the new manager to open an envelope and follow the instructions only when an impossible-to-solve problem occurs.

Several weeks go by and the project problems seem overwhelming to the new project manager. Everything is behind schedule, and the new manager must explain the failures to the steering committee in a review meeting. Not knowing what to do, the project manager decides to open the first envelope before going to the meeting. The note inside instructs, "Blame it on the last project manager." The new manager decides this is a way off the hook. In the meeting she points her finger to the last manager's inept handling of the project. The committee agrees and reluctantly approves more time and money to complete the project.

Time goes by, and the project once again becomes stalled. Without a clue as to how to handle the problems, the manager must approach the steering committee for more project moola. Opening envelope number 2, she is advised to blame the problem on the inept project team. Again, this tactic proves successful, and the grumbling committee caves in and approves more time and more money for the project. Upon leaving the meeting, the committee admonishes the project manager with "This better not happen again!"

Six months fly by with winter changing to spring. Again overwhelmed with problems, the project manager feels trapped and helpless. The project is late again, is way over budget, and is probably doomed to failure. She pauses, takes a deep breath, and then opens the third and final envelope. The instructions are simple: "Prepare three envelopes …"

Remember this story when faced with the fatalism that infects some projects. Before you give in and write your envelopes, remember that almost anything can be fixed, but not if you blame the wrong source for the problems. You, as the leader, must use what you know about project management to pull the rabbit out of the hat that others are assuming won't appear. If you do your work to plan and scope the project at the beginning and keep track of things as they go along while always keeping communications open, you'll probably never need the three envelopes. Yes, you'll have problems, but they will probably be solvable or at least not fatal.

The Least You Need to Know

- Ask questions, listen, observe, and communicate with candor and clarity. If you do these four things, you'll reduce the impact of almost every project problem.
- Remember that problems and change go hand-in-hand. Change may cause new problems, but change handled well can often be the best solution to keeping a project on track.
- Always be honest (but not brutal) in your assessment of project problems, and always support your honest appraisals with documentation.
- Tell your boss or customer as soon as you know something is wrong. Waiting will only delay the inevitable and make the problem worse.

Part 6

The Close-Out Phase

Whether it's a summer vacation or a visit to the dentist, there comes a time when all things (good or bad) must come to an end. Likewise, your project must move through the close-out phase so that you can wrap up the details, pay the bills, evaluate what you and your team learned, and move on to the next project with a sense of satisfaction. That's what the two chapters in this part are all about—showing you the steps to bring a project to the proper conclusion.

Chapter 27

Will the Last One Out Please Turn Off the Lights?

In This Chapter

- Life after the project ends
- Reasons to close out a project
- The steps for closing a project
- Evaluating the lessons learned
- Conducting an after-implementation review
- Releasing the workforce

If you've successfully completed your project, the close-out phase is a time of celebration and accomplishment. Not every project ends gracefully, but all projects should have a distinct ending. Without a proper closing, some projects seem to just drift into operations without any formal recognition that the project completed its mission.

In this chapter, we'll show you how to close out any project, especially those that finish successfully. But we'll also talk about those that die prematurely and the more annoying ones in which team members never seem to want to let go! Closure is important because it's the point at which, while wiping your sweaty brow with relief, you can say to yourself, "It's over." (And regardless of the outcome, break out the chilled champagne—you deserve it!)

Is There Life After Project Termination?

As the end approaches, some project members get nervous while others are glad that the end is in sight. The nervous ones may wonder what their next assignment will be. Particularly if they are contractors, they may wonder if there will be a next assignment at all. Unfortunately, this morale problem occurs with the worst possible timing—when a project is almost complete. The problem runs deeper than just the risk of unemployment or a new assignment in another part of the company. It means the end of budding friendships, interesting after-hours at the tavern playing poker for pennies, and the other good times that accompany a well-run project. Your people will miss it. You will, too—really.

> **Words from the Wise**
>
> When projects veer off course or no longer meet strategic needs, companies must know when and how to let go.
>
> —Dr. Xiaojin Wang, PMP, Yuman University, Kumming, China

Why Is a Close-Out Phase Necessary?

We know several good reasons for a formal closeout to a project. Some involve people issues, and others involve you personally learning from the experience and recording what you've learned. You need to acknowledge people for goals they have achieved in order for them to feel the work is complete. Because you as a project manager need to evolve your skills for managing projects, analyze the techniques, processes, and procedures used on a project so you can adapt and improve them in the future. These are the most fundamental and underlying reasons to formally close a project. You may also want to hold similar closing, acknowledgement, and review meetings at the close of major milestones or phases in a longer project as well.

The Final Shutdown

Make the following tasks part of the final termination process for most projects, as they are necessary to bring them to the final closure:

- Meet with stakeholders to get their final approval of the project deliverables. Because they are the reason for the project existing in the first place, their approval signals the project's completion. For larger projects, you may want to request a formal memorandum acknowledging the completion of the project by the project sponsor or customer.

- Finalize all contractual commitments to vendors, suppliers, and customers. This may include reports or final payments. It may also include letters thanking vendors for a job well done when appropriate.
- Transfer responsibilities to other people if required. For example, the end results of some projects are inputs for operations (remember Chapter 23?) or new projects to be managed by other people. Consider our case study of All-Star Cable. Once the project is finished, the company's operations group will take formal control of Movies-on-Demand. The team members for development of the billing database will finish and turn over the maintenance of the database to the information systems department. The team members who were responsible for answering customers' questions during the pilot test will turn over the ongoing responsibility to customer relations to handle future questions. These activities are all part of the final termination of the product design project.
- Reassign people in the project, and redirect efforts to other priorities or projects. You may return people to their functional areas, assign them to new projects, or both. Follow the human resource plan you developed earlier for rolling people off the project.
- Release nonhuman resources, such as equipment and materials, so they can be disposed of or used for other work. Some construction and manufacturing projects also require cleanup tasks to prepare the facilities for new activities.
- Complete the final accounting of the project. This includes totaling the costs, paying all the bills, and closing the books on the project.
- Document the results of the project and make recommendations for the future. If you have been documenting as you go, this is not as daunting a task as you might think. The amount and detail of final documentation will vary based on the size, importance, and issues associated with each project.

Risk Management

Before you close out a project, make sure you have delivered all the project deliverables according to the requirements of and approval by the sponsor. Begin these discussions informally in advance of the formal closeout. Shame on you if you are surprised that the key stakeholders refuse to accept the project deliverables!

Projects that aren't formally closed may continue to consume resources required elsewhere. Most projects should end as soon as you have achieved the goals or you recognize there's no hope for success.

Closing a Small Project

For small projects, the formal closing (also called termination by some project managers) can be a simple matter of having a meeting with the team and the stakeholders to acknowledge attainment of the project goals and writing a brief final report on the project. The closing meeting should focus only on the accomplishments of the completed project so that people feel satisfied with the work performed.

Closing a Large Project

For large projects, the closing phase can be a time of stress and anxiety. Team members may have developed friendships and a sense of family. Some team members will be going their separate ways, adding to the anxiety. Termination of a long project with a close-knit team is always difficult and can be complicated. However, you can reduce the frustration if you acknowledge the team members for their current accomplishments and then give new assignments and challenges as soon as possible. It's also a good idea to have a formal celebration to close down the project.

Because some people fear leaving the security of an established project team or changing roles after the project is complete, it is often difficult to get the final details of a large project completed. People may continue to work on insignificant tasks. Remember your work authorization system! If they are working on work packages that you haven't given them, then you need to stop that work, gently of course.

As a project manager, it is your responsibility to see that the project ends by helping the people involved move forward into new challenges and opportunities. To reduce the stress associated with project termination, remind your team members of the overall goals they have achieved and the fact that the stakeholders consider the project completed. Emphasize the importance of the project to the business and their contribution in meeting the project objectives. Then remind them of new goals and objectives they have yet to achieve on other projects and assignments.

In addition to having a formal meeting or even a party to acknowledge project completion, many projects involve other formal termination tasks, some of which we mentioned earlier: reassigning personnel, auditing the final expenses and closing the books on the project, archiving any files and other project materials, passing the end results of the project on to another organization (for example, setting up a product for manufacturing or installing the final product at a customer's site), informing other departments (including purchasing, finance, manufacturing, or whoever needs to know) that the project is finished, and completing other miscellaneous documentation of the project. And of course there will be an extensive final report.

The closing tasks for a large project are not always clear-cut. When such a project is almost complete, often some small details need to be resolved. The project manager must decide when a project is "finished" so it can move into the termination phase. Don't drag out the close-out phase and clean-up details to keep the project alive. This is a common problem in large projects. Get on with it and turn the final details over to the operations group to finish.

Because of loose ends, the termination of a large project may be a mini-project in its own right, demanding schedules, priorities, and budgets. Identify the major steps in the project closeout, and implement them as quickly as possible. Follow all the steps and methods for managing any other project.

For many projects, large or small, a checklist is useful in determining the requirements for termination. Later in the chapter we provide an example of a termination checklist for a complex product development project to demonstrate the kinds of tasks that might be required to terminate a large project. Of course, the checklist you develop may include entirely different elements that require shutdown, but our example should give you the basic idea of what to consider.

Write Out Your Lessons Learned

Closure is also the point at which management evaluates your success in meeting the goals and your skills as a project manager. In project management circles, this is part of a process called "lessons learned." Was your project a big success? A dismal failure? Usually it is neither of these but somewhere in between. Writing down the specifics will help you and your team capture the information you need regarding lessons learned during the project. All of the following questions apply to each focus area.

Focus Areas: Project Management, Communications, Schedule & Budget, Training, Quality, Issues, Human Resources, Support Templates

- How did we do? ______________________________
- What did we do well? ______________________________

- What did we do poorly? ______________________________
- What should we improve? ______________________________
- How? ______________________________
- What else did we learn? ______________________________

  ____
- Recommended actions: ______________________________

  ____

Write out what you and your team learned during the project, what worked well, and what would you do differently if you had to do it all over again. These types of reports can be very helpful for you in the future, but they can also help other project managers who may read your report as they tackle a similar project in the future. At least they won't make the same mistakes you did; they can find some of their own!

Some Additional Details for Project Shutdown

The cleanest closure of a project comes when all work is done and team members already have other work or have returned to their permanent jobs. The easiest project to close down is the small one in which tangible (visible) results demonstrate completion to one and all. For example, when the All-Star Cable Movies-on-Demand project is finished, everyone will know because customers will be able to order movies on their TV!

On the other hand, closing down the project of building a large refinery in Houston is much more complex. Not only are there multiple subplans, but for the uninitiated project manager, reaching the state of completion may seem impossible. Yes, the plant itself may be up, but all the little details may seem endless. In addition, some work may linger on. After completion, repairs may be on the project manager's shoulders as necessary. In a sense, the project continues rather than winding down in a planned and predictable process. Although 99.8 percent of the work is complete, remnants of the team must address that other .2 percent or hire outsiders if former team members are no longer available.

To shut down a project, here are some additional details on the steps to take toward an orderly closure. On a large project, shutdown may occur in phases, although in most cases the tasks can be done in parallel. One major component of the project may be completed earlier than others as projected in the project plan. Treat shutdown of each facet similarly to the termination of the entire project. After all, each of these facets amounts to a project unto itself and deserves the celebration that accompanies completion of any project. The steps to project termination are as follows:

1. **Decision to close out.** Make sure that operations has accepted the project and you are finished. For All-Star Cable, that means that the project manager has received the decision from the sponsor that operations will take over Movies-on-Demand and he is finished.

2. **Task list.** Make a list of small tasks that need to be accomplished and get them taken care of. For example, if the project requires user documentation and it's not fully "user ready," then do it now!

3. **Consensus.** You, the team, and the other project stakeholders agree that the project has met its goals. Have your project sponsor or the chair of the steering committee sign a project completion memorandum stating that the project is completed and that it meets their requirements.

4. **Meetings.** Hold individual meetings with team members and team managers who have reported to you. Thank them for their contribution. Take notes on what they thought of the project's highlights and lowlights and your leadership (take a deep breath first). If you don't already know their intentions, find out what they would like to do in the future.

5. **Communication.** Instruct all team personnel in writing as to when the project will end. This puts pressure on the stragglers who need a little more time to complete their role. If you suspect that more time is needed, set the end date several weeks into the future and give weekly reminders of the drop-dead date. For real problem people, visit them daily to assess their progress and remind them of the date.

6. **More communication.** You must notify outside suppliers and vendors that the project will cease to exist in X number of days, weeks, or months. Since the project is ending, tell them you will not accept bills received 30 days after the termination date. (Be flexible on this one. It's really a tactic to get the bills coming in the door from vendors with tardy billing practices. It also saves you interest charges, and really prompt payment may knock a percentage off the total project bill.) If possible, check purchase orders to see what's outstanding.

7. **Even more communication.** Inform managers of "borrowed" employees, temporary agencies, and contractors in writing that the project's termination date is near. This provides the managers time to find other opportunities for these people or to move them back into their usual job responsibilities.

8. **Closing the books.** Assuming you are working with a finance department, once a project is complete, finance must close the books so that wayward bills aren't charged against a nonexistent budget. Most companies assign code numbers to accounts for projects. Assuming your project receives one or more codes, have finance render the codes invalid. That way, you can review any invoices that pop up for legitimacy prior to payment or rejection.

9. **The celebration.** Once a project is (successfully) completed, hold a team celebration. (One of Mike's customers took the whole project team to Las Vegas for the weekend!) Awards may be in order for team members who performed above and beyond the line of duty. This event is not only fun, it marks the official end of the project in everyone's mind. If the project was a flop but not because of team failure, still hold such an event even if the occasion is somewhat more subdued.

10. **Dispersal of resources.** Take an inventory of supplies and equipment. Return borrowed and rented equipment, send back unused supplies for credit where possible, and haul off trash to the recycler or landfill. If the project was large and ends up owning a lot of surplus equipment, an auction on eBay can be the ticket to parting with 12 table saws or 48 slightly dated computers. Money from such an event can go into the organization's general fund, be distributed to team members in the form of profit sharing, or be donated to charity.

11. **Handing over the keys.** Transfer responsibilities to the operations team. In the All-Star Cable Movies-on-Demand project, the operations team will be people at All-Star Cable who will run Movies-on-Demand once the project is complete. They must now take responsibility for the day-to-day running of Movies-on-Demand.

Risk Management

The formal ending of a project should take you off the hook for the budget. However, make everyone concerned fully aware that the project is completed. Otherwise, miscellaneous charges may pop up and be assigned to your now-closed project accounts. Should bills be unavailable upon termination of a project, ask whoever handles finances to build separate accounts for each one for your review before payment.

Checklist for Closing a Large Project					
DESCRIPTION	NEEDED? YES	NEEDED? NO	REQUIRED DATE	RESPONSIBLE PERSON	NOTES
Identify Remaining Work	☐	☐			
Closing/Termination Plan	☐	☐			
Personal Evaluations	☐	☐			
Close-Out Work Orders	☐	☐			
Audit Final Changes	☐	☐			
Pay All Vendors	☐	☐			
Close-Out Books/Audit	☐	☐			
Final Delivery Instructions	☐	☐			
Customer Training	☐	☐			
Notify Purchasing of Completion	☐	☐			
Equipment Redeployed	☐	☐			
Materials Returned to Inventory	☐	☐			
Staff Reassigned	☐	☐			
Close-Down Procedures	☐	☐			
Engineering Documentation	☐	☐			
Final Staff Meeting(s)	☐	☐			
Final Report and Review Meeting	☐	☐			

This checklist for closing a project may not include everything you need to remember, but it should help you consider all the items that are important.

The After-Implementation Review

A common practice among experienced project managers, particularly on large projects, is to conduct an after-implementation review. A meeting is scheduled, usually between three to six months after the project is closed out, with the key team members and some of the stakeholders. The review is a discussion about what has happened since the project was turned over to operations. Often getting a little distance from the project will help everyone gain some insights on what went well and what they would do differently in the future. Also, any problems or surprises that occur will happen in those first few months, and that information can help in crafting your lessons learned.

Three Ways to Release a Workforce

Tony Soprano might have other ideas, but three ways to terminate a project are standard in the project management biz: inclusion, integration, or extinction. Choose the right method for your project, or you'll have lots of unhappy campers with nowhere to pitch a tent:

- **Inclusion** is a happy ending of sorts. Your project proved successful, and upon nearing completion, was absorbed into the organization. Again, it may become a part of the company or be run as a separate organization. In the happiest scenario, many of the original team members keep their jobs and continue to contribute. However, it may be that all staff members are replaced because they are deemed unsuitable for the post-completion phase of the project. Some team members may choose to leave anyway because, while they found the project phase exciting, the thought of running day-to-day operations makes them yawn. You may find yourself the head of a hot new company or updating your resumé and looking for another project.
- **Integration** is the most common technique for dissolving a project workforce. Team members are reintegrated into the organization from which they were borrowed. On a long project, integration becomes complex because management may have been forced to fill slots held by the team members. Now they must find a new position for each returning team member that is satisfactory to the employee and the headcount. Often new skills acquired by the project member open the door to new job responsibilities.
- **Extinction** of a project and everything and everyone related to it is an all-too-common route to unload personnel. This is obviously the least desirable outcome and one you should avoid if possible. Once a project is closed down, the people are simply let go.

Time Is Money

Leave good documentation for your successors. When you consider almost any project, you'll understand why this is a good idea. Given current job tenure across the nation, it's entirely possible that the people who worked on the project may not work there five years later.

Give It Up!

At the end of a project, especially a major one that has absorbed six or more months of your life (some take decades), ready yourself for a letdown period. It's like post-partum blues. You've spent nine months devoting your energies to a specific project (a baby). You've been so focused on that one goal that, once it is successfully achieved, you feel lost, directionless, and sad. You feel these emotions even though you know what your next project will be (raising the baby). Think how much more difficult it would be to cope if you didn't have the prospect of a new project and had to adjust to your former everyday routine.

Suddenly, you are no longer the head of a project with team members constantly seeking your advice and decisions. Instead, you return to civilian life with your normal job duties and responsibilities. You may have a period of letdown in which the project stays on your mind. You may keep thinking of improved ways to accomplish some tasks, or ideas may come to you that might have better met the project's goals. Your "symptoms" may indeed be real. But if it's your skill and desire, freelance project managers do well and make good incomes depending on their experience and success. This could be you! Be encouraged: there's always another project to manage somewhere.

Here's a simple checklist for project closeout.

Project Close-Out Phase

- ❑ A. Document project lessons learned
- ❑ B. Schedule after-implementation review
- ❑ C. Provide performance feedback
- ❑ D. Close out contracts (as needed)
- ❑ E. Complete administrative closeout
- ❑ F. Deliver project plan memorandum to decision authority

Right now you should have a celebration. Your project is done (except for the final report, which you'll learn how to write in the next chapter. You didn't think you'd get away without another report, did you?). Get your team together. Revel in your accomplishments. Then move on to the next project.

The Least You Need to Know

- Dissolving a project takes time and deliberate effort on your part.
- A key success factor for growing as a project manager is to conduct a "lessons learned" process.
- Closing down a project is a process that follows a predetermined series of steps.
- After a project is finished, team members will be included in the operations component of the project, reintegrated into the organization, or terminated.
- Conduct an after-implementation review as part of closing out a larger project.

Chapter 28

The Final Evaluation: The Short and Long of It

In This Chapter

- Understanding your successes and shortcomings
- Talking back: the final report
- Team member performance appraisals
- Assessing the bottom line

Now that your project is closed out, you may think you're finally done. But there's one more important step—the final project evaluation. The purpose of this step is to appraise your actions: what you did well and what you could have done better. Only through a final project evaluation will you learn how to better manage your next project.

Evaluating Your Project

Through an effective *postmortem*, you can efficiently apply lessons learned from this project to the next one. The final evaluation should happen whether the project achieved its goals or evolved into a dismal failure.

def•i•ni•tion

A **postmortem** for a project means a close examination of all parts of the project to determine its successes and failures.

Small leftover tasks, such as installing the built-in office coffeemaker or screwing in light bulbs, shouldn't delay the final evaluation. Large leftover tasks indicate a project that's incomplete, however, making it too early to analyze results even if the scheduled completion date has come and gone.

The final evaluation has three components: project assessment, a final written report, and team member performance reviews. A final meeting of the core team is often in order as well because this will assist you in evaluating the project and producing input for the report. The team's technical expertise and experiences may provide data you hadn't previously considered.

Meet with Core Team Members

Before you formally evaluate your completed or closed-down project, you need input from your core team. Ask for a brief written report, or provide them with a simple questionnaire to complete. Then schedule an informal meeting with key players and ask their opinions about the project and what they would do better next time. Take notes so you remember comments and confirm that you value their input.

The first question to ask when evaluating a project is whether the desired results were accomplished. Then consider the project life cycle from start to finish in order to understand what worked and what didn't. Look closely at problems and how you and your team coped with them. Picking up the pieces and successfully gluing them back together is an art. Consider when you did this well and when you could have done better.

Compare Goals to Achievements

Project evaluation has no hard-and-fast rules. Essentially, you match your achievements to the project's goals. If what you produce lines up clearly with well-defined goals, chances are you've succeeded. If you have met the goals only partway, your project may be considered a success by some and a failure by others. The toughest evaluation is one in which the goals were fuzzy to begin with. That's why it's so important to clearly define a project's requirements during the planning phase.

To evaluate your project's success (or lack of success), make a list of the project's accomplishments and place it next to the goals page(s). Study each list, checking off goals as you consider your list of accomplishments. This is the best way to evaluate your project.

With the exception of the smallest projects (and sometimes even for those), management will mandate a final report at the close of the project. The final report for a megaproject is more formal and obviously longer than for a small, simple project. As previously mentioned, reports are necessary for both successfully completed projects and those that are canceled. On a successful project, the final report may precipitate bonuses for the team members and their project manager. If the project went belly-up, the report serves to document the problems and to help others avoid the quicksand you and your team slipped into. The report can also document why a project problem wasn't your fault.

Writing the Final Report

The final report is both a history of the project and a final evaluation of performance. While the final report for a small project may be no more than a two-page memo, the report for a large project may be 10 to 20 pages in length. If you kept a project diary (see Chapter 20) and the various logs suggested in this book, producing the final report should be relatively easy.

In the project report for a simple project, cover all the topics included in the final report for a large project, only in less detail. Include these items in the final report:

- An overview of the project (primarily schedule and budget), including revisions to the original project plan
- A summary of the business case for the project
- A summary of major accomplishments
- An analysis of achievements compared to the business case objectives for the project
- Final financial accounting and an explanation of variances from the budget
- An analysis of the quality or work performed on behalf of the project against the expectations of the stakeholders
- An evaluation of administrative and management performance

- The team's performance (keep this section confidential when it applies to specific individuals and their performance)
- Special acknowledgments to team members
- Total number of approved changes and the impact of those changes to the accomplishment of the business case
- Issues or tasks that require further investigation
- Recommendations for future projects of this type
- A scheduled date for the after-implementation review (see Chapter 27)

In addition, the following elements are appropriate to include in the final reports for more complex projects:

- A summary of performance issues, conflicts, and resolutions from the issues log (see Chapter 24), the risk log (see Chapter 8), and the change control log (see Chapter 24)
- The results of each phase of the project, including actual versus forecast dates and the budget versus actual expenses (budget use, additions, and so on require thorough documentation)
- A description of ongoing activities related to transitioning the project to operations that will require further project team member participation (if any)
- Recommendations for changes to future projects so they will run more smoothly and be more compatible with the sponsoring organization
- An in-depth analysis of reporting procedures and recommendations for improvements
- An analysis of the project management process as a whole

In each section of a final report for a project, analyze the procedures used in the project. Acknowledge things that worked. Explain things that didn't work. Make recommendations for improvements in future implementations of the project methodology, and include clear examples and rationales for the changes. All core team members should either contribute to the report or review its contents for accuracy before it is finalized. You can have others write and submit their relevant portions of the final report and then, after editing, add your own comments as an overview to cement the document.

Packaging Options for the Report

Everyone involved in the project from your management to the project stakeholders should review your final report. You may want to break it into five sections, as outlined here:

- **The executive summary.** This one- to two-page document summarizes the report's content for people who need a quick briefing and don't have time or are unable to digest the entire document.
- **The report, part A.** This section contains information that can be disseminated to all team members, managers, and other interested parties. It includes a detailed review of the project and an assessment of the project's success in meeting the business case for the project.
- **The report, part B.** This section includes information for management only or that may be confidential in nature. Confidential reports are the most difficult to manage. They contain information not appropriate for team members' eyes, such as salaries, team-member performance, and recommendations for using the results of the project. It can also include the financial reports for the project or even highly confidential government and military material that your own boss isn't authorized to read.
- **The project plan.** Include the project's overall plan along with copies of the goal information. If they fit and make you look good, include the original baseline plan and the final plan so that readers can see how you met the scheduled dates.
- **Miscellaneous components.** If tangible proof of a project's success is possible, such as the opening of a new store or the discovery of life on another planet, include photos in this section, referenced from report parts A and B.

Risk Management

Keep all financial documents very secure. In CIA terms, a portion of a report may be "for your eyes only" while the rest is available for distribution. If you find yourself in the awkward situation of not knowing what to release and how to keep it secure, get advice from someone who is already privy to the report's contents.

The Political Impact of Final Reports

In a politically sensitive organization, a negative report can cause problems. Before you state emphatically that a particular vice president was the major roadblock to successfully completing the project, you had better be in line for another job or an unemployment check.

As was strongly (if wrongly) suspected of the Warren report on the slaying of President Kennedy, for political reasons there were two versions of the report: one for the public and another for high-level government officials and operatives. You may consider this tactic for presenting information to your management. However, as many people have learned the hard way, written communications have a way of circulating beyond the intended audience. You may want to provide a verbal report on the difficult VP to your sponsor, but we would discourage you from writing two distinct reports.

> **Words from the Wise**
>
> Honest criticism is hard to take, particularly from a relative, a friend, an acquaintance, or a stranger.
>
> —Franklin P. Jones, American author and humorist

Who Accomplished What and How Well?

Since your project involved people, you'll likely be called upon to evaluate the performance of each team member. This may be limited to core team members or may apply to all team members and even outside vendors, consultants, and suppliers. The evaluations can be used for anything ranging from promotions to new assignments to layoffs. In a project in which a team member's contribution is made before the project terminates, hold a review when the team member departs rather than waiting for project closure. Why? Because on any really large project, the time between an individual rolling off the project and the actual time for the review may be a considerable amount of time. It may be hard to remember exactly what points you want to emphasize if too much time has passed.

Many companies have standard evaluation procedures that must be followed, and the human resources department will also insert itself into the evaluation process. Chances are, HR will provide standard evaluation forms for both you and the employee to fill out. In a matrixed project organization (see Chapter 19), other managers who work with the team member may contribute to the written evaluations as well.

The basic criteria for appraising team member performance include the following:

- Quality of work
- Cost consciousness
- Timeliness
- Creativity
- Administrative performance
- Ability to work as part of a team
- Attitude
- Communication skills
- Technical ability
- Recommendations for improvement
- Consistency in meeting deadlines

When giving a performance review in person, try for a relaxed atmosphere away from other team members. For stellar performers, this is a good time to hand out any bonus checks (if appropriate), with the agreement that the team member will keep it quiet so as not to make other members unhappy.

The Bottom Line and You

In addition to the formal review of a project, every project manager needs to do some personal soul-searching to understand why a particular project went well or why it went poorly. After the project has been completed for a while and the emotion is gone, stand back and look at the project and your own management skills as objectively and dispassionately as possible. What did you do well? What could you have done better? What do you still need to learn? These observations, if acted on and taken seriously, will help you prosper, develop, and improve as a project manager. A good time to complete this exercise is following the after-implementation review discussed in Chapter 27.

At this point, we have exposed you to the complete process of project management. You have learned how to complete project management calculations and develop diagrams, reports, and communications that will help you plan, monitor, and control your project to a successful conclusion. Congratulations! And good luck in your role as project manager!

But wait—don't forget about the last section of this book. There you'll learn how entire organizations are realigning their operations to improve project productivity, and you'll discover the wealth of new software tools available to help you in your project management ventures.

The Least You Need to Know

- After a project ends, take stock of what went right and what went wrong.
- On most projects, management requires a final report to inform all participants and stakeholders of the project's results.
- Review performance formally or informally (depending on the organization) when team members depart the project or when the project is completed.
- Always evaluate the success of the project by comparing it to the business case.

Part 7

The Organization and Tools to Make Project Management Prosper

In this part, you'll learn the requirements for instilling the discipline of project management to project work throughout your organization. We'll start by looking at ways a company can use the lessons learned in the project management discipline (that you captured at the close-out) at the organizational level. In the final chapter, you'll learn how an empowered project-oriented organization can benefit from using project management software to help implement the planning, control, administration, and communication aspects of project management with less effort and more consistency. And you'll discover how new Internet-enabled collaboration tools can assist in facilitating interactions and work among team members, even when they are separated by international borders.

Chapter 29

The Project-Enabled Organization

In This Chapter

- Focusing your business culture on project success
- Adapting your organization to focus on projects
- Establishing a portfolio management strategy
- Creating the "project office" for supporting projects
- It's all about leadership

Project management offers many opportunities for creating consistency in meeting business goals that can be applied to entire organizations. Organizations will often think of project management for a large Information Technology deployment or for the building of a new facility, but they rarely think of its use beyond those areas. However, as mentioned in Chapter 1, project management techniques can be just as useful in implementing a new strategy or rolling out a new product.

In addition, firms that have adopted *Six Sigma* as their quality approach now view project management as one of the necessary components for achieving dependable, quality results. They have discovered that the consistent, defined processes of project management are a foundation for improving not only quality but also productivity and profitability as well.

So now let's look at some of the steps an organization can take to move from ad-hoc project control to becoming an efficient, projectized organization.

Understanding the Benefits of Formalizing Project Management

In Part 1, we specified several general factors that contribute to the success of projects and project managers alike. Consider how these factors apply to the work in your organization:

- Agreement among the stakeholders on the business goals of the project and the measures of success
- Support by the senior management of the organization for the project priorities and resources required
- Effective, consistent, quality communication between the project team and the stakeholders involved in the project
- A project plan that describes a clear path and unambiguous responsibilities that can be used as a baseline for measuring progress as the project proceeds through time
- A clearly defined scope that is both controlled and understood by project stakeholders

def•i•ni•tion

Six Sigma is a disciplined, data-driven approach and methodology for eliminating defects (driving toward six standard deviations between the mean and the nearest specification limit) in any process—from manufacturing to transactional and from product to service.

—From www.isixsigma.com

Is Your Organization Ready to Be Projectized?

If projects are becoming a larger and more important aspect of the work in your organization, project management offers potential for increased quality and efficiency. To determine the degree to which your organization can benefit from consistent employment of the project management discipline, ask yourself some tough questions about your current organization:

- What's your organizational style now and should you change it to better match your priorities? The organizational models presented in Chapter 19 (functional, pure-project, matrix, and mixed) can include a wide range of organizational styles.
- Has your company favored one project and overlooked others? Every company has projects and ongoing operations. In most cases, favoring one comes at the expense of the other.
- How much of the budget is spent on projects now? If you spend the majority of your cash (or earn most of your money) on projects, then a project-oriented structure makes sense.
- Do your projects include multiple functions such as IT personnel, accounting staff, engineers, and marketing experts? Do you have to borrow these resources from the functional departments? If so, the time and cost of communicating and coordinating with these functional areas (if you work in a functional organization) is increased. The more frequently you need to depend on the functional areas for support, the more a project-oriented style will improve efficiency.
- How large are the projects in your organization? The larger the projects, the more sense it makes to organize around them. Measure size in terms of duration (projects lasting a year or more are considered large), level of resource utilization (if most of the team members are employed by the project on a full-time basis, then it's a major project), the size of the project team (any project with more than 50 team members is a large project), and the size of the budget in proportion to your organization's total budget. Obviously, when a project consumes a large portion of an organization's budget, it demands more focus. (In all these examples, an "organization" could be a department, a division, or an entire company. Project size is always relative to the size of the organization you're considering becoming *projectized*.)

> **def•i•ni•tion**
>
> **Projectized** is the word used by the Project Management Institute (PMI) to describe an organization in which most of the resources are focused on project work.

- How similar are the projects in your organization? Projects are always unique, as you've learned already, but in some firms, a great deal of similarity exists among projects. The more similarities there are, the greater the opportunity to manage projects as ongoing operations. For example, Mike had a client that drilled wells regularly (about 30 to 40 per year). While they referred to these activities as "projects," they were really part of their ongoing operations. And the company was really good at it! The more projects produce unrelated or dissimilar results, the more the project-oriented structure makes sense.

- How complex is the work, and how important is knowledge transfer from one project to another? This is an especially important question in engineering-oriented organizations. The complexity and size of major engineering endeavors often favor projectized organizations. However, in functional organizations, people organize their careers and expand their expertise within that function; the knowledge is maintained within the company. In a project-oriented structure, knowledge transfer from one project to the next requires conscious effort. If this isn't done (and it often isn't), technical innovations or special skills may be lost when the project is over. Thus the benefits of a projectized organization can result in losing valuable institutional knowledge unless a structure and process is designed within the larger organization to prevent this from happening.

As you consider your own project experiences and forthcoming endeavors, remember these factors and determine whether your own organization should become more or less project-oriented. The size and complexity of modern corporations defy a definitive recommendation for an organizational style. Any organizational format has strengths and weaknesses. The key is to adapt the organization of projects at the right level and in the right way for the organization in question.

Define the Organizational Boundaries First

The first decision in projectization is defining the organizational boundaries for the change. Should projectization occur at the project, department, division, or corporate level? In your analysis of organizational change, use the risk management techniques you learned in this book. Ask yourself how much risk there would be of losing the information gained from one program to the next if each were being managed as an independent project organization? What is the risk of losing quality and productivity if you don't organize in a project-oriented manner?

These three examples of projectized organizations demonstrate how different organizations can incorporate the project-oriented approach at different levels.

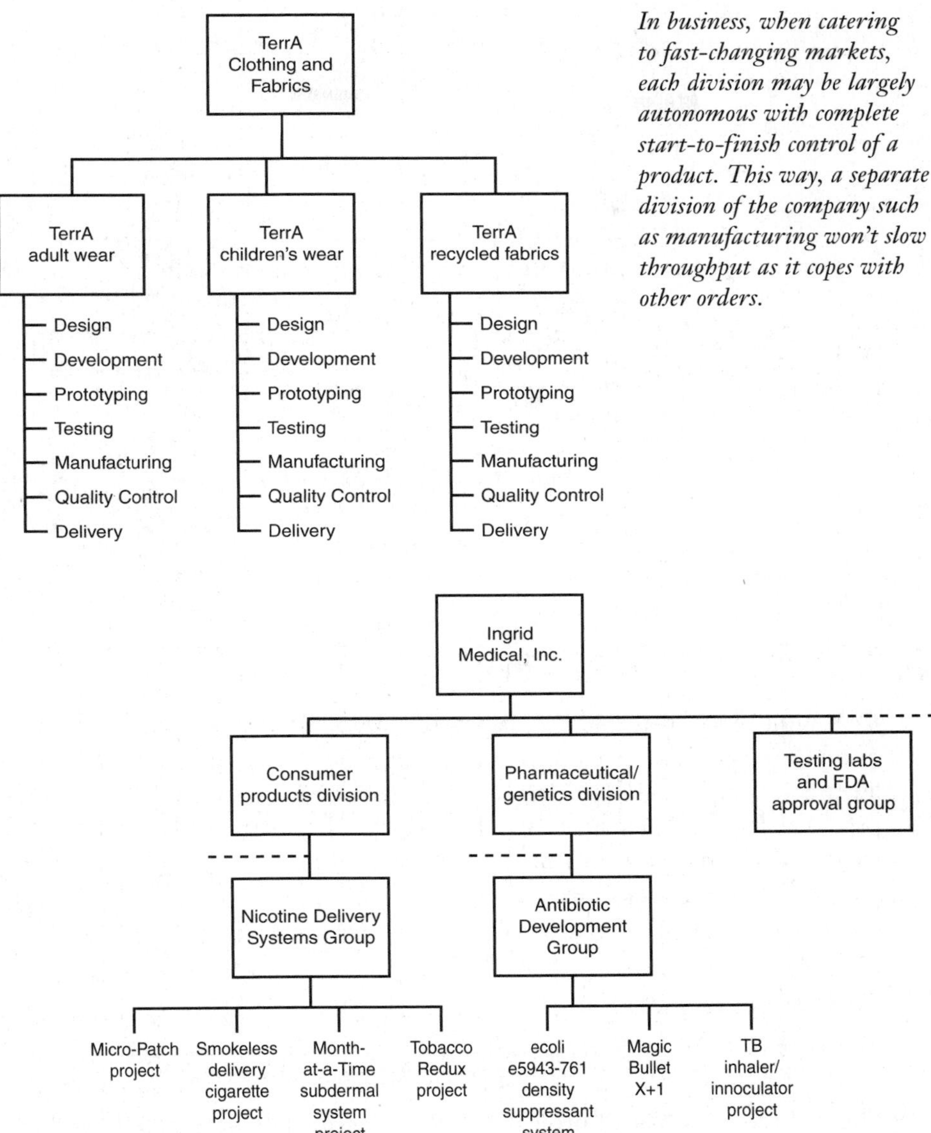

In business, when catering to fast-changing markets, each division may be largely autonomous with complete start-to-finish control of a product. This way, a separate division of the company such as manufacturing won't slow throughput as it copes with other orders.

Not all organizations can use the "top-down" project development management scheme. There may be too much expense to completely duplicate all functions. Instead, one or more elements—here, the testing and FDA components—are shared. This reduces expenses but also creates a potential bottleneck for all parties if not properly implemented.

Many manufacturing and software-development houses run development on one side and operations on the other. The key to this kind of project is communication, often a thankless task handled by the most senior person (where the "org" chart trees grow together). This system has the necessary economies of scale to both market and deliver existing products while developing new ones.

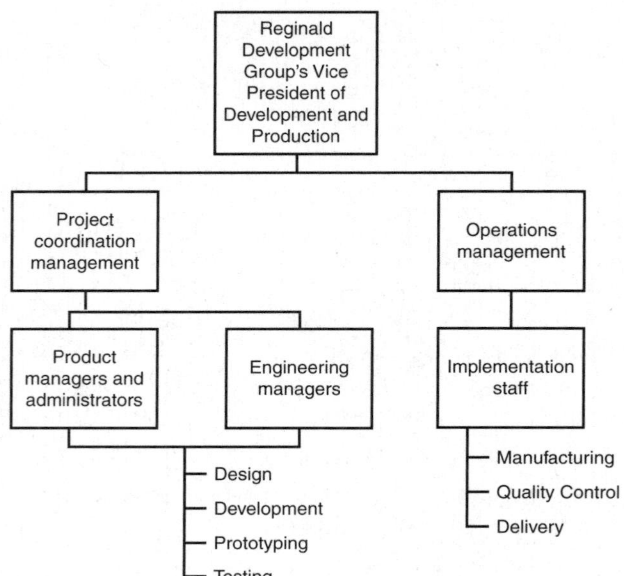

Now Come the Standards

Once you've decided that the projectization of all or part of your organization is a good idea, work on developing consistent procedures for implementing project management. This book can help you do that, but be forewarned. You can't buy *standard* practices for your organization in an off-the-shelf format; you need to adapt the standards to your own projects and organizational preferences. And don't be surprised if your project "standards" are interpreted as "bureaucracy" by others (remember Chapter 23 on preparing operations).

def•i•ni•tion

Standards often begin as guidelines that describe a preferred approach. As these standards enjoy widespread adoption, they become *de facto* regulations. Regulations, on the other hand, are rules for which compliance is mandated. It's important in discussing requirements for projects to differentiate between standards (which enjoy some flexibility in implementation) and regulations (which are dictated and absolute).

As you develop the procedures for your own organization, consider these procedures and support tools:

- **Common project authority levels and responsibilities for the project manager and other key players.** Who will have the authority to approve a project or cancel it? Who will assign people (or remove them) from a project? To whom does the project manager report? What responsibilities do the functional managers have, if any? What exactly is the sponsor's, working committee's, and steering committee's role and responsibility to the project? Who will have the ultimate authority to approve major changes to the project scope? Don't be vague in these definitions. Don't leave authorities and responsibilities subject to interpretations.
- **Support staff for projects.** Will you have a formal project office (discussed a little later in this chapter) to assist with administrative duties and coordination? Or will you have a full-time staff for each project? Maybe you'll borrow staff time from the functional areas. Whatever is appropriate, clearly document it in your standards.
- **Standard formats and criteria for project deliverables.** This will often consist of templates for the statement of work, work plans, project plans, status reports, and other deliverables; multiple sets of templates might be required for projects of different sizes. For example, the standards for complex projects in multiple locations with multiple customers and the employment of outside resources would require more standardization than small, internal projects.

Where Do Standards Come From?

Reading a number of books, including this one, can furnish ideas for project standardization. The best sources for standards, however, are the project histories from your own organization and those from expert project managers who you may call upon to help you as you projectize your organization.

People who have been project managers in your organization in the past can help you define the success factors and problem areas in past projects. That's why the documentation in the close-out phase of the project is so important: it provides key information for improving processes in the future. By addressing both success factors and problem areas in your standards, you'll be able to emphasize the processes that will lead to triumph within the culture of your company.

Establish a Life Cycle Standard

Remember the discussion of project life cycles in Chapter 4? All efforts at improving project management start with the definition of a consistent life cycle. This life cycle definition can help you define consistent project management practices for each phase in a project. However, you might need two or three different life cycle definitions for different types of projects in your organization.

In the four phases life cycle discussed in Chapter 4 (definition, planning, execution, and close-out phases), each phase emphasizes a certain type of activity, and each phase requires approval from the key stakeholders to move on to the next phase (often called the stage gate).

You can also have a life cycle with as few as three phases, defined as initiate, implement, and close-out. A single approval and the initiate phase might be appropriate for a small project that must be done quickly.

Then again, you might want a life cycle with five, six, or even seven phases that require more approvals at each life cycle phase to help reduce risk in a complex project or to add time to hire project staff.

The following diagram of different types of life cycles used in different industries gives you an idea of the type of life cycle that might make sense for your projects.

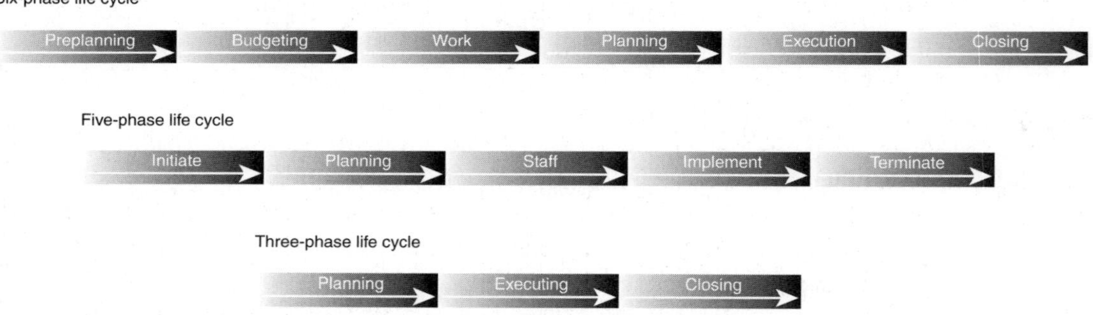

Three life cycle possibilities with common project deliverables by phase.

Make your life cycle more than just words on paper. Include a clear definition of deliverables, stakeholder roles, and approvals required at each phase. In your life cycle definitions, create a document that answers questions like these:

- What must you achieve to move to the next level?
- Who will approve your movement into the next phase?
- What criteria will the stakeholders use to make this approval?

You may want to bring in outside resources with the experience and expertise to assist in building a project life cycle tailored to your organization.

Manage Projects Like an Asset for Your Future

A major institutional step in developing a consistent project management framework is to begin managing projects as a portfolio, just as you'd manage a portfolio of assets. This means you'll need to develop a systematic approach for choosing, monitoring, and canceling projects. Projects, like assets that are underperforming, are eliminated, while projects that are performing well deserve additional investment. To do this, accurate information, consistently formatted, is required from every project.

Managing your projects as a portfolio also requires clear authority for the steering committee or governing board who have been granted authority to manage the portfolio (which includes initiating, reviewing, canceling, and continuing projects).

Furthermore, project portfolio management requires clear operational and strategic goals for evaluating projects and a disciplined process that requires regular review of projects and clear guidelines for proposing, reviewing, and approving them.

Risk Management

Don't weigh your projects down with excessive amounts of bureaucracy. Guidelines appropriate for a project to build All-Star Cable's Movies-on-Demand would be inappropriate for a project to develop a training program for the sales force. Standards are important, but make them flexible enough to accommodate the differences in projects of varying size and complexity.

Portfolio management also depends on the use of a quality project reporting system or enterprise resource management system. (You'll learn more about project management software for this purpose in the next chapter.) In defining the right type of information systems to support the portfolio management process, you'll need to ask questions like these:

- What information do we need?
- Who needs the information and for what purpose?
- Where do we get the information?
- How often do we need the information?
- Does the information exist already or do we need to create it?
- How can we make the information consistent so we are comparing "apples to apples"?

Without a portfolio management system in place, these simple questions are almost impossible to answer.

Putting a Project Office in Place to Support the System

Without visible and ongoing support for project management, standards and policies will likely degrade and return to their previous, unproductive state. One common way to prevent this from happening is to employ a group for continuous development and support of the standards, practices, and information systems that define project management. This group is often known as the project office, but may also be called the project management office (PMO), the project center of excellence, the business program office, or the project support office. In general, the project office is responsible for various levels of planning, budgeting, scheduling, and hiring assistance. The objective is to help people put good project management practices in place.

The project office can be assigned various levels of authority for a project, from basic guidance to complete authority. In some cases, project offices are temporary; they exist only during the development of a long program. In other cases, project offices are at the top of the authority structure and oversee all the functional or cross-functional projects in an organization.

The responsibilities of the project office (regardless of its name) will vary based on the degree to which the organizational structure favors projects and embraces project management processes. Some of the responsibilities that a project office can assume are:

- Maintaining project management standards
- Providing training on project management
- Consulting on technical and procedural issues
- Scheduling assistance
- Creating and tracking budgets
- Providing staff, including project managers, for the organization
- Providing enterprise-level project information
- Supervising project managers
- Procuring resources (people or equipment)

Words from the Wise

There are two things to be considered with regard to any scheme. In the first place, "Is it good in itself?" In the second, "Can it be easily put into practice?"

—Jean Jacques Rousseau, French political philosopher and writer

- Participating in project portfolio management
- Making project management decisions

The most successful project offices will provide expertise in the discipline of project management and enthusiasm for its value in getting things done on time, with the right quality and within the budget. The simple presence of a project office in any form helps breathe life into the organization's commitment to project management principles.

In the End, It's Leadership That Makes It Work

To organize project management, it's critical that you understand the nature of your organization's projects. It's even more important, however, that management supports the changes required to reap the benefits for the long haul.

Joining the Project Management Institute (PMI) can be a great way to start. If there is a local chapter in your area, attend monthly chapter meetings to learn more about PMI and chat with other project managers. Also a professional certification from PMI, called the Project Management Professional (PMP), signifies both knowledge and experience in project management. Some organizations are requiring senior project managers to have the PMP certification as part of the requirements for attaining that title.

In the United Kingdom, the professional group that supports project management is PRINCE2. They also have a professional designation called Practioner that signifies a level of knowledge in project management methodology and terminology.

No matter what you do, change won't happen overnight. There are few higher-risk projects in business than consciously attempting to change the cultural and operational practices of an organization. It will take both discipline and commitment. If you make the standards optional, that's exactly what you'll get: optional project management and optional results. But if you provide authority and funding to the endeavor, you'll win cynical employees over to your side.

Time Is Money

Red Zone Management by Dutch Holland (Dearborn Trade Publishing, 2001) has an excellent chapter on making organizational culture changes.

People will take project management standards seriously if the authority of the project managers and the project office is taken seriously. This means the organization must grant enough authority to the project managers to be taken seriously. While this might sound obvious, it's not easy. Project managers must have a career path that's well-defined and well-rewarded. Nothing speaks louder about management commitment than what's rewarded.

Even enthusiastic supporters of the organizational changes may be bogged down as things proceed. Learning a new process can be tedious, especially when ordinary work must get done in the process. To eliminate this frustration, break the projectization process into phases—just like any other project—so the work is doable. Also supply people with appropriate training and support.

Changing the organization to embrace project management can entail significant risk if people aren't convinced of the need to use the processes. Thus, your critical task in this endeavor is to win those people to your side through leadership, training, and persistent communication. (Sounds a lot like project management work, doesn't it?)

The Least You Need to Know

- Reorganizing for project management requires planning, management support, assigned authorities, training, and time for implementation.
- Projectized organizations employ consistent standards to help guide their projects to success.
- The structure of a project-oriented organization will vary based on the products produced, the size and frequency of the projects, and the culture of the organization.
- The forms and names for project offices may be different, but the support functions, in terms of planning, budgeting, and staffing assistance, are similar.
- The authority level of the project office will vary depending on the degree of projectization of the organization.
- Without management support for the processes, a projectized organization is doomed to return to older, less efficient ways of getting things done.

Chapter 30

Software for All Projects Great and Small

In This Chapter

- The things software can do to help your project
- Elements to consider when buying software packages
- Virtual project management
- The types of project management software
- Choosing the right software for your projects
- Limitations of software

Creating a detailed project plan and keeping it up-to-date for most nontrivial projects can be a very time-consuming process if done manually. The complexity of figuring in vacations, holidays, weekends, early-starts, and other factors can be overwhelming to someone inexperienced in project management techniques. The details involved in producing networks and work breakdown structures seem daunting, and assembling a budget can be tedious. Just producing the plan is a lot of work for a project. And, as you've hopefully concluded by now, project management entails more than just creating a good plan. Producing the reports, updating the charts, and incorporating changes to a project plan along the way add complexity and more paperwork. Of course, if you need to manage multiple projects at the same time, the calculations, graphs, and reports can seem impossible.

Just like any job you do, having the right tools can make it easier. That's what project management software really is—a tool for the project manager to use. This chapter covers the basics of selecting and using computerized project management programs so you won't give up on project management before you get started.

Software That Simplifies the Details

All the graphing, changing, and reporting in project management can drive you crazy. Some naïve managers simply reject project management methods because of the reports involved. Instead, they choose to manage projects with intuition and keep the details in their heads. The benefits of project management methods are too important to ignore just because the charts and graphs take time to produce. And there are just too many details to keep track of in your head. There is a better way.

> **Time Is Money**
>
> With the right project management program and information system, you can concentrate on the management of the project, leaving you more time for thinking and planning. Let the computer provide tactical support in the form of charts, graphs, schedules, resource allocations, and virtual communication capabilities.

Today, thanks to computers and the Internet, solutions are available that enable everyone to benefit from using project management methods. Anyone can master easy-to-use project management programs, such as Microsoft Project, in a few hours. Also, highly sophisticated systems can integrate projects across the organization and can help teams collaborate on their efforts from all over the world.

What Can Project Management Programs Do?

Project management programs range in capabilities from simple scheduling programs that produce Gantt charts to prodigious software applications for engineering and aerospace projects that are integrated with the corporation's budgeting, marketing, manufacturing, personnel, and other management information systems, such as Enterprises Resource Planning (ERP) systems.

The underlying methods supported by most project management programs are similar to those presented in this book. Depending on the capabilities of the program, you enter task sequences, resources, dates, and costs, and the program calculates or modifies the schedules, budget, or resource utilization for you. Most programs even draw the networks or can convert one network format into another. Most of the time, you'll enter your project data into a form that looks like a spreadsheet with columns and rows; this allows you to define WBS levels and to describe tasks, precedence, resource requirements, and almost anything else that's relevant, including resource calendars, labor costs, and overhead allocations.

In addition to helping you calculate schedules and costs, project management programs produce a wide variety of reports, from simple to comprehensive. If you have a special project management requirement, such as a custom report or chart, there is probably a program out there with the capability to produce the output you need.

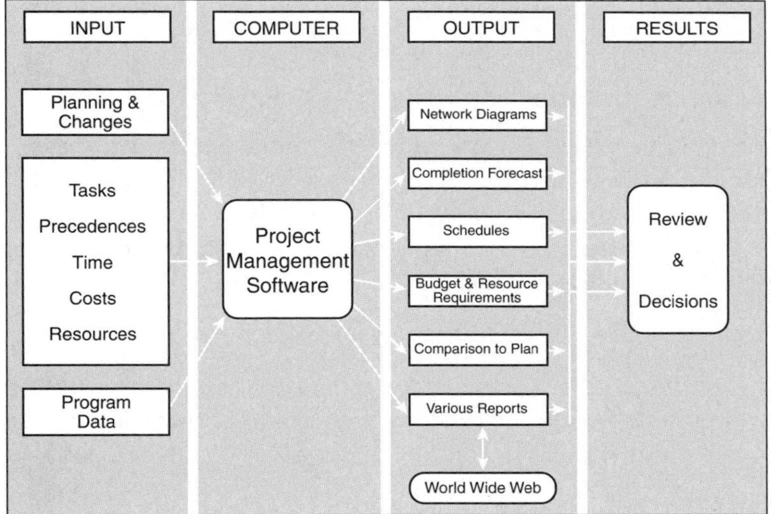

Here's how project management software works. You enter various information on the left and the software organizes it and allows you to see various information and reports. The final step on the right is to review the information and reports to make decisions.

Even though the most sophisticated software package is a substitute for competent leadership and skilled decision-making and, by itself, can't correct any task-related problems or human-centered conflicts, project management software can, however, be a terrific boon to the project manager tracking interrelated variables, schedules, resources, costs, and tasks that come into play. Software development companies are continually improving project management tools that can enhance communication among team members and can facilitate collaborative problem solving. Although not all programs do everything, most of them can help you do some or all of the following:

- Graph costs, schedules, and resource utilization using Gantt charts, histograms, line diagrams, and a variety of other charts.
- Create standard and custom reports, including standard accounting and tracking. Some programs will even produce special report formats required by government agencies such as the Department of Defense.
- Maintain resource and project calendars that record the availability of staff and equipment. These internal program calendars are used to create optimum schedules. This feature allows the project manager to establish workweeks based on actual workdays and to specify non-work periods such as weekends, holidays, and vacations. The project calendar can be printed out in detail or in a summary format.
- Make schedule changes based on a variety of resource-leveling parameters (for example, no overtime!) and priority scheduling attributes.
- Maintain skills inventories that match resources to task requirements.
- Track and schedule multiple projects at the same time. Some packages feature a single, comprehensive database that enables cross-project analysis and reporting (the project office would want that ability). Cost and schedule modules share common data files that allow integration among projects and minimize problems of schedule inconsistencies and redundancies.
- Allow multiple people to access, input, and report on project data at the same time.
- Collapse the view of projects by work breakdown structure or organization structure, subproject, or milestone.
- Calculate and display the critical path for a network.
- Display alternative schedules, task assignments, and cost criteria so you can evaluate the immediate impact of schedule, sequence, and resource changes.
- Assign early-warning parameters that let the program inform you of potential trouble including schedule problems, resource conflicts with other projects, and cost overruns.
- Integrate with material management, purchasing, and accounting systems to assist in ordering materials, supplies, equipment, and contractor services.
- Produce presentation-quality graphics for making reports to management and customers about the plans and status of a project.

- Display actual and planned data simultaneously.
- Summarize data in a variety of ways, including expenditures, timing, and activity data.
- Complete cost analyses, cost accounting, and variance analyses.
- Create free-format reports with an integrated word processor or other report generator for incorporating personalized project annotations.
- Display relevant information on the web or corporate intranet so that project team members can view the status and schedule of the project and their own assigned tasks.
- Communicate and collaborate with the project team across dispersed project locations.

The Virtual World of the Project Needs Virtual Tools

A virtual project is a collaborative effort toward a specific goal or accomplishment based on "collective yet remote" performance. Some experts have called this "working together, apart." This increasingly common mode of work needs information management tools that enable communication and coordination at a distance.

Today's "teams" often have team members scattered across various cities, states, or even continents. The solution is to follow project resources virtually rather than physically; you need not leave your office to do it.

Virtual project management (VPM) is possible because of the rise to dominance within organizations of Internet-based collaboration tools that offer many possibilities for group-based and web-based project management. Virtual project management requires several layers of information system support:

- **Multimedia communication** incorporates e-mail, text messaging, instant messenger, phone calls, memoranda (hopefully as e-mail attachments but possibly as paper), and other media.
- **Collaboration** goes beyond basic messaging to sharing information, often done using the collaboration capabilities of Internet tools like Webcast and Netmeeting.
- **Tracking and leveling of resources** are functions performed by traditional project management products that must be shared across spatial boundaries and time zones in virtual project management systems.

- **Access to project-related information systems** by allowing project team members access to shared drive folders and data is advantageous. For complex projects, this project information may reside in specialized repositories, such as CAD programs, CASE tools, simulation software, and data warehouses, in addition to the information contained in project management software.

Regulation or self-imposed standards require some organizations to use a specific methodology (such as the Capability Maturity Model, or CMM) for software development to maintain complete configuration control over project deliverables. The new virtual tools should also help with maintaining this ongoing documentation.

The Power of Networking

Drug manufacturers and bridge builders weren't exactly on hold until the advent of distributed computing. Pencil and paper and human ingenuity have handled all the activities mentioned so far for years. How do electronic information systems change this? How do web-based applications in particular add value? The answer lies in the power of networking and the Internet.

Because of networking, e-mail allows ideas to flow asynchronously (that is, without parties online at the same time), enabling work to flow across time zones. E-mail doesn't require incremental labor and provides a searchable audit trail, which is key to many formal project processes.

Networking also enables remote collaboration. With modern client/server technology, it is possible to work in collaboration with people all over the globe on a project. However, to be effective, you will need to have shared drives that all project members can access and set up a protocol for controlling the editing of various documents. A growing number of client/server collaboration products are coming to market that allow multiple contributors to share and add content to project information. Some of these products allow project members to collaborate directly from a web-based browser.

Increasingly, companies are using web-based portals to allow project teams access to integrated environments that bridge project domains and applications. The goal of integrated process management through a suite of cooperating tools is becoming the standard in large-scale project management.

So What's in It for Me?

One of the most powerful benefits of using software to assist in the implementation of project management methodology is the "what-if" analysis capabilities facilitated by interactive software products. Even the products that aren't web-enabled allow you to do this. Changes can be made to the time estimates of individual tasks, and a new schedule is immediately displayed for review. The sequence in tasks can be changed and then put back the way it was almost instantaneously. The same thing can be done with costs and resources. Imagine trying to do that with a pencil and eraser. It would take hours. With a computer, it takes seconds!

To facilitate what-if analyses, many programs establish a separate, duplicate project database, often called a "sandbox" or test environment, before changes are entered. The software then performs a comparative analysis and displays the new against the old project plan in tabular or graphical form. This makes it fast and easy for managers to review the impact of changes and come to better, more-informed conclusions.

Simple vs. Complex Projects and the Software They Need

If you manage your projects by using manual techniques, you will probably limit yourself to Gantt charts and simple precedence or PERT networks. Early project management programs were also limited to these simple displays because they used "character-based" graphics. The imprecise resolution of character-based project management graphics makes it hard to build projects and more difficult to view results.

For a project management software program to be considered for general business use today, it must facilitate interactive changes and support high-quality graphics. And, by modern standards, it must have the ability to use collaborative capabilities provided by networks and the Internet.

Traditionally, project-driven organizations preferred client/server software. Organizations that were less project-driven looked for less expensive, personal-computer software either networked or not, depending on the size and consistency desired in project management procedures.

The Types of Project Management Programs

For purposes of easy classification, we can divide project management software products into three categories based on the functions and features they provide. These include single-project programs, corporate-level programs, and mega-project programs. Let's take a closer look at each of these.

Single-Project Programs

Full-featured software packages designed for managing single projects are a step up in sophistication from scheduling programs. These products are still relatively simple and easy to use, and their output is easy to understand. Most of them provide the ability to produce Gantt charts in a variety of formats, network diagrams (either PERT or precedence), and a number of standard reports. These programs sometimes offer simple resource management and cost control capabilities.

Single-project programs are best for projects with fewer than 200 tasks because they provide only a limited analysis of the data. And since programs at this level often fail to provide automatic rescheduling based on specific resource changes, they are not useful for projects that require extensive staffing changes and what-if analyses. Programs in this category cost as little as $200 and are almost always less than $500. You can receive big discounts for larger purchases these days since software vendors are often in financial straits.

Corporate-Level Programs

There are many programs in this category. These corporate-level programs extend the features already discussed for single-project software, and many run on personal computers. Others run on servers, and their manufacturers often provide a personal-computer version for smaller projects. These programs typically allow sophisticated cost accounting, resource leveling, charting, and what-if analyses. Most provide some sort of web-based reporting. The specific features vary considerably, as do their ease-of-use, flexibility, and reporting capabilities.

If you intend to regularly manage projects with 100 or more tasks or if you coordinate programs that include multiple projects, look at software in this category. Some corporate-level programs offer a beginner's and an expert's mode that allow you to start out simple and add functions and capabilities as your project management skills develop.

Corporate-level programs begin at $1,000 for each licensed user. Network, multiuser, or minicomputer versions, when available, can be considerably more expensive. The most sophisticated programs in this category may offer add-on modules for contract control or specialized reporting functions that rival the capabilities of the mega-project programs.

Mega-Project Programs

Mega-project programs, which may or may not have more features than the most sophisticated desktop computer programs, are typically web-based or designed for use on servers. Mega-project programs can handle thousands of tasks and hundreds of resources. They almost always have sophisticated cost-accounting modules and resource-leveling functions. Although they are sometimes difficult to use and can certainly be difficult to install, they offer advantages in processing speed and information exchange, including advanced collaboration capabilities. Most important, their success depends on a commitment from management to standardize the program and use it consistently across projects.

Mega-project packages (with sophisticated accounting and cost-analysis modules) are priced from $50,000 to $150,000; and that doesn't count the equipment, training, and other implementation costs for a complex system. Some of these programs come as modules for different functions so you can buy just the modules you need or add more as you learn to use the first ones.

If your project management requirements include the management of thousands of tasks or complex multiple projects with shared resources, adherence to government contract specifications, and integration with corporate accounting and information systems, then one of these mega-programs may be necessary.

How Do You Choose?

After you determine the category of software you need for your project management efforts, carefully consider several critical factors for evaluating software before you make a purchase decision. Complete the software requirements checklist shown a little later in this chapter and then consider the factors in the following sections.

As you research which software package to buy, there are several key considerations. We'll work through some of them, but ultimately you will need to decide which package best fits your needs.

Pricing

Obviously, pricing is a key consideration. There is not any direct relation between price and performance in most project management programs. You will find products from well-known software developers and others that sell directly to the consumer (you) from their websites. The main consideration for price is getting the features you require at a price your project (or company) can afford. Don't be fooled by slick advertising or list prices. Most vendors will negotiate prices for a well-known customer or one they believe will be a long-term customer.

Total Number of Activities and Resources

The question here concerns the number of activities (tasks) the program can handle for both the major project and any subprojects associated with it. Find out what limits the system has. Also, find out if the program is limited by the main memory within the computer you plan to use to track the project. With memory expanding rapidly, this shouldn't be a problem, but you need to ask!

Remember, when we are talking about resources, we are not just talking about people. If you need to track equipment, materials, and so on, you'll need a program that can handle the amount you have in mind. Also, remember the skills matrix we talked about in Chapter 14? Many software programs will allow you to assign that matrix to individuals if you ask!

Direct Cost Assignment and Tracking

When you review a software package, ask how the package assigns direct costs for materials, equipment, and supplies. If you must provide detailed accounting for the project, make sure the package can give you what you need for your reports (such as amortization, fixed payments, or performance bonuses at milestones) and what choices the package offers. Also, you will want the ability to record actual costs incurred as the project progresses for exception reporting.

Resource Scheduling and Leveling

Make sure any package you consider will allow you to see any overloaded (or underutilized) resources so you can correct the situation. Coupled with the ability to move noncritical tasks within the float available will be invaluable to you as you attempt to build your baseline schedule and then change it over the course of project execution.

Flexible Calendar Functions

These functions will be necessary if you are managing a project that has people scattered in locations across various time zones. Global projects, where even the work week may vary, require a combination of features to help you manage the work.

Import and Export Functions

A common practice among project managers is to keep some information on spreadsheets or other documents. If you find yourself in that type of situation, the ability to either import data to the project management software or attach documents to specific tasks or resources will be very useful.

Requirements Checklist for Project Management Software

Scheduling Programs

- ☐ Schedules
- ☐ Gantt Charts
- ☐ Presentation

Single-Project Programs

- ☐ Network Diagrams
- ☐ Simple Resource Tracking
- ☐ Actual versus Planned Reports

Corporate-Level Programs

- ☐ Tracks Multiple Projects
- ☐ Internet/World Wide Web Publishing
- ☐ What-If Analysis
- ☐ Task Splitting
- ☐ Sub-Project Tracking
- ☐ Variance Reports
- ☐ More then 200 Tasks per Project
- ☐ More then 50 Resources per Project
- ☐ Multiple Operating Systems
- ☐ Email/Group/Network Communications
- ☐ Multiple Budget Types
- ☐ Reporting by Resource
- ☐ Reporting by Milestone
- ☐ Multiple Calendars
- ☐ PERT-Least to Most Likely Projections
- ☐ Integration with General Applications
- ☐ Resource Leveling
- ☐ Audit Trails

Mega-Project Programs

- ☐ Integration with Corporate Mainframe Programs
- ☐ Over 2,000 Tasks to Be Coordinated
- ☐ Government Requirements for a specific Program or Report
- ☐ Advanced Cost and resource Accounting

If you check boxes at more than one level, choose a product in the highest category checked.

An example software requirements checklist.

Infrastructure Requirements

Finally, look at whether you will need special infrastructure, such as a dedicated server, to house the program. Is it web-based so users from any location can access it, or must they be tied into the corporate network?

Documentation and Support for the Program

When learning how to use a product, your first point of reference when looking for a solution to a problem is the manual (whether it's online or printed in a book). So check the documentation and help menus carefully before you purchase.

Study the documentation carefully. The information should be well-organized, have a detailed index, and offer plenty of screen shots showing how the product works. A lengthy troubleshooting section doesn't hurt either. Keyboard templates, quick-reference cards, and disk-based sample projects are also useful. Avoid complex products with skimpy manuals at all costs. Also, make sure the company offers training options for the program that are commensurate with the complexity of the software.

Reputation of the Product Manufacturer

If you are purchasing an expensive product that will get considerable day-to-day use, check out the company that designed the product. If the company discontinues the product or closes its doors, you'll be on your own with the software. Look for a stable company with a strong track record of designing useful software and providing regular updates and bug fixes. Once a product becomes incompatible with the current version of your computer's operating system, project plans that could have been revamped for future use become unavailable if the software is not updated.

Word-of-Mouth Experience

Talk to other users of a particular package to get feedback on how well the product performs with real-world projects. Query users who use the package for projects similar in scope to the ones you plan to carry out. If you call references provided by the manufacturer, take anything less than a glowing tribute to mean that the product performs less adequately than expected.

Technical Support

When considering any software product, evaluate the technical support provided by the manufacturer. Find out if it's free or if you must pay an annual fee after 90 days or a per-use fee after a certain number of calls. Do they provide a toll-free number? Must you listen to an automatic telephone system recite a long list of options before connecting you to a technician at your expense? Dial the number and see what happens. Check out the technical support information on the company's website. If you're fortunate enough to have other users to ask for recommendations, query them on the quality of technical support.

So which computerized tool is best for you? The one that meets your feature requirements with the most flexibility, with an acceptable learning curve, from a reliable and supportive vendor, and at a price you can afford. (This is pretty much the standard formula for choosing any software or computer product, not just project management software.)

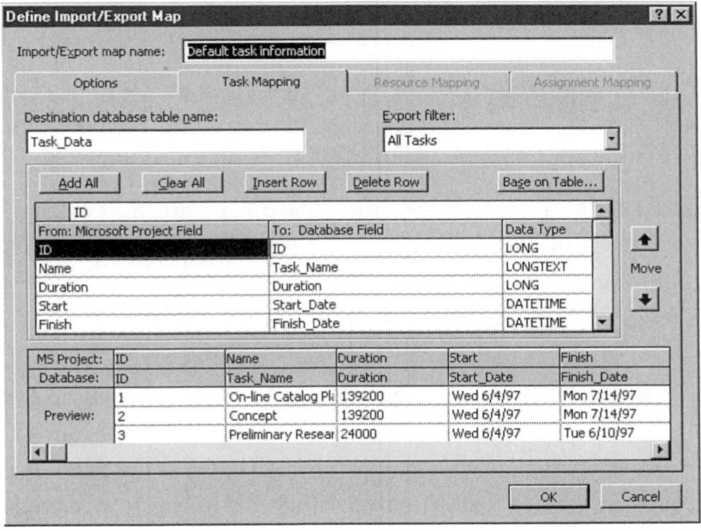

Software makes creating network diagrams and schedules a breeze. You also can easily update precedence and task relationships as the project proceeds. Here you see a project that's sending information to a corporate database.

Things Project Management Software Can't Do

As powerful and efficient as project management programs are, many aspects of the project management process are not within the computer's realm. Using computer-assisted project management streamlines administration, reporting, analysis, and even communication, but the following are things the computer can't and shouldn't be allowed to do:

- **Project management software can't gather data.** You'll have to decide how much and what type of information you need to manage the project. You or members of your team will still need to gather data regarding the project status, as described in Chapter 22. The computer only helps compute and display the information after you gather and enter it.
- **Project management software can't make decisions.** The computer can make it easier and faster to look at alternatives, but ultimately you and your project team will have to make the choice between the alternatives and take responsibility for the decisions.
- **Project management software can't solve problems that require subjective judgments.** Sometimes human intuition is the most important ingredient in project management, especially when dealing with people. People require understanding. Software is programmed and is not intuitive. It only gives back what you put into it. You still have to manage the risks, solve the problems, and use your own judgment.
- **Project management software can't find the errors in your input.** If you put biased, incomplete, or erroneous data into the project management program, it will output biased, incomplete, and erroneous project reports. Don't blame the computer for human error. The best way to eliminate this problem is to check the reports and entries a couple of times before you distribute them.
- **Project management software can't communicate for you.** Software is great at producing reports that look good and contain a wealth of detailed information, but reporting on a project is more than sending out the report. You still need to communicate with people face to face, build interfaces between people and departments, and listen to what is going on around you.
- **Project management software won't save money by reducing the need for project personnel.** Automation almost never really reduces the personnel costs on a project. The software can make you more efficient and make decision-making more effective because the information is better, but project management software will not significantly reduce the need for project management people. In fact, in a large projectized organization, you'll probably need to add a person or two as project analysts just to help keep the computerized project definitions and website up-to-date and the project personnel supported when they have questions.

Go Get Yourself Some!

Now that we have introduced you to the features for selecting project management software to meet your needs, start talking to store personnel, reading computer magazines, and asking friends and colleagues about the programs they use. Then select a program and get started in computer-assisted project management. Follow the step-by-step guidelines for implementing the project management process you have read about. As your projects come in on time and within budget, you will have achieved membership in the league of successful project managers, and the opportunities available to you and your company will take on new perspective. With each success, you will contribute to the business, the economy, and your own career—no mean feat for just learning a few project management skills. Go for it!

The following companies sell or distribute project management software, although this is by no means a comprehensive list. Many other companies and products are out there, and more are added every day. The companies listed here offer products that have been recently reviewed in computer literature. A listing in this book should not be considered a testimonial for the functionality or suitability of any of these products; it is only provided to get you started in your search for project management software.

Company	Project Management Products
AEC Software, Inc. www.aecsoft.com	Fast Track
Artemis Management Systems www.artemissoftware.com	Powerplay, GlobalViews, Artemis
Ballantine & Company, Inc. www.ballantine-inc.com	QuickGantt and QuickAssist
Enact www.enact.cc	Project collaboration tools
Microsoft, Inc. www.microsoft.com	MS Project, Project Professional
Primavera Systems, Inc. www.primavera.com	Primavera Project Planner and others
Project Invision International www.projectinvision.com	Project Invision and Portfolio Management

The Least You Need to Know

- Project management programs exist for projects of all sizes and complexities and run on most common personal computers.
- Project management programs incorporate network-based and web-based communication tools to assist with collaboration, data gathering, and ongoing reporting.
- To get the most benefit from its features, choose your project management software carefully.
- No software program can replace the communication, negotiating, assessment, and other management skills required to manage a project.

Web Resources for Project Managers

The following World Wide Web resources provide general information about project management or offer special training programs for project managers.

Project Management Institute
130 South State Road
Upper Darby, PA 19082
Website: www.pmi.org

The Project Management Institute (PMI) is a not-for-profit organization dedicated to the advancement of project management methodology and the training of project managers. The quarterly *Project Management Journal*, published by PMI, includes timely articles about project management procedures, experiences, and techniques. The institute holds regular seminars and meetings for members. PMI also offers a certification program for people who want to verify and document their project management expertise. As of this writing, the membership fee is $119 per year. A subscription to *Project Management Journal* and *PM Network* is included as part of the membership fee.

PRINCE2
The OGC Service Desk
Rosebury Court
St Andrews Business Park
Norwich, UK
NR7 0HS
Website: www.get-best-practice.co.uk

Since its introduction in 1989, PRINCE2 has been widely adopted in the United Kingdom for project management and the management of change. OGC offers two examinations for the professional certification in PRINCE2.

Project Management International
Website: www.infoser.com/infocons/pmi/

This site provides information on project management activities and standards around the world.

PM—Project Manager: The Industrial Project Management Site
Website: www.project-manager.com/

This site provides links to a wide range of industrial project management resources.

The SMG PM IQnet
Website: phl.smginc.com/smginc/marketing/pmiqnet/demo/

The demo of the PM IQnet from SMG (Strategic Management Group) illustrates the training, consulting, and other resources available from SMG to help develop project management skills within the corporation.

Index

A

B

C

M

N

O

P

Q

R

S

T

U–V

W–X–Y–Z